REGULATION IN PERSPECTIVE

HISTORICAL ESSAYS

regulation in perspective

HISTORICAL ESSAYS

•

Thomas K. McCraw
EDITOR

Morton Keller
Ellis Hawley
Samuel P. Hays
David Vogel

Gerald P. Berk
RAPPORTEUR

•

Division of Research
Graduate School of
Business Administration
Harvard University   Boston 1981

Distributed by
Harvard University Press
Cambridge, Massachusetts
London, England

Contents

Introduction

THOMAS K. McCRAW

•

In recent years, the explosion of interest in government regulation
has produced a huge volume of new research. Studies have poured
forth from universities, private research organizations, legislative
committees, and business associations. The principal cause of this
phenomenon, no doubt, has been the rapid growth of regulation
itself, not only in the United States but in other market economies
as well.

Two additional reasons lie behind the proliferation of research,
and each is important to an understanding of the approaches
taken by the authors of this book. First, the issue of government
regulation embraces a number of themes inherent in the study of
industrial society: the cultural and ideological tension between
individualism and communitarianism, the inescapable tradeoffs
between efficiency and equity, and the contest—real and imag-
ined—between economic growth and environmental quality. The
debate over regulation and deregulation, as broad as it is, implies
a still broader debate over the advantages and disadvantages of
adversarial business-government relations compared with cooperative ones, and even over the preponderance and relative legitimacy of the two at any given time. Regulation, then, is
a complex and sometimes intractable topic, but nonetheless an
irresistible one.

Its irresistibility has beckoned students from numerous disciplines, and this is the second source of the profusion of research.
Scholars in economics, political science, law, business administration, sociology, and other disciplines have staked claims over all

or part of the regulatory turf and have assiduously mined the rich seams and lodes that lie beneath. New journals have arisen to spread the new learning, and often—as with the *Bell Journal of Economics,* the *Journal of Law and Economics,* and *Regulation*—ironically to argue for less regulation. Privately supported research organizations, notably the Brookings Institution and the American Enterprise Institute, have carried to completion major inquiries into the nature of the regulatory cosmos.

The present collection of essays should be regarded, in the first instance, as a modest rivulet into this existing flood of scholarship. The word "historical" in the subtitle is important. Four of the five essayists are professional historians, the fifth being a historically minded political scientist. By their nature, historical scholars are inveterate empiricists. What they care most about is getting the story and the record straight. They are not often given to sweeping generalizations or to overarching theories about the nature of man and his works. They are comfortable with indeterminacy in large questions even as they seek certainty in small ones.

Within this guild of careful empiricists, on the other hand, the present essayists are noted for certain additional characteristics. They tend to generalize more confidently than do many of their colleagues. Several are acknowledged pathbreakers who have re-defined their specialties: Ellis Hawley and the political economy of both the "New Era" of the 1920s and the New Deal of the 1930s; Morton Keller and the legal manifestations of cultural and economic change in the decades spanning 1900; Samuel P. Hays and the environmental movement and its politics throughout the twentieth century. All five essayists, furthermore, tend toward institutional approaches. None is primarily a quantifier or clio-metrician. Legatees of Weber, Veblen, Schumpeter, Parsons, and other institutionalists, they are less interested in numbers and equations than in organizational patterns and structures. They have typically chosen to study bureaucratic adaptations to cultural movements and have often focused their research on the thought and behavior of professionals operating within complex organizations or doing battle against them from without. Of necessity, they have read widely in sister disciplines and have absorbed

Introduction

methodologies from law, political science, economics, and organizational theory.

I should add that these remarks must not be taken so as unduly to homogenize the contributors, some of whom, given the opportunity, might not subscribe to such characterizations. Moreover, as the reader will discover, some essayists have a more pronounced institutionalist bent than others. They will be seen in this book to disagree in many particulars, even on such basic matters as the optimal methods of studying and explicating the topic of regulation.

The topic itself, as suggested earlier, is an exceedingly broad and diffuse one. The essays reflect this inherent breadth, and the authors have made no attempt to coordinate their focus on particular sub-themes. All five essays, however, share elements of both the closeup snapshot—the historian's characteristic choice—and the photograph from the orbiting satellite. Historians are at their best when they insist on this dialectic between the particular and the general, and when they make it the core of their approach to the measurement of change across time. In these respects, the present essayists each rely heavily on the comparative method. Several of them make systematic efforts to exploit the comparative approach not only by counterposing the particular with the general, and one period of time with another, but also one country with another by reference to regulatory patterns in other market economies. The aim in every case has been to serve the goal explicit in the title of the book: to place the phenomenon of regulation in perspective. Given this goal, the comparative approach may be seen as not merely advantageous but indispensable.

A sixth essay, which concludes the book, records the responses of the initial readers of the first five, which were presented at a Harvard Business School conference in 1980. It goes beyond this, however, to inquire still further into the nature of regulation and the best means of its study. In doing so, the concluding essay draws on the collective wisdom of the original conference participants, a group of thirty scholars from history, political science, business administration, and law.

Rethinking the Trust Question

THOMAS K. McCRAW

Harvard Business School

•

I. ELEMENTS OF A FRESH ANALYSIS

Old Debate and New Departure

Three generations have now passed since the Wilson-Roosevelt-Taft-Debs presidential campaign of 1912. That election marked the climax of more than two decades of intense public controversy over the trust question, and in so doing it fixed the essential ideas and clichés through which subsequent generations encountered the issue. To this day, much of the vocabulary we use to discuss big business and antitrust remains frozen in the lexicon of 1912.

In recent years, we have learned a great deal about related themes such as the association movement of the 1920s and the persistent tensions within New Deal economic policy between antitrusters and advocates of business cooperation.[1] For the trusts themselves, however, our point of reference remains 1912. We habitually rehearse the Wilson-Roosevelt debates on the apparent assumption that new insights might emerge from endless repetition of the same words—even though we know that these words were steeped in ambiguity even as the candidates spoke them. What could Wilson have meant by being "for big business" but "against the trusts"? How could Roosevelt tell the difference between "good" trusts and "bad"?[2]

I believe it is now possible to transcend the old ambiguities and strictures. I am convinced that three generations of experience with the American business system, together with the flowering

1

of new research in business history and the evolution of a more rigorous vocabulary in economics, now permit us to move decisively toward a new historical conceptualization.

This essay, accordingly, is an attempt to rethink the trust issue. It begins with a brief review of the fundamental reason behind the rise of the trusts. It then introduces a vocabulary drawn from several disciplines, principally economics, and suggests how such a vocabulary can facilitate a reconceptualization. Next the essay focuses on the evolutionary patterns of large companies both before and after 1912 and—most important—both in the United States and other major capitalist economies. Finally, in a section comprising about half its length, the essay shifts to an extended example of this new conceptualization through a close look at the thought and career of Louis D. Brandeis. Brandeis was the most incisive critic of the trusts during his generation. He served as Wilson's chief economic adviser from 1912 until 1916, and he was regarded as the chief architect of the Federal Trade Commission and other Wilsonian initiatives. In addition, of course, he became the godfather or patron saint of a major wing of the American regulatory tradition.

Overcapacity and the Rise of the Trusts

The trust movement—that is, the powerful tendency of businessmen to cooperate with competitors in associations or mergers—grew out of a particular problem of industrialization. This was the problem of periodic industrial overcapacity tied to the boom-and-bust cycles of the late nineteenth century economy. Just as worldwide overcapacity lies behind the periodic "sickness" of such contemporary industries as steel, fibers, footwear, and automobiles, so in the late nineteenth century industrial overcapacity plagued the economies of all developed nations.

The underlying reason was the industrial revolution, which initially took the form of a revolution in production. Corresponding progress in distribution, marketing, and consumer purchasing power lagged behind production, and sometimes far behind. This created a serious periodic imbalance between nations' capacity to produce and their ability to consume. In some respects this sequence was natural and inevitable. The rise of the department store (1870s) could hardly have preceded the invention of the sewing machine (1844). Cyrus McCormick's reaper, invented in the 1830s, spawned the national and international system of commercial grain agriculture; but this new system did not develop until a national rail network emerged for marketing the grain (there were 23 miles of track in America in 1830, and 208,152 by 1890).[3] And the vast array of consumer goods that poured forth from thousands of American factories could not flow to their end users until a corresponding revolution had occurred in packaging and wholesaling. The "Uneeda Biscuit" in its wrapped packet, for example, could not replace the cracker barrel until delicate packaging machines had been perfected.

The sewing machine, reaper, and machines for wrapping biscuits are but three examples of a profound, pervasive, worldwide revolution in productivity. The revolution substituted machine tools for human craftsmen, interchangeable parts for hand-tooled components, and the energy of coal for that of wood, water, and animals. In labor-short America, capital invested per worker in manufacturing grew from about $700 in 1869 to about $2,000 in 1899. Total capital invested in manufacturing multiplied from $2.7 billion in 1879 to $8.2 billion in 1899, and to $20.8 billion in 1914.[4]

The resultant explosion in production, as is so often the case in any period for individual industries, was accompanied by sharply declining prices. The wholesale price index, which stood at 193 in 1864, dropped to 82 by 1890, even though real per capita gross national product rose sharply during the same period. But the truest measure of what was happening during this era, just as it is the truest measure in our own time, was productivity. The best estimates suggest that the annual increase in total factor productivity, which had held remarkably steady at roughly 0.3 percent for most of the nineteenth century, began to rise very rapidly in the closing decades. So violent was this spurt that the figure for 1889–1919 reached nearly *six times* the rate that had prevailed for most of the nineteenth century. During this phase, then, the industrial revolution was primarily a revolution in production and productivity.[5]

With rising productivity came overcapacity, not only in the United States but throughout the industrialized world, as reflected in the worldwide price declines characteristic of the period. And among businessmen in every industrial nation, the natural initial response to overcapacity, especially in periods of recession and depression, was to combine with each other to limit the total output of their plants, maintain the price levels of their goods, and discourage the entry of new firms into their lines of business.

Such tendencies of business executives are more or less universal. They are discoverable in all industries, all countries, and all periods of time. Adam Smith's famous description of the phenomenon was already trite when he made it in 1776. "People of the same trade," wrote Smith, "seldom meet together, even for merriment and diversion, but the conversation ends in a conspiracy against the public, or in some contrivance to raise prices."[6] But the tendencies Smith observed in 1776 were mild indeed compared with the manic compulsions stimulated by the revolution in production. That revolution dramatically changed the orders of magnitude involved, and in two ways. First, the huge new volume of output made the potential rewards of industrial success far greater than had been the case in Smith's era. Second, and for the trust question more important, the immense capital investment tied up in a large modern factory or string of factories raised the cost of failure beyond anything Adam Smith could have contemplated. The failure of, say, a large steel company would cost tens of millions of dollars in idled physical plant and would throw out of work thousands of employees. Thus, industrialists felt a powerful urge to maintain a market for their products, if necessary by temporarily selling below costs, if possible by cooperating with each other for the mutual protection of their capital and their own survival of gyrations in the business cycle.

In Europe, this inclination to combine in self-defense against overcapacity had very different results from those in the United States. The response was by no means identical all over the Continent, but in general Europeans accepted business combinations far more readily than did Americans. Price and production cartels, set up in every country and in many different industries in response to the overcapacity problem, usually enjoyed the official sanction of the state. The law was actually on the side of cartels, and the machinery of the state could be used to enforce contractual articles of cartelization against rebellious price cutters. In Europe, with its large public bureaucracies long in place, and where government had always had a prominent role in the affairs of business, industrial overcapacity was in this sense simply another new problem for a mature state to help manage. The official sanction of cartels was a convenient way for governments to keep peace within troubled industries and among the major sectors of the economy—manufacturing, transportation, wholesaling, retailing. The rise and success of cartels in these sectors tended to soften and stabilize the industrialization process by protecting the vested interests of participating firms. Direct harm to individual companies was thereby minimized. Consequently, in Europe there were fewer of the internecine business wars so characteristic of the more fluid and indeterminate American context.[7]

This is not to say that industrial peace prevailed on the Continent during the late nineteenth century. It is clear, however, that in Europe the typical political battles pitted a fairly united business community against a powerful but factionalized labor movement. In the United States, by contrast, with its less mature proletariat, the labor question—despite periodic strikes and violence—was less salient. Instead, the customary political warfare found one group of businessmen faced off against another: carriers versus shippers, commodity farmers against mortgage bankers, small wholesalers and shopkeepers against large firms whose marketing divisions were displacing traditional jobbers and retailers. Again in vivid contrast to Europe, the tiny size of the United States government meant that no public bureaucracy existed to manage these conflicts. (In 1871, on the eve of the trust movement, only 51,020 civilians worked for the federal government, of whom 36,696 were postal employees. These few thousand governed a country whose population exceeded 40 million.) Within such a context, the emerging overcapacity problem, compounded by the boom-and-bust business cycle, moved immediately into the realm of public controversy. And to a degree sometimes underestimated by scholars, it underlay nearly every major economic issue of the period: not only the trust question, but also the perennial and divisive battles over the protective tariff, the railroad rate problem, and the imperial quest for foreign markets to absorb surplus production.[8]

The initial response to industrial overcapacity in America took much the same form it took in Europe. American businessmen, like their counterparts abroad, energetically combined with each other in loose cartels designed to limit production, maintain prices, and divide markets so that all could survive. The array of formal and informal associations erected for this purpose within the United States in the 1870s and 1880s soon numbered in the thousands. Seldom, however, did these early cartels accomplish their purpose, because they encountered intractable legal obstacles. The common law and the national culture were so inveterately opposed to "monopoly" and "restraint of trade" that American courts refused to enforce cartel arrangements against recalcitrant members.[9] Thus, in a fashion that would have been difficult in Europe, American businessmen participating in cartels were free to cut their prices in violation of the agreements or sell their products outside areas demarcated by the cartel. The passage in 1890 of the Sherman Antitrust Act formalized the common law's hostility and compelled the Department of Justice eventually to be an active opponent of cartel behavior. Despite the indifference of the first attorneys general who dealt with it, the act was soon to have an enormous and in part unexpected impact.

The New Vocabulary

In order to analyze that impact and its many ramifications, it is appropriate to set forth the terms necessary to such a discussion. Most of these terms were not contemporary with the trust movement but have evolved in the years since from several streams of research in economics and business administration. In using such terms in historical analysis, it is important to keep in mind that we are in a position something like that of modern astronomers studying the pre-Copernican theories of Aristotle or Ptolemy. That is, we are testing the assumptions and insights of an earlier generation of observers through the use of methods developed in a subsequent scientific revolution to which they had no access.

The requisite vocabulary has a minimum of nine relevant terms. Of the nine, the most important is "efficiency," which has different meanings and must be split into two parts.

1) Productive efficiency. This term means maximum useful output per given input. The concept is common in mechanical engineering, as in the comparison that steam engines are more efficient than internal combustion engines because they deliver more work per unit of fuel consumed. In the economic sense, the meaning of productive efficiency is much broader. It means anything—organizational, technical, or whatever—that businesses do either to reduce the cost or improve the quality of their products without a corresponding offset; that is, anything they do that will reduce the cost without reducing the quality or will improve the quality without raising the cost. The readiest examples of productive efficiencies are economies of scale and machine mass production on assembly lines, but there are innumerable other instances.[10]

2) Allocative efficiency. Under maximum allocative efficiency, no rearrangement of distribution, inputs, or outputs within the economic system could possibly make one consumer better off in terms of his own desires without making another worse off in terms of his. Allocative efficiency is served when resources are directed where they will generate the greatest productive efficiency. Allocative inefficiency results when greater amounts of resources are claimed without a corresponding increase in productive efficiency, as in the OPEC oil cartel. With the highest allocative efficiency, individual consumer welfare tends to be maximized. No one pays more than is necessary for any given item and everyone is therefore able to choose how to spend his own money optimally for his own individual satisfaction.[11]

Consumer welfare, it should be added, is obviously not the only criterion against which all public policy should be measured. Neither is economic growth. Both of these goals apply chiefly to "economic man" and say little—at least directly—about aesthetic values, ideological preferences, or any number of other legitimate concerns. In the argument of this essay, however, and in economic theory generally, any policy that promotes growth and consumer welfare carries a strong favorable presumption. Conversely, any policy tending to diminish them should, if it is to be justified, bring with it extremely strong offsetting benefits of a noneconomic nature.

This is not to imply, of course, that in the making of public policy economic growth and consumer welfare are themselves precisely the same thing. All governments—democratic, monarchical, communist, socialist—purport to promote growth through their economic policies. High government regard for consumer choice and consumer welfare, on the other hand, has been closely correlated in modern times with democracy, and low regard with totalitarianism.

3) *Economies of scale.* Some industries, such as railroads and oil refineries, tend to have higher productive efficiencies with large physical plants than with small ones. In the case of railroads, the longer the trip and the larger the number of cars in a given freight train, the lower the ton-per-mile cost of moving a given item of cargo. In industries that involve the flow of liquids or gases, such as oil refining, economies of scale derive from certain circumstances of geometry. The volume of a pipe, for example, multiplies by the square of its radius. If the radius is doubled, the volume is quadrupled. Thus, the bigger the plants, the more efficient, all other things being equal.

A second type of scale economy derives from what Adam Smith called "the division of labor." The more particularized an operation is, the more efficiently it can be done by a specialized tool, machine, or skilled worker. (Cardiac surgeons can perform arterial by-passes better and more quickly than can general surgeons, let alone general practitioners.) All other things being equal, the larger the undertaking, the more numerous and specialized its constituent labor force and machinery can be. As Adam Smith put it in a further observation, the division of labor was limited only by the extent of the market; and by about 1890 the United States had the largest domestic market in the world, which meant that it had the largest potential scale economies from the division of labor. (The European Common Market, set up in the 1950s, was an effort to replicate the American system.)

4) Long production runs. Another type of productive efficiency is the cost reduction gained from long production runs in so-called continuous process industries such as oil refining, chemicals, and steelmaking. Continuous process operations can run day and night, day in and day out, without shutting down. Oil is refined, steel and chemicals are compounded not by labor-intensive operations requiring hundreds of workers, but by giant distillation columns or retorts running on constant heat and supervised by a small but very specialized labor force. Huge savings derive from the simple practice of never putting out the fires beneath such plants but instead keeping the operations running around the clock without the need for new warmup periods.

A similar productive efficiency can be achieved from the moving assembly line. The faster the line moves, the greater the number of units produced per hour. More important, however, is the constancy of the movement, together with the possibility of making very large quantities of identical items in long production runs. The moving assembly line represents an effort to duplicate for the mechanical manufacture of such items as automobiles and firearms the continuous process methods inherent in oil refining or steelmaking. Through extremely long production runs, Henry Ford reduced the price of his Model T from $590 in 1911 to $260 in 1924 (a period of sustained inflation), and simultaneously improved the quality of the car. In later years, business managers began to speak of the "learning curve" or the "experience curve," by which they meant the phenomenon of progressively lowered unit costs as a firm's output rose and as the firm gained experience over time in making the product.[12]

9

5) Transaction costs and economies of speed. The functioning of a market economy depends on innumerable transactions between buyers and sellers. In addition to transactions between retailers and end users, an immense range of intermediate transactions occurs between wholesalers and retailers, manufacturers and subcontractors, assemblers and parts producers, and between transportation companies and nearly everyone. Each of these millions of transactions has a certain cost for the parties involved. Such costs—administrative, informational, legal, and many others—are entailed as the parties locate each other, negotiate the price and quality of the items to be exchanged, assess the reliability of the other party in fulfilling his contract, and schedule desired deliveries to coincide in time with shipments from other sources. The more complex the business, the greater the risk of interruption of the flow of materials from one stage to another, and therefore the greater the potential transaction costs.[13]

As transaction costs are lowered by efficient management, (or as transactions with identical costs are done faster and more reliably), "economies of speed" tend to increase.[14] Again, one characteristic of Henry Ford's assembly line provides a suitable illustration. For the line to move without undue interruption, hundreds of parts had to arrive at the appropriate site at just the right time to be assembled by the right kind of worker. These needs—which were not just desirable but absolutely essential to the operation of the line—meant in turn that numerous external and internal transactions must be expedited administratively in order to make certain that machinery, materials, and workers were properly coordinated. Without such administrative coordination, the line would slow down or even stop. With such coordination, the line could move faster and faster and huge economies of speed could accrue to the company.

The flow of parts and semifinished goods through a factory represented the final stages of a long series of transactions stretching back to the construction of the factory, the hiring and training of an appropriate labor force, and the acquisition of each component of the final manufactured product. And even after the manufacturing phase was completed, very large transaction costs remained in the distribution and marketing of the product. For many types of business, such as mass retailing by the giant mail order houses, the reduction of transaction costs in these later phases yielded far greater productive efficiencies than did those in the production phase. The coordination of flows in Sears, Roebuck's processing of more than one hundred thousand orders per day sharply reduced the unit costs of distributing a wide range of consumer goods, and therefore reduced the selling prices of those products.

6) *Vertical integration.* One approach to the problem of transaction costs was for a company to minimize its market relationships with intermediaries and instead to do all its business operations itself, from the derivation of raw materials to the selling of finished manufactured products at retail. Such a company is said to have achieved complete "vertical integration."

No company enters business in fully integrated form. The process occurs through incremental decisions to extend the functions performed by the existing business. An oil-refining company, for example, might decide to purchase tank trucks to transport its gasoline to market and service stations from which to retail the gasoline. A fully integrated oil company would own exploration and production equipment for the finding and pumping of crude oil, tanker fleets and pipelines to transport it, refineries to turn it into gasoline, kerosene, and heating oil, tank trucks from which to wholesale its products, and service stations from which to retail gasoline. The largest integrated oil company, Exxon, started out as John D. Rockefeller's Standard Oil Company, which did nothing except refine crude oil. Rockefeller and his associates first integrated "forward" into transportation and wholesaling, then integrated "backward" into crude oil supplies.

The reason they did this had to do with reducing transaction costs and thereby improving economies of speed and the overall productive efficiency of the company. They wanted to be able to guarantee a constant source of crude oil and a constant market for their final products. And their surest means of guarantee was to go into these new lines of business—transportation, retailing, and so forth—themselves. Only in this way could they take full advantage of the scale economies in their refineries and, later, in their pipelines. They did precisely this, and achieved enormous economies of speed by a series of vertical integrations. Broadly speaking, they aimed at matching the capacity of every stage of their business to that of every other stage. Instead of remaining content with the type of structure depicted on the left below, they moved to construct the vertically integrated type on the right:

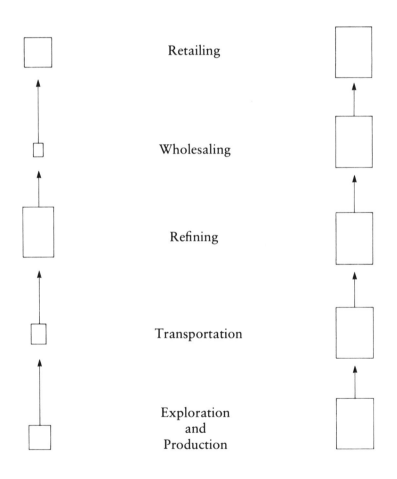

Under the first model, the scale economy potential in refining (which derived from the pipes' volumes being squared as their radii doubled, together with the economies of long production runs) stood to be interrupted randomly by a host of unforeseen events. These might come in the form of an abrupt stoppage of crude oil supply, a sharp rise in its market price, the unavailability of transportation at a critical time, a collapse of the distribution system, or some other sudden bottleneck in the movement of the product from one stage to another. Under the second model or structure, on the other hand, with Standard's own managers and its own facilities involved, a continuous flow of the product at high speed and at sharply declining marginal costs could almost be assured. (If it were not, middle managers would be fired.) Assuming a steady market—which in Standard's case the fortuitous emergence of the automobile guaranteed—then the inherent risks of the oil business could be thoroughly hedged. In short, the result of Standard's vertical integration was to smooth and speed the flow of the product by internalizing the complex management tasks involved in the refining of different grades of crude oil into different types of products for different markets. This minimized external transaction costs. The result was an enormous gain in the productive efficiency of the company, to the disadvantage of its competitors.

Within the framework of the trust question, the important point is that the chief purpose of vertical integration historically has been to promote productive efficiency, even though it can also serve as a competitive weapon to preempt supplies or markets. Vertical integration usually works well as a business strategy only for those industries that possess a significant scale economy at some stage of the production or marketing process. The business integrates vertically for the purpose of ensuring that its advantage from the scale economy is maximized and not interrupted. On the other hand, vertical integration has the disadvantage of putting all a firm's eggs in one basket and risking the entire basket to the contingency of a declining market for its products.

7) *Horizontal combination.* As outlined in the early part of this essay, the nineteenth century was characterized by an unprecedented outburst of technological innovation, which led to a productivity revolution. Together with the boom-and-bust business cycle, this resulted in an overcapacity problem across a wide range of industries. As manufacturers began to apply the new technology and new sources of energy in their factories, shops, and refineries, they discovered to their astonishment that production had suddenly become the least of their worries. They could produce huge quantities of oil, steel, sewing machines, cigarettes, and hundreds of other items. But could they sell this enormous new production? If so, at what price?

The revolution in productive efficiency, in other words, precipitated a host of new problems having to do with marketing and price levels. The result was a powerful stimulus to "horizontal combination"—agreements among producers either to limit production or to keep prices up or both. Horizontal combination could take numerous shapes. At its simplest, it might consist of an informal agreement among the coal dealers in a single city to fix the price of a ton of coal above a certain minimum. In more complex form, it might be a European-style cartel of ten steel companies sharing output quotas and price agreements. The ultimate in horizontal combination appeared in huge firms such as the American Tobacco Company, which was the final stage in a series of mergers of every important cigarette company into one industry giant. This "tight" form of horizontal combination, involving actual mergers, is known as "horizontal integration." [15]

In most cases, the motives for horizontal combination, unlike those for vertical integration, had little to do with reducing transaction costs and achieving productive efficiencies. Instead, the usual motives were self-protection. Decisions to participate in a horizontal combination might be defensive (to protect one's company against price cutting by a competitor), or offensive (to drive a rival to the wall). In either case, total output was restricted, prices were held up, and allocative efficiency was diminished.

In the case of tight horizontal integration, however, two additional organizational adjustments often yielded such productive efficiencies that they more than offset potential reduction of allocative efficiency. When a large number of companies in a given industry merged, the managers of the new giant firm usually concentrated production in the most efficient (least cost) plants involved in the merger. This had the effect of reducing the production costs of the company as a whole, thereby permitting lower prices to consumers. Second, and again in contrast to loose horizontal combination, tight horizontal integration was very often followed by a series of vertical integrations, as the new giant firms moved to protect their scale economies by reducing external transaction costs.

For contemporary observers—men such as Roosevelt, Wilson, Brandeis, and a host of journalists, lawyers and common citizens—this was an extremely confusing spectacle to watch as it unfolded in successive stages between 1880 and 1920. It was impossible for them to assess the causes and consequences of vertical integration, to gauge the difference between loose and tight horizontal combination, to forecast the ultimate destination of the movement (some predicted one great national "trust" embracing all businesses), or—most important—to understand the overall effects of these organizational changes on consumer welfare. The most baffling aspect of all was that a large number of firms—American Tobacco, Standard Oil, Carnegie Steel, and many others—engaged widely in both horizontal and vertical integration. The common pattern was a series of horizontal mergers followed by a slower vertical integration aimed at increasing productive efficiency.

Over the retrospective of three generations and with the benefit of a vocabulary and of research unavailable to contemporaries of the movement, it is now clear to a degree impossible to achieve at that time that business combination both helped and hurt consumers, depending on the details of the particular situation and the stage of the drive toward vertical integration. In the case of cartels and other loose horizontal combinations, which reduced allocative efficiency and brought no offsetting productive efficiency, prices remained artificially high and consumer welfare suffered. In the case of vertical integration, on the other hand, consumers usually benefited by the rise in productive efficiency through reduction in transaction costs and corresponding gains in economies of speed. In the case of tight horizontal integration, consumers were helped to the extent that production was concentrated in the most efficient plants involved in the merger.

For example, between 1882 and 1885 the Standard Oil trust concentrated production in the twenty-two most efficient of its fifty-three refineries, closing the least efficient thirty-one. This "rationalization" of production facilities reduced the company's average cost of refining a gallon of oil *by two-thirds,* from 1.5¢ to 0.5¢. Similarly the American Tobacco Company, after its various consolidations and rationalizations, reduced the average wholesale price of its cigarettes from $3.02 per thousand in 1893 to $2.01 per thousand in 1899.[16]

The cost savings from these productive efficiencies could be passed onto consumers, or they could be used to augment the company's profit margins. Augmented margins in turn could go into shareholders' dividends or, as retained earnings, into research and development. From the historical record it is difficult to tell which of these uses predominated, because all were powerfully affected. Standard Oil, American Tobacco, and Ford Motor made very large profits, but the prices consumers paid for their products also dropped steadily. In the vocabulary of this essay, the question may be posed as to whether the productive efficiencies deriving from economies of scale, speed, long production runs, and concentration of production in least-cost plants were, on the whole, greater than the allocative inefficiencies attendant upon horizontal integration. This is an enormously complicated historical and economic question, and it may well be unanswerable empirically.

On the other hand, it is possible to make several lower-order generalizations. One is that tight horizontal integrations often benefited consumers in a way loose horizontal combinations never did, and indeed could not do. Another is that the successful persistence of certain types of large horizontally and vertically integrated firms over very long periods of history, in the face of competition both domestic and foreign, constitutes strong evidence that such companies habitually moderated their profiteering on the wise principle of keeping the golden goose alive. A third generalization is that the fundamental strategy of these companies categorically emphasized the constancy of production far more than it did the fleecing of consumers or the building of monopolies. As an executive of Du Pont expressed it in 1903, commenting on the firm's production of gunpowder, "If we could by any measure buy out all competition and have an absolute monopoly of the field, it would not pay us. The essence of manufacture is steady and full product. The demand for [sic] the country for powder is variable. If we owned all therefore when slack times came we would have to curtail product to the extent of diminished demands. If on the other hand we control only 60% of it all and made that 60% cheaper than others, when slack times came we could still keep *our* capital employed to *the full* and our product to this maximum by taking from the other 40% what was needed for this purpose. In other words you could count upon always running full if you make cheaply and control only 60%, whereas, if you own it all, when slack times came you could only run a curtailed product." The great steel titan Andrew Carnegie put it even more bluntly. During one period of slumping demand, he asserted that "the policy today is what it has always been in poor seasons; 'scoop the market,' prices secondary; work to keep our mills running [is] the essential thing."[17]

8) *Center firms.* Standard Oil, American Tobacco, Carnegie Steel, and a few hundred other companies that grew to large size during this period *and remained so* tended to have a common set of characteristics.[18] Most of these "center firms" were technologically advanced in the sense that their production facilities were dominated by continuous process production (Standard Oil, American Sugar Refining, Carnegie Steel), or by some combination of large batch production with machine mass production (Singer Sewing Machine, American Tobacco, Quaker Oats, Pillsbury Flour, International Harvester). Consequently most of them enjoyed some significant scale economy in the production or packaging process, and nearly all were vertically integrated.

A second characteristic of center firms was their long-range perspective. Because of the enormous investments they represented, survival was a far more important goal than short-run

17

profits, and by the turn of the century many center firms had begun to plan systematically on the basis of five-year horizons. In addition, they had begun to engage in research and development of new products to make and sell in ever expanding markets. And to manage their many internal functions, they began to develop complex managerial hierarchies.

A third characteristic was that most center firms were capital intensive, employing a high ratio of machinery or other physical equipment per employee. Very few center firms have ever been labor intensive, with the partial exception of those specializing in retailing. And even the greatest of these—Sears, Roebuck— centralized its distribution through immense and expensive mail order facilities located in Chicago.

9) *Peripheral firms.* Peripheral firms were everything center firms were not. Typically they were small, labor intensive, managerially thin, and bereft of economies of either scale or speed. They perforce looked to this year's profits more than to five-year plans. Peripheral firms were not necessarily unimportant, however, and many were major sources of employment for the national economy. Such industries as textiles, furniture, clothing, food service, building materials, hotels, and automobile repair were and still are characterized by a large number of relatively small firms. These firms compete with each other very much in the fashion of Adam Smith's classical model, which is still the model of economics textbooks. Such industries, along with numerous others ranging from restaurants and family retail outlets to specialized parts manufacturers and subcontractors for the center firms, form the backbone of small business in all capitalist economies.

Because of their characteristics, peripheral firms were ill suited to vertical integration. Some peripheral firms were suited to horizontal combination, but there was one problem. The kinds of horizontal combination most appropriate to their needs—that is, local price-fixing arrangements—were very easy to detect and were illegal under the Sherman Antitrust Act. This circumstance caused much grief to progressive insurgents and others who admired small business and wanted to help it in its battles against bigness. The major point, however, is that *center firms and peripheral firms are two fundamentally different types of business.* Seldom have center firms become peripheral or peripheral firms center, either in the United States or elsewhere. Indeed, the situation has been called "the dual economy," and an emerging literature in economics and sociology has been devoted to its exploration and theoretical refinement.[19]

Old Assumptions and New Research

To many members of the generation coming to maturity during the 1880s and 1890s—that is, the generation of Woodrow Wilson, Louis Brandeis, William Jennings Bryan, Theodore Roosevelt, Henry Demarest Lloyd, Edward Bellamy, Ida Tarbell, and Lincoln Steffens—center firms seemed somehow illegitimate or unnatural. This generation, like its predecessors, had grown up in an era occupied almost exclusively (the railroads being the sole exception) by peripheral firms, whose meager resources and lack of political power posed no threat to the country's democratic heritage. Center firms, on the other hand, brought new and alarming conditions and practices: degradation of human labor in the steel industry, unscrupulous manipulation of stocks and bonds in the railroad industry, and sudden loss of community control not only over industries but over individual center firms whose resources dwarfed those of city and even state governments.

Center firms seemed to be mutations, the consequence of some sinister tampering with the natural order of things. They seemed not merely economic entities but powerful new political forces which must be opposed in the name of American democracy. This sort of conclusion was especially compelling given the ruthless methods employed in the formation of such companies as Standard Oil and American Tobacco. Unlike loose cartels, which protected the interests of all participating companies, these tightly organized, horizontally and vertically integrated giants had swallowed up numerous competitors and pushed aside traditional wholesalers and retailers. Irrespective of the benefits they brought to consumers through low prices, these very prices directly injured large numbers of competing small producers, wholesalers, and retailers.

Perhaps the central assumption shared by contemporary critics was that the trusts were unnatural, the bastard offspring of unscrupulous promoters. Without the benefit of a vocabulary that distinguished conceptually between center and peripheral firms, productive and allocative efficiency, vertical and horizontal integration, economies of scale and transaction costs, these observers had only their personal sensibilities and political ideologies to guide them. And both their personal and political values concerning the nature of liberty, the meaning of opportunity, and the promise of America were directly threatened by the trusts.

Only the passage of time, together with a special kind of research, could test with any conclusiveness the question of whether center firms were "unnatural." In the years since 1912, steady progress within the discipline of economics has been of great help, especially in supplying part of the necessary vocabulary. In some ways, however, the discipline has been misleading. Mainstream microeconomics still tends to assume that only the peripheral economy is part of the natural world; it speaks of the center economy in such negative terms as "imperfect competition," "market failure," "barriers to entry," and "vertical restraint." Despite important advances in the subdiscipline of industrial organization, the theory of oligopoly has not progressed very satisfactorily. In addition, mainstream microtheory tends to accord little importance to the efficiency effects of organizational change, including even vertical integration.[20]

The crucial research has come not from economics but from history, and specifically from the world's leading historian of business, Alfred D. Chandler, Jr. In a series of articles and books stretching from the 1950s to the 1980s, Chandler, together with his students, has systematically examined the evolution of the business system in the United States and in other major capitalist economies as well. From his study of more than one thousand center firms has emerged an enormous body of information about their evolution, structure, business strategies, and methods of internal governance.

Rethinking the Trust Question

The implications of Chandler's work are too far reaching for even a brief summary here. The principal message, however, is simple and forthright. As the economist Robert Heilbroner described Chandler's Pulitzer Prize-winning book, *The Visible Hand,* "[It] is a major contribution to economics, as well as to 'business history,' because it provides powerful insights into the ways in which the imperatives of capitalism shaped at least one aspect of the business world—*its tendency to grow into giant companies in some industries but not in others.*"[21] For the purposes of this essay, three of Chandler's propositions bear directly on the reconceptualization of the trust issue:

First, the industry structure characteristic of the American center economy evolved largely during the forty-year period between 1880 and 1920. The shakeout of center firms and peripheral firms into a more or less stable configuration did not end abruptly in 1920, but the major phase of the shakeout clearly was complete by that time. As evidence of one aspect of this stability, Chandler has discovered the following remarkable facts about the makeup of the 200 largest U.S. manufacturing firms (measured in assets) in 1917 as opposed to 1973:

a. In 1917, 22 of the largest 200 companies were in petroleum.
   In 1973, 22 of the largest 200 were still in petroleum.
   Mostly they were the same 22.
b. In 1917, 5 of the largest 200 companies were in rubber.
   In 1973, 5 of the largest 200 were still in rubber. Four of these five were the same (Goodyear, Goodrich, Firestone, and Uniroyal). The fifth, Fisk, merged with Uniroyal—then called United States Rubber—in 1939.
c. In 1917, 20 of the largest 200 companies were in machinery.
   In 1973, 18 of the largest 200 were in machinery.
   Mostly they were the same companies.
d. In 1917, 30 of the largest 200 companies were in food products.
   In 1973, 22 of the largest 200 were in food products, and several other food companies were still in the top 200 as parts of conglomerates.
e. In 1917, 26 of the largest 200 companies were in transportation equipment.
   In 1973, 20 were in transportation equipment, down partly as a result of mergers from 26 in 1948.[22]

These numbers suggest, among other things, that the inherent characteristics of certain types of industries are such that the first companies to succeed in them enjoyed overwhelming advantages over later entrants. These advantages included scale economies and lower unit costs achieved through long production runs and the "experience curve." If the companies also rationalized their production process by concentrating operations in their lowest cost plants, and then proceeded to integrate vertically, thereby compounding and multiplying the advantage they held in production—and most of these companies did precisely this—then they were inordinately difficult for competitors to dislodge. When one considers that the companies maintained their position over a very long period which included two world wars, the Great Depression, and a series of profound changes in American society, then the question of "natural" versus "unnatural" takes on a different aspect.

A second proposition suggested, though not highlighted, by Chandler's research is that companies in nearly every manufacturing industry attempted the same sort of growth strategy described above. That is, the combination movement was just as attractive to peripheral industries as to center ones. Only the outcome was different, and therein lies the significance.

Try as they might, businessmen in peripheral industries simply could not make their combinations work, precisely because of the nature of those industries. Their experience—an experience of failure unrelated to talent, entrepreneurship, or dedication—is one of the forgotten aspects of the trust movement, unfortunately for subsequent understanding of the issue. Everyone remembers the United States Rubber Company, which succeeded, but nobody remembers the United States Leather Company, which did not. American Tobacco thrived, but American Cattle failed. Standard Oil became one of the world's most successful corporations, but Standard Rope and Twine soon perished. The National Biscuit Company became, as Nabisco, a household word, but National Cordage disappeared.

These failed combinations are of crucial analytical significance. By comparing their experience with those of the successful combinations, and in particular by comparing their inherent economic characteristics with those of the companies involved in successful mergers and subsequent vertical integrations, it is possible to isolate the likely determinants of success or failure. Recent research by Chandler and others indicates that the failed trusts typically had a high ratio of variable to fixed costs, that they were labor intensive, that they lacked any important scale economies in either production or marketing, and that they were easily overtaken by new entrants whose smaller size gave greater price and production flexibility.[23]

Perhaps the only way such combinations might have succeeded is through the cartel route. That is, they might have been able to maintain themselves in loose combinations had they been able to enforce industrywide price controls and production quotas. The antitrust laws made it difficult for them to do this for very long, however, and in that sense antitrust ironically added to the disadvantages of peripheral firms vis-à-vis center firms.

A third of Chandler's propositions central to the argument of this essay has to do with business evolution abroad. After having established that certain patterns characterized the structure of American industry in the twentieth century, Chandler has gone on to discover that the very same patterns obtain, with surprisingly few modifications, in other major market economies, despite different sources of supply, markets, and political cultures. That is, the numbers cited above concerning the stable makeup of the largest 200 American manufacturing companies over more than fifty years are closely similar to numbers compiled for the same period in the economies of Germany, France, Britain, and Japan. Only the pace and timing of appearance varied, and even these did not differ radically.[24]

Furthermore, the industries themselves tend to be similar, as the following list shows. This list applies to all manufacturing companies worldwide which as of 1973 had at least 20,000 employees each. Included in the tally are a total of 379 companies, approximately half of which were in the United States and half abroad:[25]

Regulation in Perspective

	U.S. (192 companies)	Abroad (187 companies)
Transportation Equipment	22	23
Electrical Machinery	20	25
Stone, Clay, and Glass	7	8
Tobacco	3	4
Chemicals	24	28
Rubber	5	5
Textiles	7	6
Petroleum	14	12

These very striking similarities between the U.S. experience and that of major market economies abroad suggest strongly that *the inherent economic and technological characteristics of given industries almost force them to assume either a center or peripheral configuration and to maintain that configuration over a long period of time. These inherent characteristics seem much more important than different legal systems or different national cultures in determining the relative size and organizational structure of firms within those industries. This is a fact of surpassing importance in assessing the historical record of the evolution of big business in the United States and the conceptualization of the trust question from the late nineteenth century to the present day.*

II. TESTING A PREVALENT ANALYSIS: LOUIS D. BRANDEIS
AND THE ANTITRUST TRADITION

Brandeis and His Values

The thought of Louis D. Brandeis illustrates especially well one of the earliest conceptualizations of the issue, and one still remarkably influential three generations later. Brandeis's career as a practicing lawyer, which began in 1878 and ended with his appointment to the Supreme Court in 1916, coincided almost precisely with the major phase of the rise of center firms, which occurred between about 1880 and 1920. As the "People's Lawyer" of the Progressive Era, Brandeis symbolized the insurgent revolt against the domination of the nation's economic life by the new center firms. He watched the business revolution as it unfolded, tried his best to understand it, and found it, on the whole, hostile to his own central values of autonomous individualism. For that reason he fought it, and in his crusades against what he called the "curse of bigness" he was a formidable champion indeed.

Brandeis's values had been shaped by several different forces in his background. His Bohemian Jewish parents had fled Europe during the suppression of the democratic movements of 1848. Settling in Louisville, Kentucky, the family had prospered in the grain merchandising business but had suffered setbacks during the depression of the 1870s. Louis Brandeis, an intellectually gifted child, was educated at the German and English Academy in Louisville and, later, at the Annen-Realschule in Dresden. He entered the Harvard Law School in 1875 at the age of eighteen, and made a phenomenal record which still stands as the highest in the school's history. After graduation, he spent a year practicing law in St. Louis, but he soon returned to Boston, for whose intellectual life and Puritan values he had developed an intense affection.[26]

For twenty-five years, Brandeis practiced in Boston as a commercial lawyer. As an outsider and a Jew, he did not attract the largest clients available to local firms: the major banks and insurance companies, the railroads headquartered in Boston, or the new center firms arising from the reorganizations and mergers of the period. Instead his typical clients were small and medium-sized manufacturers of boots, shoes, and paper, together with prominent Jewish wholesalers and retailers such as the Hechts and the Filenes. Brandeis came to know these clients intimately, impressed them with his knowledge of their businesses, and acted as their counselor and adviser on a wide range of legal and business problems. It was his work on their behalf that made him a millionaire. Ultimately, Brandeis identified with their interests politically, and some of his later campaigns as "People's Lawyer"—in particular his approach to the trust question—can be traced back to the problems and interests of these clients, interests which in any case were fully consistent with his own values.[27]

Though himself a millionaire, Brandeis was repelled by materialism. He disliked most other rich people, being profoundly disturbed by their ostentatious consumption. He was nearly incredulous, for example, when he read newspaper reports in 1911 that Elbert H. Gary of U.S. Steel had presented his wife with a pearl necklace valued at $500,000: "Is it not just the same sort of thing which brought on the French Revolution?"[28] Brandeis had an active revulsion against such modern devices as automobiles and telephones. He disliked spectator sports and other passive amusements. He practically never went shopping, even for his own clothes; he simply reordered suits and other items that had served him well in the past.[29]

His passionate sensibilities led him, like so many others, to a hatred of advertising and from that to a contempt for the manipulated consumer. Ironically, the premise that people could be persuaded to believe things they would not believe in the absence of persuasion was central to Brandeis's own career as publicist and muckraker, and it underlay his great promotional campaigns for causes ranging from savings bank life insurance to Zionism. "All law is a dead letter without public opinion behind it," he wrote in 1890. "But law and public opinion interact—and they are both capable of being made. Most of the world is in more or less a hypnotic state—and it is comparatively easy to make people believe anything, particularly the right."[30]

The trouble was that they could be made to believe the wrong as well, and in Brandeis's view that was what usually happened with advertising. Besides, nationally advertised brands undermined the relationship between consumers and local retailers and thereby broke down the individualism and localism that lay at the heart of Brandeis's ideology. Dependence on advertising revenues also caused newspapers and magazines, in Brandeis's view, to be less "free" than they should be. By the 1920s, when he was an associate justice of the Supreme Court, his dislike for advertising had matured into abhorrence. "The nationally advertised branded goods make the retailer practically an automatic machine, instead of an expert to whom the consumer pays, in profits, compensation for expert services and trustworthiness. . . . In a large part of the field there is no social justification for the national widespread market for very many of the trademarked articles." Brandeis urged that journalists "teach the public" such lessons as "to refuse to buy any nationally advertised brand & to look with suspicion upon every advertised article."[31]

The consumer himself Brandeis judged to be "servile, self-indulgent, indolent, ignorant." Even worse, the consumer had abrogated his role as a countervailing power against bigness. "Isn't there among your economists," he once inquired of Felix Frankfurter, "some one who could make clear to the country that the greatest of social-economic troubles arise from the fact [that] the consumer has failed absolutely to perform his function? He lies not only supine, but paralyzed & deserves to suffer like others who take their lickings 'lying down'. He gets no worse than his just deserts. But the trouble is that the parallelogram of social forces is disrupted thereby. It destroys absolutely the balance of power."[32]

The consumer, then, was not Brandeis's ideal American, and Brandeis himself was never the type of "consumer advocate" so prominent in later years. Again, the reason had less to do with economics than with personal values. At bottom, it was a matter of taste, reminiscent in some respects of Nietzsche's aphorism that it was taste and not reason that had driven him from Christianity. Nietzsche, unable to endure the posturing, the vulgar piety, the manifest hypocrisy of conspicuously professing Christians, turned on and denounced Christianity itself. Brandeis, similarly repelled by the flaunting materialism abroad in America, angrily denounced conspicuous consumption and in so doing drifted imperceptibly into an attack on consumer preference, a principle that lay at the very basis of the market economy. Consumers had in effect betrayed him, had refused to follow his precepts against bigness, had showed their true nature by passively purchasing the endless stream of goods that flowed from the center economy. They had guaranteed thereby the success and permanence of the center firms he so detested; and for that it was difficult to forgive them.

Brandeis and the Evolution of the Trusts

Brandeis became seriously interested in the business revolution in the 1890s, during the severe economic depression of that decade and at a time when he himself was nearly forty years old. A major influence was a book he encountered at this time, Henry Demarest Lloyd's *Wealth Against Commonwealth,* a classic muckraking analysis of the Standard Oil Company. Brandeis's correspondence with a reviewer of Lloyd's book illustrates his awakening sense of the subject, his emphasis on the small competitor rather than on the consumer, and his characteristic interest in methods of molding public opinion.

"I cannot quite agree," he wrote, "that 'Wealth against Commonwealth' is the 'Uncle Tom's Cabin' of the industrial movement." The problem was that Lloyd had not pitched the argument to a sufficiently broad audience. "The great trouble with the efforts against the trusts are [sic], that these efforts are not backed by the people. The American must be educated. The man who has consciously suffered from the trust is the individual competitor, and, in some instances, the producer. The public as a whole have perhaps suffered in many instances, but not suffered consciously. Our people still admire the Captains of the trusts." [33]

At about the same time, Brandeis was preparing a series of lectures for a course on business law at the Massachusetts Institute of Technology. One of the topics he chose was the trusts, and the text of these lectures, never published, provides an unusually precise measure of his understanding of the issue. "The term *trust*,'" Brandeis noted, "is commonly used in a broad, and perhaps inaccurate, sense as including all kinds of combinations of concerns engaged in the same line of business." The combination might use territorial restriction, or it might specify some other means for limiting competition. Whatever the means, the end was clear: "Its general purpose is usually and mainly one of monopoly and the difference is merely the extent to which it is carried out."[34]

To rephrase Brandeis's conclusions in the vocabulary suggested in the preceding sections of this essay, all combination was horizontal, with the aim of reducing competition. Productive efficiencies were neither intended nor achieved, and since the aim was monopoly, allocative efficiency was by definition reduced. Center firms were merely combinations of peripheral firms.

In his lecture notes, Brandeis went on to characterize four different varieties of trusts and to argue that these four had evolved sequentially. The first class, he wrote, "presents the cases of several competing manufacturers, producers or traders agreeing not to sell their product below a certain price." In this variety of horizontal combination, historically the first to appear in America, the agreements were informal, the participants posted a deposit of money to be forfeited in case of a violation, and a grievance committee adjudicated disagreements. Such a form of combination through contract, though clearly "in restraint of trade" and therefore unenforceable at common law, in many respects appealed to Brandeis. In comparison with other forms, this one offered its members "absolute freedom" in the management of their businesses in all respects other than those covered by the agreement. For him, this was a vitally important point. He was concerned primarily not about the welfare of consumers but about the autonomy of producers, wholesalers, and retailers—that is, the preservation of the independent identity of the small firm. What Brandeis sought to maximize, in other words, was not allocative or productive efficiency, both of which suffered under this first type of agreement, but instead the absolute number of individual business units.[35]

The second variety of trusts Brandeis identified "is presented by agreement creating some central body, created with the design of equalizing prices," and administered by "some neutral party, as trustee, committee or corporation." Brandeis noted that this form of trust often materialized as a "joint selling agency" in such industries as salt, lumber, and coal. (Each of these was a naturally peripheral industry with numerous individual competitors and no great inherent economies of scale or speed.) "Here too freedom in production is ordinarily preserved," which for Brandeis was the most important point. And here too, the arrangement, being a horizontal combination in restraint of trade, was unenforceable in court.[36]

"The third class of trade combinations," Brandeis continued, "is the trust proper." This was a tighter form than the first two. "Now under the trust arrangement, all of the stockholders in a corporation transfer all of their stock to certain individuals, generally three or more, as trustees. These individuals then holding the stock, possess the voting power of the stock, and have the absolute power to elect any officers they please." In this way, twenty or thirty separate corporations might combine under "practically omnipotent" central management. "These trustees then determine whether the factory of one of these corporations shall be run or not; they purchase the goods and sell the goods for all the corporations, and as you have this unity of management, there is no possibility of a breach of agreement. This was the original form of the Standard Oil Trust and the Sugar Trust."[37]

In retrospect, it is clear from the empirical research of Chandler and other scholars that this third type of horizontal combination was usually successful only in center firms and industries. To be viable, it required important scale or transaction cost economies. Since its primary aim was to control prices by controlling output, it tended to distort allocative efficiency. On the other hand, because it usually resulted in the concentration of production in the most efficient plants, it increased the productive efficiency of the industry as a whole. Very often, too, it was a prelude to progressive vertical integration, a process which brought substantial additional economies. For all these reasons, the net effect, over time, might well be the reduction of prices and the enhancement of consumer welfare.[38] But this complex mixture of effects was not at all clear to Brandeis and other contemporary observers, who naturally paid more attention to the ruthless methods of such companies as Standard Oil (methods made possible because of Standard's much lower unit costs), and the gradual disappearance of small, autonomous oil refiners than to long-term trends in the price of petroleum products. On the other hand, it was clear to Brandeis that the tight "trust" form failed in some industries as often as it succeeded in others; but he had little way of understanding the reasons why.

The fourth form of combination set forth by Brandeis was actual merger of many companies into "one huge corporation." In this tightest of all combinations, Brandeis observed, "all semblance of individual activity is removed. This is the form of the Diamond Match Company, of the present Sugar Trust, the Standard Oil and other trusts." Brandeis noted that the four-stage evolution "has been historical, in the order mentioned, and you will see how the law hastened this development."[39]

What had started out as loose federations based on mutual agreement soon succumbed to self-interest, as one or another member of the federation (types one and two in Brandeis's taxonomy) broke the agreement because of economic necessity. Meanwhile, the other parties to the agreement, unlike their counterparts in Europe, had no legal recourse against the violators. As a consequence, in America these combinations nearly always disintegrated. As Brandeis put it, "You see in all the cases I have referred to, the combinations were broken up by virtue of civil remedies, that is, by denying to the parties the ability to enforce legally their contracts, or to maintain their organization."[40]

When the loose agreements did break down, Brandeis wrote in his lecture notes, the parties entered tighter combinations such as his categories three and four. And even category three, the "trust proper," sometimes ran afoul of the limitations of what a corporation could do legally under its charter. The only remaining step was category four, the tight combination achieved through merger or acquisition of formerly competing firms into one huge enterprise with unified management and obliteration of the individual identities of the constituent parts. In other words, the legal limitation on loose combinations promoted tighter combinations in a way Brandeis found unfortunate, since his primary goal was the maximization of the total number of autonomous business units. Even though tight combinations—especially after they became vertically integrated—might serve the consumerist goal of allocative and productive efficiency, they at no time served the Brandeisian goal of maximizing individual identities.[41]

Although for the most part Brandeis's analysis was very perceptive, his portrayal of the trust movement as a single four-stage process was mistaken in one important particular. It is clear in retrospect, as it could not have been at the time, that the combination movement had not one but two separate and distinct patterns of origin, a reflection of the fundamental differences between center industries and peripheral.

Among center firms, Standard Oil had pioneered the movement with its trust of 1882. This had been followed by the American Cotton Oil Trust in 1884, the National Linseed Oil Trust in 1885, and the Distillers and Cattle Feeders Trust ("Whiskey Trust") in 1887. The greatest wave of actual mergers came in the period 1897–1904, during which 4,227 American firms merged into 257 combinations. By 1904, some 318 "trusts"—most of which were center firms—were alleged to control two-fifths of the nation's manufacturing assets.[42]

As noted earlier in this essay, companies in the great majority of all manufacturing industries attempted this sort of horizontal integration, either as trusts, holding companies, or mergers. A very large number of such attempts failed, however; and their failure is extremely important in understanding the historical and economic patterns of the combination movement as a whole. Many of these combinations perished despite very capable management and despite everything financiers and others could do to save them. Fundamentally, the architects of failed trusts were trying to construct center firms in naturally peripheral industries. All the successful center firms—Standard Oil, Carnegie Steel, American Tobacco, United Shoe Machinery, National Biscuit— had major inherent economies of either scale or speed or both. Most were vertically integrated, with highly organized functional divisions. Most combined mass production with mass marketing. By contrast, the unsuccessful trusts—Standard Rope and Twine, United States Leather, United States Button, American Glue, American Cattle, National Novelty, National Wallpaper, National Starch, National Salt, National Cordage—had no major inherent economies of scale or speed. Few resources were required to enter any of these peripheral industries, and in consequence the new trusts were immediately vulnerable to competition from still newer entrants. Such competition quickly arose and did the trusts in. The attempts of peripheral firms to merge into center configurations simply did not work, and such combinations were soon dissolved.

Meanwhile, under a distinctly different second pattern of combination, other peripheral firms were forming innumerable loose horizontal associations. These combinations materialized when local, regional, or even national groups of businessmen entered into agreements in self-defense against their sudden collective overcapacity rooted in new technologies and periodic economic downturns. The number of loose combinations—pools, trade associations, cartels, and other formal or informal agreements— numbered in the thousands, far exceeding the few hundred successfully merged center firms (some of which, of course, had begun their evolution into center firms as loose associations under this second pattern). These very numerous cartels and pools fell into Brandeis's categories one and two: loose horizontal combinations of peripheral firms whose arrangements with each other were unenforceable but which, to the extent that they effectively limited production and kept prices high, were anti-consumerist.[43]

Brandeis took the experience of the failed trusts as evidence of the inefficiency of bigness. He reasoned that if size alone sufficed, then all trusts would prosper. Here he was on the edge of a breakthrough, but he soon got off the track because of his antipathy toward bigness. Instead of concluding that firms in some types of industries gravitated toward large size and firms in others toward atomistic fragmentation, he asserted that bigness in general was inefficient, mistook cause for effect, and ended up arguing a tautology. As he expressed it in testimony before a House committee in 1911, "In the first place, most of the trusts which did not secure a domination of the industry—that is, the trusts that had the quality of size, but lacked the position of control of the industry, lacked the ability to control prices—have either failed or have shown no marked success. The record of the unsuccessful trusts is doubtless in all your minds." Brandeis recounted several historic failures, then brought his analysis down to the present period. "Consider other trusts now existing, the Print Papers Trust (The International Paper Co.); the Writing-Paper Trust (The American Writing Paper Co.); The Upper Leather Trust (the American Hide & Leather Co.); the Union Bag Trust; the Sole Leather Trust; those trusts and a great number of others which did not attain a monopoly and were therefore unable to fix prices have had but slight success as compared with their competitors." [44]

Some of the examples Brandeis cited were vivid in his mind because of his personal experience with them in New England. His clients included a number of paper companies and an even larger number of shoe manufacturers who had dealings with the leather trusts. Yet it escaped his notice that few of these industries had any important economy of scale or speed. Few if any of the firms he mentioned were vertically integrated. Combinations in such industries were almost certain to fail, and bigness in their case was indeed a disadvantage because it sacrificed flexibility without achieving corresponding gains in productive efficiency. To this extent, Brandeis's analysis was correct.

The pivotal point for him, however, was that these grain, leather, paper and other trusts had simply failed to secure control of their markets. Again he was correct. The problem was that he confused cause with effect: "Now, take, in the second place, the trusts that have been markedly successful, like the Standard Oil

Trust, the Shoe Machinery Trust, the Tobacco Trust. They have succeeded through their monopolistic position." [This statement is a tautology.] Nor, Brandeis went on to say, was there anything secret about their success. "They dominated the trade and were able to fix the prices at which articles should be sold. To this monopolistic power, in the main, and not to efficiency in management, are their great profits to be ascribed."[45]

As a final comparison, Brandeis offered the evidence of two firms which in his view were in the same industry, transportation. The first was the International Mercantile Marine, a steamship combine financed and sponsored by J. P. Morgan and Company. This steamship trust failed miserably, despite the great resources and business expertise of the Morgan firm. In contrast, Brandeis cited the Pullman Palace Car Company, which enjoyed a monopoly of the sleeping cars popular among railroad passengers. Pullman, said Brandeis, enjoyed "profits so large as to be deemed unconscionable." He attributed the difference in the two companies' experience to their control or lack of control of their markets. In the case of International Mercantile Marine, he said, even good management could not save a trust which failed to gain such control. With tight control, on the other hand, the Pullman Company prospered.[46]

It is clear, using the lines of analysis proposed in this essay, that the Pullman Company was not only in the transportation business but was also a metal-working and machinery firm, a manufacturing company with inherent economies of scale, speed, and long production runs. It was more analogous to International Harvester or Ford Motor than to a steamship line. Furthermore, although steamships were expensive, the shipping industry was peripheral, without important scale or speed economies except in manufacturing (as the Kaiser company, a center firm, proved during World War II with its Liberty ships). Any company with one ship could go into business and compete with the Morgan transportation combine. By contrast, to compete with the large, vertically integrated Pullman Company would require an immense initial investment in a substantial factory, the assembly of a large group of skilled workers, and very careful management, all on the off-chance that the new company could undersell Pullman or that the market for sleeping cars was or could become larger than that which Pullman was presently satisfying.[47]

The "trust" or "monopoly" question, then, comprised two fundamentally different types of consolidation, though Brandeis and his contemporaries did not realize it. It included on the one hand several hundred tightly integrated center firms (many of which were integrated vertically as well as horizontally), and on the other tens of thousands of peripheral firms associated with each other in a few thousand loose horizontal combinations. As Brandeis's future campaigns showed, his inability to grasp the distinctions between center and peripheral firms and between vertical and horizontal integration fed his confusion concerning how and why big businesses evolved, which business practices would or would not help consumers, and which types of organizations were or were not efficient.

Politics, Economics, and Bigness

Brandeis had convinced himself once and for all that big business became big only through illegitimate means. His constant references to the "curse of bigness" meant, among other things, that bigness itself was a mark of Cain, a palpable sign of prior sinning. "I think that if the methods pursued in business are proper," he once told a Senate committee, "and businesses too are allowed to grow, as distinguished from forcibly combining a large number of businesses, there is no such likelihood of any one business acquiring a control as to be really dangerous."[48] Throughout his life Brandeis believed bigness to be unnatural: "If the Lord had intended things to be big, he would have made man bigger—in brains and character." As for the alleged efficiency of large units in some industries, Brandeis was derisive: "I am so firmly convinced that the large unit is not as efficient—I mean the very large unit—is not as efficient as the smaller unit, that I believe that if it were possible today to make the corporations act in accordance with what doubtless all of us would agree should be the rules of trade no huge corporation would be created, or if created, would be successful."[49]

Rethinking the Trust Question

Although Brandeis and his contemporaries often discussed the trust question in economic terms, their opposition to big business was based on their perceptions of its political implications. And indeed the center firm component of the trust question actually *was* primarily a political issue having to do with the distribution of power in a democracy. The peripheral firm component, in contrast, posed primarily an economic issue having to do with the reduction of allocative efficiency and consumer welfare.

In the absence of an adequate theoretical framework, Brandeis, like many later reformers, had only his personal and political sensibilities to guide him. His intense predisposition in favor of small units led him to endorse loose, horizontal, productively inefficient, consumer-injuring associations for the suppression of competition. Correspondingly, Brandeis opposed horizontally tight, productively efficient, consumer-helping, vertically integrated center firms on the grounds that their giant size and central management destroyed the individuality of their merged constituent companies and posed a threat to democratic society. Whereas center firms helped the economy but appeared to threaten the decentralist American polity, loose combinations of peripheral firms injured the economy but tended to protect the polity.

For Brandeis, the choice between the two was not difficult. He unhesitatingly opposed the rise of large firms, whatever their benefits. "I have considered and do consider," he said, "that the proposition that mere bigness can not be an offense against society is false, because I believe that our society, which rests upon democracy, can not endure under such conditions."[50] His response shows vividly the dominance of political considerations over economic ones in his thinking. But however dominant the goal was in his own mind, the subsequent record in all major capitalist economies has made clear one fact that Brandeis had no way of predicting: that the movements toward large size by firms in center industries—that is, the power of the economies of scale, speed, long production runs, and lowered transaction costs which impelled them toward merger and toward vertically integrated structures—were very likely inexorable. Concomitantly, to tear apart all these center firms, when economic forces held them together so powerfully, would likely require action by the state bordering on the totalitarian. This, of course, would be the precise negation of Brandeis's deepest values.

Four Companies and Their Lessons

When Brandeis denounced the "trusts," or "monopoly," he usually meant tight horizontal integration. This image remained the basis of his conception of big business all the way from the 1890s to his emergence in 1912 as Woodrow Wilson's chief economic adviser and beyond. Within the limits imposed by his legal practice, Brandeis had made as close a study of the trust question as he could. In particular, he focused his attention on four giant center firms. Three of these—American Tobacco, United States Steel, and Standard Oil—were the three largest companies in America. The fourth—United Shoe Machinery—was a Boston firm which Brandeis himself had helped to set up and on whose board of directors he served. From his analysis of each one of these companies he took certain lessons, all derived from his hostility toward bigness, which turned out to be mistaken as economic propositions.

The first of the four, the American Tobacco Company, had grown through a series of mergers followed by partial vertical integration. The economies of scale inherent in the tobacco industry lay primarily in the machine manufacture and packaging of cigarettes and the heavy advertising of national brands. Beginning in the 1880s and assisted by their exploitation of a new cigarette-making machine, James B. Duke of Durham, North Carolina, and his fellow entrepreneurs consolidated the industry through a series of more or less ruthless business deals in which they bought out or merged with all important competitors. Eventually the American Tobacco Company became a nearly perfect monopoly, and the Department of Justice consequently brought suit against it under the Sherman Antitrust Act. In a landmark Supreme Court decision of 1911, the company was ordered dissolved.[51]

As attorney for a group of small tobacco firms, Brandeis himself was involved in the dissolution decree. His approach to the case—

evident from his legal brief and from his subsequent public statements—reflects a fundamental confusion over several major
issues, a confusion he shared with many of his contemporaries
and with many future opponents of big business.

Brandeis took the position that the tobacco industry had no
scale economies: "Efficiency does not demand great concentration. In other words, in the tobacco business (unlike, for instance,
steel) the efficient unit may be relatively small." He elaborated the
distinction further, in an effort to show that bigness was unnecessary: "In one branch of the business there are a great many
independents who have survived—that is, in the cigar industry—
because it has been the feature of the Tobacco Trust, and it has
in some respects been extremely wisely planned and administered," to go one step at a time. First, the trust would gain control
of cigarettes, then chewing tobacco; "and the cigar manufacturers
were those who in this tobacco fight were most persistent in their
efforts to secure an adequate [dissolution] decree, because they
felt that it was now their turn to be attacked by the monster
organization."[52]

Brandeis was very close to a conceptual breakthrough here, but
again his antipathy toward bigness prevented his taking the final
step. In the American Tobacco story lay one of the clearest possible illustrations of the principle that with an important scale or
speed economy bigness was almost inevitable, but that without
such an economy bigness was almost impossible. The heart of the
distinction lay in the remarkable fact that cigarettes and cigars
were two very different lines of business from a production viewpoint. Cigarettes could be made by machine mass production at
a speed and on a scale unimaginable prior to the 1890s. During
that decade cigarette-manufacturing machines in only two of
American Tobacco's factories supplied the entire export market
of the company, which by 1898 amounted to 1.2 billion cigarettes
annually. This was an extraordinary economy of scale, speed, and
long production runs, a classic example of these phenomena.[53]

Cigars, on the other hand, could not be manufactured satisfactorily by machine. The leaf came from a variety of sources in the
Caribbean and Connecticut, and had to be handled with great

care. Finished cigars were distributed in small quantities to specialized tobacco dealers familiar with the idiosyncratic tastes of their customers. Most important of all, cigars came not from machines but from skilled craftsmen who were physically able to roll only a small number per day. Where cigarettes were a capital-intensive industry dominated by machines, cigars were extremely labor intensive.

In other words, cigarettes belonged to the category of center industries but cigars were clearly peripheral. Nor was Brandeis the only analyst to make the error of assuming that the two were the same. The American Tobacco Company itself made the equivalent error and expended enormous resources in an effort to integrate the cigar industry in the fashion it had done with cigarettes. Despite the company's expertise, experience, and unscrupulousness, the effort proved futile.[54]

A second erroneous lesson, in this case having to do with European cartels, emerged from Brandeis's analysis of the United States Steel Corporation. In this industry, as he admitted, economies of scale were clear. In addition, Brandeis admired the technical genius of Andrew Carnegie, who in the late nineteenth century had built the vertically integrated and eminently successful Carnegie Steel Company. Carnegie Steel could outproduce and underprice every other steel company in the world, and it was universally admired for its efficiency.

In 1901, however, in an unprecedented $1.4 billion transaction, Carnegie Steel merged with other large firms to form the United States Steel Corporation. This giant horizontal consolidation yielded immense profits to J. P. Morgan and other financial promoters. One condition of the merger was that Carnegie himself retire from the field, which he was happy to do because he now wished to devote his energies to philanthropy.

As Brandeis saw it, the financiers had "bribed" Carnegie, paying him the excessive price of $400 million in order to get him out of the way. They and their henchmen could then operate the great corporation undisturbed, charging whatever prices for steel and other products they wished. And indeed they did institute a series of price-maintenance schemes—the so-called Gary dinners, the Pittsburgh-plus rates to standardize national steel prices—that gave them a measure of control over the industry. These devices did not persist forever, and though it took U.S. Steel an unduly long time to rationalize its production process (more than twenty years), the company eventually did so in response to competitive pressures from both domestic and foreign rivals. But Brandeis's time horizon for analysis was short, and he could not foresee the future. Furthermore, he deplored U.S. Steel's system of working its immigrant laborers very long hours for low pay.[55]

Labor problems aside, Brandeis's economic error lay in contrasting American business organization unfavorably with the cartel system. Cartelization, as noted earlier in this essay, was the typical European response to the overcapacity problems that plagued all market economies in this stage of industrialization. For Brandeis, the cartel—which is inherently hostile to consumer interests because its purpose is to restrict output and keep prices up—represented a preferable alternative to the tight integration characteristic of American center firms. In his view, cartels preserved the individual autonomy or at least the identity of the member firms: "Whatever may be said in regard to the [German] cartel, in the main it leaves competition free—that is, you have competition in production. The only things you have not freedom in is the price at which you sell; and to a certain extent the quantity you sell may be limited as to the proportion of the whole business you can handle." Even though the cartels set and enforced a common price for all their members, Brandeis insisted that "they leave otherwise competition free, and you have all the benefits in that respect of the small businesses with the individual opportunity of increasing your profits, provided you can produce cheaper than your neighbor." It is clear that Brandeis's test was not allocative or productive efficiency, not consumer welfare, but individual autonomy. It was, in short, an aesthetic/political argument and not an economic one: "Each one of those thirty-six German concerns, which are federated for certain purposes, are free and independent in other respects. They are restricted as to selling price and quantity of production (these being fixed by the syndicate), but they are absolutely independent as to internal management. . . . The German Steel Trust preserved competition in large part. The United States Steel Trust destroyed competition."[56]

This line of analysis contained several fallacies. First, the notion that firms whose prices and production quotas are fixed by an outside authority are "free and independent" seems sentimental at best. Second, a cartel is by nature a producers' protective organization whose purpose is to keep prices high. If it is effective, then allocative efficiency suffers, and with it consumer welfare. As with OPEC, the most successful cartel in history, consumers are certain to pay more than they would have to pay in the absence of the cartel. Third—a more subtle point—tight horizontal integration of the U.S. Steel variety was almost always followed by vertical integration and the progressive retirement of the less efficient plants involved in the original merger. In contrast, the European cartel system often preserved these less efficient plants and allocated to them a certain production quota.[57]

Although Brandeis's analysis assumed a static organizational structure at U.S. Steel, in fact the company—like virtually all center firms in America—went through a number of extremely important organizational changes as it adapted to shifting market conditions and different supply situations. American center firms have historically been more flexible organizationally, and more innovative, than have European cartels, many of which were inherently defensive mechanisms designed to maintain the status quo. In the years since 1900, American center firms have been characteristically forward looking organizations, much more prone than European cartels to such adaptations as vertical integration and internal structural change of the organization.[58]

For a number of reasons, however, Brandeis did not like to focus on organizational issues. He had little first-hand experience with great organizations. He never really understood how functions were divided and authority was split among line and staff officers or among division chiefs. Though he did set up a modern law office, it never attained large size and Brandeis himself liked to work alone or in tandem with junior associates. The largest organization in which he ever worked full time was the United States Supreme Court.

At heart, and again because of his distaste for bigness, Brandeis was antiorganizational. "Man's work," he wrote in 1912, "often outruns the capacity of the individual man; and no matter how good the organization, the capacity of an individual man usually determines the success or failure of a particular enterprise—not only financially to the owners but in service to the community. . . . As the Germans say, 'Care is taken that the trees do not scrape the skies.'"[59] Steeped in this anti-bigness ethic, Brandeis had little sense of how organizational arrangements such as vertical integration could achieve economies of speed by matching each part of the functions of a particular center firm to every other part. In vertical integration he saw not the reduction of transaction costs and the creation of productive efficiency but the immersion of individual autonomy in the impersonal organization.

This is clear from his critical analysis of Standard Oil, another center firm. "What does the Standard Oil Co. do with all of its hundreds of millions of dollars and capital and business?" he asked a House committee in 1912. The answer was that the company integrated forward into marketing, so that it could be more certain of selling its products. "There is none too mean to be the direct customer of the Standard Oil Co. Their wagons will travel over the prairies and they will travel over the deserts of Egypt to sell you a gallon of oil for 14 or 15 cents." In Standard's action Brandeis saw the disappearance of the independent wholesaler and retailer of oil. If something were not done to stop this trend, he added, there would evolve "the substitution of agents' arrangements for the ordinary barter and sale which in most respects leave the citizen of the small town of Arkansas or Texas and the other places a free man."[60]

Brandeis deeply feared that other big businesses, following the example of Standard, would set up their own marketing organizations for the wholesaling and retailing of their products. This would destroy the independence of the thousands of small wholesalers and retailers whom Brandeis so admired. It struck him as unfair, furthermore, because only the very large manufacturer could do it. "In the first place, he has the capital. In the second place, he has the organization. And in the third place, he has a volume of business which enables him profitably to establish an agency [i.e., a sales organization] which otherwise he could not do."[61]

Again, his analysis suggests that Brandeis's chief goal was not consumer welfare through productive efficiency—which in this particular passage he seems to concede to the center firm—but instead individual identity. He was concerned about the loss of identity as the individual jobber or retailer was metamorphosed into the mere agent of a vertically integrated corporation.

Still another illustration of the hegemony of politics and personal ethics over economics in Brandeis's thought emerged in his attitude toward the United Shoe Machinery Company, a Boston firm. The manufacture of shoe machinery (that is, the making of machines which in turn would make shoes) was a natural center industry, with economies of scale in the design, production, and servicing of its product. The making of shoes, on the other hand, was a peripheral industry, with hundreds of small and medium-sized competitors. The United Shoe Machinery Company, founded with Brandeis's personal legal advice in 1899, was a horizontal merger of several shoe machinery firms. The new company leased its machines to hundreds of shoe manufacturing companies throughout the United States and abroad. These lease arrangements were managed so as to maximize the commercial advantage of the center firm, sometimes at the expense of the peripheral firms. The peripherals, including a number of Brandeis's own clients in and around Boston, were in turn united in loose combinations for the management of the market for shoes.[62]

Brandeis saw nothing wrong with either type of combination, at least for the seven years during which he served as a director of United Shoe Machinery. "First," he wrote, "it is entirely true that in April, 1906, I believed the policies and methods of the

United Shoe Machinery Co. were legally and morally unobjectionable and that its activities were beneficial to the public, and as a director of the company I appeared before the Massachusetts legislature to oppose a bill seeking to compel a change in these methods [the bill would have made some of the company's leasing arrangements illegal]." At the time, Brandeis added, he himself was "of the opinion that under some conditions monopoly in industry could operate beneficially to the public; or, in other words, that there were 'good trusts' as well as 'bad trusts.' I believed, not unnaturally, that this company, which was managed by men in whose ability and judgment I then had confidence and with which I was myself connected, was such a 'good trust.' The particular ground upon which I based my opinion that the shoe-machinery monopoly operated beneficially was that it appeared to help the small manufacturer and thus, while itself a monopoly, promoted competition in shoe manufacturing."[63]

In other words, Brandeis thought a center firm in shoe machinery would maximize the number of peripheral firms in shoe manufacturing. "In the first place everybody, big and little, was to be treated alike: there were to be no discounts for quantity; so that the small manufacturer had the same chance as the large manufacturer, both in respect to service and to royalty. The company adopted a system of leasing, which gave an opportunity to the small manufacturer with little capital to go into the business, and the company gave them as good service as the large manufacturer." As for the association of small and medium-sized shoe manufacturers—that is, the loose horizontal combination of peripheral firms, a combination which included some of Brandeis's own clients and over which he himself occasionally presided—there was nothing wrong whatever. "You have a situation in that business where there is not the slightest danger at the present time of the suppression of competition."[64]

These quotations suggest two additional aspects of Brandeis's thought. First, they indicate the quite natural confusion of standards when the economic test of consumer welfare was subordinated to faith in personal participation. On this occasion and several others, Brandeis emphasized the doer more than the deed.

More important, the remarks show that for Brandeis the test of whether a combination was good or bad was not whether it suppressed *competition* (which both of these horizontal arrangements in the shoe machinery and shoe manufacturing industries did), but whether it reduced the number of *participating companies*. If the combination directly or indirectly preserved intact the existing shoe manufacturing firms, then it might be a "good trust." Calling anything a "good trust" was a very strong statement for Brandeis, who almost never conceded such a point. But with United Shoe Machinery, as with the European cartels, if it could be shown that the absolute number of firms would not shrink, he was in favor of the combination irrespective of its effect on prices and consumer welfare.

Price Fixing, the Consumer, and the Petite Bourgeoisie
One of Brandeis's most characteristic campaigns was his energetic work on behalf of resale price maintenance (that is, price fixing or "fair trade"). This controversy began in 1911, when the U.S. Supreme Court, in the case of *Dr. Miles Medical Co.* v. *John D. Park & Sons Co.*, ruled wholesale and retail price fixing illegal under both the common law and the Sherman Antitrust Act. The Dr. Miles company was a manufacturer of popular patent medicines which it sold through a network of 400 wholesalers and 25,000 retailers. The company's contracts with each of these dealers required that its patent medicines not be sold for less than a price specified by the company. If a wholesaler or retailer would not sign such a contract, the Dr. Miles company declined to do business with it.[65]

John D. Park & Sons, the victorious defendant in the case, was a wholesale drug company which had refused to sign but instead had procured Dr. Miles products from another wholesaler at cut prices for the purpose of reselling the products below the figure desired by the manufacturer. In finding for Park, the wholesale druggist, and against Dr. Miles, the patent medicine company, the Supreme Court opened a new era in the competitive pricing of retail goods. It also unleashed one of the longest, most relentless, and best organized business lobbying efforts in American history.

Brandeis became the early spearhead of this effort. He lent his name to the crusade to overturn the Court's decision, wrote articles and delivered speeches in opposition to the new doctrine, and drafted a bill to exempt small wholesalers and retailers from the Sherman Act so that they could resume their practice of fixing retail prices at uniform levels nationwide.[66] The episode shows again his preference for the maximization of the absolute number of business units over his concern for consumers and the high prices they would have to pay under the plan. It shows perhaps better than any other episode precisely for whom Brandeis spoke and why in many ways he was less the "People's Lawyer" than the petite bourgeoisie's lawyer. It also shows the dilemmas in which he found himself as a consequence of his preference. He was compelled to do battle on behalf of a particular interest group in opposition to broader-based consumer interests. And he found it very difficult to draft legislation that would permit price fixing by small retailers without also legalizing price fixing by all businesses, including the center firms against whom he was fighting.

The Supreme Court did not stop with the *Dr. Miles* case, but tightened the screws against price fixing still further. In response, Brandeis grew more and more frustrated at the irony that the antitrust movement to which he himself had contributed so much appeared to be hitting the wrong targets. To the secretary of commerce he wrote, "The [Court's] decision plays into the hands of the capitalistic undertaking the chain of stores of the great concern [*sic*] which, like the Standard Oil, can retail an article as well as manufacture [it]." "It seems to me very important," he wrote Senator Robert M. La Follette, "that we, who are endeavoring to maintain the competitive system in business, should do our best to erect barriers against the excesses of competition, and draw very clearly the distinction between those restrictions upon competition which are harmful, and those which serve to preserve competition. . . . We are much in the situation of those who love peace so much that they are ready to fight for it. There must be reasonable restrictions upon competition else we shall see competition destroyed."[67]

In other words, Brandeis saw this new series of decisions, taken by the Court under the Sherman Act, as promoting bigness. He believed the decisions would drive manufacturers of goods that no longer could be "fair traded" into setting up their own outlets—that is, integrating forward into wholesaling or retailing or both. This, he thought, would squeeze out the hosts of small druggists and other storekeepers on whose behalf he habitually spoke. Again in modern terms, he was willing to sacrifice allocative efficiency and consumer welfare to the maximization of the number of "independent" storekeepers. And he would do so under the banner of protecting competition, even though it was precisely competition that he was seeking to stifle.

In this sense Brandeis hated the vertically integrated center firm more than he loved the consumer, who was only too happy to avail himself of the low prices available through chain stores, mail order houses, and department stores. Brandeis valued individualism more highly than price competition, and he sought by legislation to maximize the absolute number of individual shopkeepers under the apparent misconception that in so doing he was maximizing competition. As he said of one consumer product, the Gillette safety razor, which prior to the Supreme Court's decision could be sold at fixed prices: "Now, the fixing of that price has possibly prevented one retail dealer from selling the article a little lower than the other, but the fixing of that price has tended not to suppress but to develop competition, because it has made it possible in the distribution of these goods to go to an expense and to open up another sphere of merchandizing which would have been absolutely impossible without a fixed price. The whole world can be drawn into the field. Every dealer, every small stationer, every small druggist, every small hardware man, can be made a purveyor of that article . . . and you have stimulated, through the fixed price, the little man as against the department store, and as against the large unit which may otherwise monopolize that trade."[68]

There remained the difficult task of drafting legislation that would exempt from the antitrust laws resale price fixing in small stores without also exempting price fixing in what Brandeis called "capitalistic" concerns. In order to prepare the way, he proposed a series of muckraking articles to Norman Hapgood, editor of *Harper's Weekly*: "There probably ought to be three, not very long, articles; the first, 'Competition that Kills'; the second, 'Efficiency and the One-price Article'; the third, in substance, 'How Europe deals with the one-price goods.'" Brandeis coordinated his effort with that of the American Fair Trade League, a pressure group sponsored by small retailers and their many trade associations. The League distributed to opinion leaders thousands of copies of Brandeis's "Competition that Kills," and promoted an excerpted version in twenty national magazines.[69]

The text of the article represented Brandeis at his muckraking best. He brought every symbol and ideological appeal to bear, turned every conceivable argument to his advantage, and invested the whole with his distinctive moral passion. "The prohibition of price-maintenance imposes upon the small and independent producers a serious handicap," he argued. And he predicted that the fateful next step was vertical integration. "Some avenue of escape must be sought by them; and it may be found in combination. ... The process of exterminating the small independent retailer already hard pressed by capitalistic combinations—the mail-order houses, existing chains of stores, and the large department stores—would be greatly accelerated by such a movement. Already the displacement of the small independent businessman by the huge corporation with its myriad of employees, its absentee ownership, and its financier control, presents a grave danger to our democracy." Worst of all, Brandeis argued, the wound was self-inflicted. "It is not even in accord with the natural laws of business. It is largely the result of unwise, man-made, privilege-creating law, which has stimulated existing tendencies to inequality instead of discouraging them. Shall we, under the guise of protecting competition, further foster monopoly by creating immunity for the price-cutters?"[70]

So stirring was Brandeis's rhetoric that it is difficult to keep in mind what he was in fact proposing: that small retailers be exempted from the antitrust laws and permitted, in concert with each other, to fix the prices of consumer goods. He posed the undesirable alternative of low-price chain stores and mail order houses, together with forward integration into marketing on the part of frustrated manufacturers now forbidden by the Supreme Court to fix the retail prices of their products.

Brandeis continued his appeal in testimony before the congressional committee considering the bill he had drafted. These hearings produced some of the closest questioning Brandeis had ever endured, and he had much rougher sledding here than in his usual appearances before other committees, the courts, or the Interstate Commerce Commission. He told the committee that he had written the *Harper's* articles to educate both Congress and the voters. "The moment you allow the cutting of prices you are inviting the great, powerful men to get control of the business," he warned. "Retailers the country over have been finding out that price cutting is one of the causes of dwindling success; and one retail association after another, national, State, and local associations, have gone on record, demanding that this illegitimate competition be put to an end to. . . . Big business is not more efficient than little business. It is a mistake to suppose that the department stores can do business cheaper than the little dealer."[71]

Brandeis insisted that the only reason department stores could undersell their smaller competitors was that they bought in bulk and availed themselves of quantity discounts. This practice, he told the committee, was odious because it gave advantages to bigness per se. Congressman Alben Barkley of Kentucky was not sure he had heard Brandeis correctly, since quantity discounts were as old as business itself. But Brandeis was adamant; he predicted quantity discounts soon would be outlawed, being "fraught with very great evil. The practice of giving quantity discounts menaces the small retail business." Again one sees the heart of Brandeis's concern. He was willing to go to the extreme of outlawing the ancient and universal practice of charging less per unit for large quantities than for small ones, in order that he might maximize the absolute number of retailers. The injury they suffered was ipso facto a legitimate grievance against which there ought to be a law: "It is because they are injured that they demand relief. It is because of their inability to maintain standard prices that they have been injured. . . . My point is that if the practice did not hurt them they would not be here complaining and they would not have endeavored elsewhere [through state laws] to secure this right; they would not have been spending large sums of money throughout the country endeavoring to protect their rights. They are not dreaming or imagining, but they have learned from experience." [72]

As for consumers, Brandeis saw them as "misled by these cut-price leaders to buy other goods for more than they are worth, and they lose time in their search for cut-throat bargains." [73] On the issue of consumerism and high prices, he seemed thoroughly at sea, and again for one reason. His single-minded distaste for bigness forced him into the odd position of defending high profit margins as a means of defending small retailers. This reasoning in turn led him to an attitude toward consumers which bordered on contempt. Consumers naturally preferred low prices to high ones, and they could be counted on to do so forever and in almost all circumstances.

One particular exchange during the hearings highlights this dilemma and shows the uncharacteristically elitist posture into which Brandeis's logic led him:

BRANDEIS: The practice of cutting prices on articles of a known price tends to create the impression among the consumers that they have been getting something that has not been worth what they have been paying for it.

CONGRESSMAN DECKER (D., Mo., who avowed that he had been "raised on a farm"): That is presuming that the people have not much sense.

BRANDEIS: Well, everybody has not as much sense as some people.

CONGRESSMAN DECKER: Some people have more sense than other people think they have. [74]

For Brandeis and other insurgents, it was extremely difficult to be simultaneously anti-bigness and pro-consumer. In the historical experience, the consumer preferred to avail himself of the inexpensive products that center firms—including center chain stores or mail order houses such as Sears and Montgomery Ward— produced or distributed. In Brandeis's battles over price fixing, then, the two warring alliances were between consumers and center firms on the one hand, against peripheral firms trying to use the power of government, on the other. It was this second alliance that Brandeis represented. At its base was an aversion to bigness which in his case was primarily ideological but which in the case of the peripheral firms themselves was rooted in stark self-interest. As Congressman Barkley wearily told Brandeis, explaining once again why the committee was giving him such a hard time, "I am constitutionally and inherently opposed to class legislation and legislation on behalf of special interests."[75]

A price-fixing bill along the lines Brandeis desired finally did become law in 1937, as the Miller-Tydings Act. It prevailed as a national policy for thirty-eight years until it was finally overturned by the Consumer Goods Pricing Act during the severe inflation of 1974–1975.[76]

Regulation and the Brandeisian Tradition

"We are confronted in the twentieth century," Brandeis wrote in 1911, "as we were in the nineteenth century, with an irreconcilable conflict. Our democracy could not endure half free and half slave. The essence of the trust is a combination of the capitalist, by the capitalist, for the capitalist." Like the antislavery abolitionists before him, Brandeis was led by his own fervor to advocate radical solutions. "For their by-products shall you know the trusts," he declared, and he insisted that the only way to eliminate the by-products was to assault the center firms themselves, to tear at them root and branch.[77] He brought to bear, as a great advocate would, every piece of artillery that stood even a remote chance of hitting the target. He denounced center firms for their price cutting, their exploitation of labor, their gulling of investors, and their promotion of conspicuous consumption. He drew on every weapon available, and the weapon of an appeal to human decency was immensely powerful in the hands of a moralist who was simultaneously a peerless advocate. Much as he had drawn in his earlier legal cases on any tool that would contribute to victory, much as he had shifted the argument to any terms that might rout the enemy, so he was driven to include in the Brandeis brief against bigness any and all plausible arguments. Given his task, he had no choice but to argue that big business became big only through unfair methods. Positing bigness to be unnatural, he was compelled to discover illegitimate means of its evolution. And this is what he did.

By one of his fundamental values, he was correct. The center economy *was* inherently threatening to the atomistic common-wealth of Brandeis's imagination. On the other hand, it was not necessarily hostile to the values he saw as damaged by its "by-products." It might have reassured Brandeis to see into the future and to know that a very large number of enterprises (most, in fact) are natural peripherals, with only an infinitesimal chance of becoming big business. It did indeed reassure him in the 1930s to see securities legislation bring a virtual end to frenzied finance and achieve substantial new protection for investors. Brandeis's old age was gladdened too by the New Deal's National Labor Relations Act, which gave explicit federal protection to the right of workers to organize. In rare moments Brandeis was even pleased by the limitations on consumption imposed by the economic depression of the 1930s.

But even as these events occurred and even as the center-peripheral pattern appeared in country after country, they consti-tuted a step-by-step demolition of his brief against bigness, be-cause they demonstrated that it was not bigness that had brought these abuses, and that bigness per se was no barrier to their abolition. In fact, for some of the abuses bigness was a positive advantage. It was far easier for regulators to enforce the Wagner Act and similar legislation against one huge corporation such as General Motors and U.S. Steel than against thousands of small sweatshops. And recent research has confirmed that center firms pay their workers significantly more than do peripheral firms.[78]

Only the mistaken notion that what Brandeis termed "by-products" derived from one root cause made them part of the trust question at all. As Louis Hartz once remarked, "We think of the trust as an economic creation of American history, and we fail to see that it was just as much a psychological creation of the

American Progressive mind." Brandeis, in this sense as in so many others—his moralism, his fixation on the redemptive value of "facts"—may be seen as preeminently a man of his time.[79]

In the last analysis, Brandeis's emphasis on bigness as the essence of the problem doomed to superficiality both his diagnosis and his prescription. It meant that in his own thinking he was led irresistibly away from the organizational issues where the real revolution lay. It meant that he perforce must argue against vertical integration and other innovations that enhanced productive efficiency and consumer welfare. It meant conversely that he must favor cartels and other loose horizontal combinations which protected individual businessmen against absorption into tight mergers but which also—by definition—raised prices and lowered output, thereby diminishing allocative efficiency and consumer welfare. It meant that he must promote retail price fixing as a means of protecting individual wholesalers and retailers, even though consumers again suffered. It meant, finally, that he must become in significant measure not the "People's Lawyer" but the mouthpiece for retail druggists, small shoe manufacturers, and other members of the petite bourgeoisie. These groups, like so many others in American history, were seeking to use the power of government to redress or reverse economic forces that were threatening to render them obsolete. And in Brandeis they found a great advocate.

On each of these crucial points, then, Brandeis's aversion to bigness simply overwhelmed his analytical powers, as great as they were. Whenever he approached a conceptual breakthrough, as in his analysis of failed trusts, he shrank from taking the next step. Such a step would have shown that in order to reach a mature understanding he would have to separate the issue of bigness from the issue of efficiency. This he was never willing to do, and that is one reason why so many of his regulatory solutions made so little sense.

Brandeis himself, however, endures as an American saint, a properly revered symbol of individualism, integrity, self-reliance, and willingness to fight hard for cherished values. In the argument of this essay, he also symbolizes one of the characteristic short-

comings of the American regulatory tradition: a powerful disin-
clination to persist in hard economic analysis that may lead away
from strong ideological preference.

One sees the shortcoming in the subsequent tangles of antitrust
policy in the twentieth century; in the continuing institutional
schizophrenia of agencies such as the Federal Trade Commission;
and in the frequent unwillingness of legislators to act on the
principle that protection is inherently anticompetitive and anti-
consumerist even if it is small business that is being protected.
Insofar as regulation has been protectionist—as it was with "fair
trade" laws and with most of the policies of regulatory bodies
such as the Civil Aeronautics Board, the Federal Maritime Commission, the Interstate Commerce Commission, and a host of state
licensing boards—it has been anticonsumerist. In this sense, economic regulation typically has been not the ally but the enemy of
competition.

Because of the preference for small enterprise shared by so
many Americans, this has been a fact sometimes difficult to grasp,
even for thoughtful and disinterested observers. With three generations of experience with the business system that Brandeis did
not have, numerous American intellectuals still have difficulty
disentangling their personal predispositions from their otherwise
democratic economics. At its worst, this triumph of taste and
prejudice over economic analysis verges on sentimentality and
anti-intellectualism. But for these reasons too, Brandeis's canoni-
zation has been a rich and altogether fitting reflection of American
culture.

The Pluralist State: American Economic Regulation in Comparative Perspective, 1900–1930

MORTON KELLER

Brandeis University

•

... our government is the most successful contrivance the world has ever known for preventing things from being done.

Charles Evans Hughes

It is a truism that the United States more than any other Western country subscribes to the precepts of laissez faire. It is also the case that American economic regulation—including legislation, regulatory agencies, and the activity of the courts—is uniquely active, extensive, and detailed. This is at once the most striking and the most puzzling aspect of the American regulatory system. To understand how and why so paradoxical a situation came to be—to understand the meaning of Chief Justice Hughes's ironic observation—it is necessary first to view the rise of modern American economic regulation in broad historical and comparative perspective.

The Nineteenth Century Background

Although state oversight of economic behavior has been a persistent feature of Western history, regulation has had different purposes in different times and places. Medieval regulation—attempts to enforce a just price or forbid usury—served religious more than

56

economic ends. In the early modern period, government provided protection in return for revenue: mercantilism was an economic policy designed to enrich the state more than to add to the national store of goods and services.[1]

The age of economic liberalism that flourished during the late eighteenth and nineteenth centuries emerged from the same matrix of ideas and interests that gave rise to the age of democratic revolution. The Enlightenment, popular sovereignty, and the free market were closely linked developments. Each served to release a particular form of human energy: intellectual, political, economic. And each came to be characterized by a distinctive form of association: the intelligentsia, the political party, the corporation.

The most revealing expression of nineteenth century liberal economic policy was the response of the state to the business corporation. Everywhere in the West, law and legislation changed the corporate charter from a specific, monopolistic grant of economic power to an entrepreneurial instrument for acquiring capital, limiting risk and liability, and protecting managers.

The antiassociation British Combination Acts of 1799 and 1800 were repealed in 1824, and the Companies Act of 1855–1856 allowed for the creation of limited liability companies through simple registration with the Board of Trade. French corporation policy underwent a similar evolution. The Le Chapelier Law of 1791 prohibiting all associations was aimed both at the Estates system of the *ancien régime* and at any body that might interpose itself between the individual and the Revolutionary state. Gradually it weakened under the pressure of liberal ideas and international economic competition. An 1833 French treatise on commercial societies observed: "The spirit of association, which has given birth to marvels in England, in America and everywhere where it is forcefully fostered, daily takes deeper root in French customs, and promises soon to provide a powerful impulse to our industries." Finally, in 1867, a law much influenced by the 1855 English Companies Act substantially (though by no means completely) freed French companies from the trammels of ministerial and *Conseil d'État* control.[2]

Regulation in Perspective

The United States, unimpeded by a guild, corporatist, or absolutist past, most fully fostered the growth of private business corporations. In a sequence of cases stretching from John Marshall's *Dartmouth College* decision of 1819 to Roger Taney's *Charles River Bridge* decision of 1837, and through progressively more liberal state laws culminating in free incorporation acts, the corporation charter became a powerful, widely accessible instrument for the release of economic energy.[3]

But the precepts of nineteenth century liberalism coexisted with distinctive national traditions of economic policy. Alexis de Tocqueville's discussion of state and corporation in his *Democracy in America* reflected the special French experience of *dirigisme,* of economic development bent to serve the purposes of the state:

> It must be admitted that these collective beings, which are called companies, are stronger and more formidable than a private individual can ever be, and that they have less of the responsibility for their own actions; whence it seems reasonable that they should not be allowed to retain so great an independence of the supreme government as might be conceded to a private individual. . . .
> If once the sovereign had a general right of authorizing associations of all kinds upon certain conditions, he would not be long without claiming the right of superintending and managing them, in order to prevent them from departing from the rules laid down by himself. . . . Governments thus appropriate to themselves and convert to their own purposes the greater part of this new power which manufacturing interests have in our time brought into the world. Manufactures govern us, they govern manufactures.[4]

In light of the American experience during the century and a half since Tocqueville wrote these words, it might seem that he could not have been more mistaken. Certainly he failed to foresee the rise of private business corporations as powers in their own right. An appropriately counterposed conclusion is that of Adolf Berle and Gardiner Means in their *Modern Corporation and Private Property,* written just a century later:

> The rise of the modern corporation has brought a concentration of economic power which can compete on equal terms with the modern state—economic power versus political power, each strong in its own

field. The state seeks in some respects to regulate the corporation, while the corporation, steadily becoming more powerful, makes every attempt to avoid such regulation. Where its own interests are concerned, it even attempts to dominate the state. . . . The law of corporations might well be considered as a potential constitutional law for the new economic state, while business practice is increasingly assuming the aspect of economic statesmanship.[5]

The relationship of state and corporation seemed very different from a twentieth century American than from a nineteenth century French perspective. But in a larger sense, both were addressing themselves to one of the great themes of modern history: the interplay of the political and economic revolutions of the nineteenth and twentieth centuries. The laissez faire liberalism of the nineteenth century was as much a policy of government as the mercantilism that preceded it. At the same time, the interplay of state and economy inevitably reflected the particularities of each nation's past history and present circumstances. This became abundantly clear when the major Western states responded to the rise of large enterprise during the late nineteenth and early twentieth centuries.

Europe Faces Large Enterprise

Nineteenth century liberal economic policy was barely in place when changes in technology, management, capital accumulation, productivity, and consumption began to shape a new economic world. Large, complex business enterprises appeared in all industrial nations (though in differing forms and to varying degrees) during the late nineteenth and early twentieth centuries. And in each country the rise of big business led to a distinctive regulatory response.[6]

Modern French business regulation rested on the early nineteenth century Napoleonic Codes, which were aimed at the restrictive conditions of mercantilism in the *ancien régime*. The Civil Code of 1804 stripped fraudulent or unlawful contracts of their legal force, and defined commercial illegality as acts "contrary to good morals or to public order." The 1810 Commercial Code regulated a variety of business practices, and the Penal Code of the same year imposed penalties on those who "effect or attempt to effect an artificial increase or reduction in the price of a product."

Nevertheless, the distinctive French *dirigiste* tradition continued. Corporate financing during the early nineteenth century was subject to the review of local authorities, the ministries of Commerce and Interior, and the *Conseil d'État*. Railroad development was substantially shaped by government policy. The nineteenth century French courts applied the anticombination articles of the Penal Code with considerable vigor, reflecting the primacy of small, family-sized units in French economic life. Trade associations came under legal restraint when they threatened local market relations, as in an influential 1851 decision against a group of Calais lumber merchants. Ancillary covenants restricting competition for limited periods and areas were allowed, but not when they stretched over too much time or distance.[7]

From the 1880s on, the competitive threat of German cartels loomed larger, and domestic pressures on behalf of business combines grew. An 1884 law legitimated professional societies, labor unions, and trade associations. Phosphate, sugar, and oil cartels (still the exception rather than the rule in the French economy) were given considerable leeway by the courts, in part because they were thought to need more freedom to meet foreign competition. But the *dirigiste* tradition continued to leave its distinctive mark on French economic policy. A review of early twentieth century French regulatory law concluded that it had been haunted by "the ghost" of "the suppression of freedom."[8] Certainly big business in France did not have the place in economic life occupied by its American and German counterparts.

On the face of things, German regulatory law closely resembled that of France. The Prussian Trade Regulation Act of 1811, which limited the power of the guilds and abolished the price-fixing authority of the police, echoed the French antiassociation statute of 1791. The German Civil Code of 1896 hearkened back almost a century to the French Code of 1804 in declaring that "a transaction in violation of good morals is void" and imposing liability on anyone "who designedly injures another in a manner violating good morals." The Statute Against Unfair Competition in the same year was based on several articles of the French Commercial Code.[9]

But just as the French *dirigiste* tradition survived the sea changes of the Revolution and nineteenth century liberalism, so did the distinctive German tradition of corporatism. United States Ambassador Andrew White properly labeled the cartels rising in response to the depression of the 1870s "some new form of guilds."[10] Authorities and courts were notably willing to legitimate cartels and their practices.

The result was a degree of cartelization unmatched elsewhere. The Bavarian *Landesgericht* held in 1888 that "it was not *contra bonos mores* for business men belonging to a branch of industry which is suffering from a depression to get together and enter into agreements regulating the ways and means of operating their industry with a view to promoting recovery. On the contrary such course of action would seem incumbent upon prudent business men." In the leading *Saxon Wood Pulp Cartel* case of 1897, the *Reichsgericht* firmly identified price and production controls with the public good: "When in a branch of industry the price of a product falls too low, and the successful conduct of the industry is endangered or becomes impossible," the result "is detrimental, not merely to individuals, but to society as a whole. . . . [I]t lies . . . in the interest of the whole community that immoderately low prices shall not exist permanently in any industry."[11]

Government fostering of cartels continued to be the norm during the pre–World War I years. Complaints there were: by socialists protesting the dominance of Berlin banks, by agrarian conservatives fearful of industrial-commercial power, by wholesalers and retailers feeling the effects of cartel price and distribution policies. Imperial commissions in 1902–1903 and 1906 looked into the cartel system, but concluded that no regulatory action was necessary. Mainstream public and political opinion accepted the cartels and their social rationale. A 1912 American discussion concluded: "The men who in other countries are sometimes called muckrakers, feel themselves estopped in Germany

from attacks on capital except in the orthodox socialistic way."
And even the socialists often welcomed cartelization as a step in
the direction of a planned economy.[12]

Defeat in 1918, postwar revolution, and economic chaos substantially (if temporarily) weakened the German cartel structure.
Industrialists Fritz Thyssen and Hugo Stinnes sought security
through new vertical combinations after 1918: what the socio-
logist Ernst Troeltsch called the "Americanization" of German
industry. And postwar political pressure induced the German
government for the first time to seek cartel controls in the American
antitrust tradition. A Cartel Court was established in 1923 to
which the government and cartel members (but not competitors
or customers) could bring complaints. The court had the power
to void cartel agreements that "endanger the welfare of the people." This German analogue to the Federal Trade Commission
heard more than 2,000 complaints during the 1920s.

But the relief that it granted rarely went beyond allowing the
aggrieved party to withdraw from the cartel. The court sustained
practices such as cartel boycotts of nonmembers and "loyalty
rebates" to customers who dealt with them alone. And after the
currency stabilization of 1923, traditional cartelization revived.
The Cartel Court did little to slow the process: according to one
estimate, there were 1,500 cartels in 1923 and 2,500 in 1925. No
organized counterforce of competing business interests, no tradition of free market competition influenced the course of German
economic policy during the 1920s.[13]

In its commitment to economic liberalism, nineteenth century
British economic policy was closer to its American than to its
Continental counterparts. And just as the United States would
have to respond to the rise of big business around the turn of the
century, so did it become necessary for British law to respond to
the fact that cartels and their contracts had become an important
part of the nation's economic life.

In two major cases, *Mogul* v. *McGregor* (1889) and *Maxim* v.
Nordenfelt (1894), modern British cartel policy emerged. The
Mogul decision upheld rebates granted by a cartel of steamship

lines to customers who dealt only with them. *Maxim* enforced an ancillary covenant between an arms cartel and the defendant, who had agreed not to sell munitions anywhere for twenty-five years. Close in time to the American Sherman Antitrust Act, these decisions were far removed in spirit from that law and its early court interpretations.[14]

The dictates of an imperial economy and international competition encouraged the judges to take an expansive view of permissible cartel practices. "To limit combinations of capital when used for purposes of competition," said one of them, "would, in the present day, be impossible—would be only another method of attempting to set boundaries to the tides." Indeed, the very structure of English society seemed to foster arrangements of this sort. As a contemporary observer put it, "Combination has been accepted without regulation in England because the entire English social system is a series of closed groups. . . . English society is stratified and cellular."[15]

Yet the legal justification for cartelization rested not on some English counterpart to French *dirigisme* or German corporatism, but on traditional common law precepts of entrepreneurial freedom and sanctity of contract. The *Mogul* judges agreed that it would be invidious to distinguish between a combination of capitalists and a single entrepreneur. While the courts were reluctant to enforce agreements among cartel members if they restrained trade, contracts between cartels and third parties were given legal standing because of the common right of parties to enter freely into contractual agreements. The thrust of the German courts was the mirror image of this: to enforce contracts between cartel participants as *pro bono publico,* but to respond more sympathetically to the complaints of third parties. Thus did differing national traditions lead to varying legal responses to the rise of large-scale enterprise.[16]

British regulatory policy changed in the wake of World War I. The war, said one commentator, "forced upon us the beginnings, at any rate, of the same sort of industrial revolution that the Germans and the Americans have been busily working out for the past thirty years and more." As in Germany, there was an upsurge of interest in the American model of business consolidation—and in what was taken to be the fostering of cooperative business practices by the United States government. The Liberal Party's "yellow book" of 1928, *Britain's Industrial Future,* called for industrial "rationalization" and state control. Conservatives hoped that the Board of Trade might play a role similar to that of Herbert Hoover's Department of Commerce, so that British industry might participate in a worldwide movement for economic "federation, co-operation, and combination." The Finance Acts of 1927 and 1930 made it easier and cheaper to merge firms; and the Companies Act of 1929 made it possible to compel a resistant minority of stockholders to give up their shares.[17]

Other British measures echoed American policy. The 1919 Trust Commission was the first British counterpart to American antitrust activity. The British Railways Act of 1921, which reorganized the nation's lines into four large regional groups but left them under private ownership, closely resembled the American Transportation Act of 1920.

But "Americanization" fared little better in Britain than it did in Germany. The legal standing given to cartels, and strong traditions of family or partnership control, slowed the pace of corporate consolidation. The common law commitment to contractual liberalism, and (far more than in the United States) the readiness of firms to resolve disputes by arbitration rather than litigation, meant that British courts had a far less active regulatory role than their American counterparts. The fifty major British industrial companies figured in only twenty-two reported cases from 1895 to 1935. These conditions produced as distinctive a regulatory ambience as did French *dirigisme* or German corporatism.[18]

American Regulation and Large Enterprise, 1887–1914
The prevailing view of twentieth century American history is that fewer and fewer institutions have come to control more and more of the life of the society. From diversity to uniformity, from individualism to social control, from localism to cosmopolitanism:

these are the regnant paradigms of modern American historical analysis. When applied to the economy, their implication is clear: big business and the administrative/bureaucratic state increasingly dominate the market and the regulatory system.[19]

No one would deny the substantial element of truth in this view. But it needs to be modified in two important respects. The first is that traditional American values—hostility to the active, centralized state, deep commitments to social individualism and economic competition—had a continuing influence on twentieth century regulatory policy. If theirs was a diminishing half-life, the rate of diminution was exceedingly slow.

The second modifying factor has been the growth in the sheer scale—the number, size, variety—of economic interests. Big business has evolved in an economic milieu constantly altered by new technology, consumption patterns, and the like. Similarly, while the instruments of the modern state (legislation, administration, the courts) have been growing in size and strength, so too has been the range of interests with demands to make upon authority.

It is within this context—one in which a diverse, complex, and constantly changing pluralism of economic interests plays a role comparable to French *dirigisme*, German corporatism, and British contractual liberalism—that the American regulatory experience of the early twentieth century may be understood.

Nowhere did large enterprise take root so readily or flourish so luxuriantly as in the turn-of-the-century United States. And in no other country was there so strong a political, legal, and regulatory response. The land of the trust was also the land of antitrust. James Bryce observed in 1905 that the leading issue in American political life "is the one least discussed in Europe: I mean the propriety of restricting industrial or mercantile combinations of capitalists."[20]

What accounts for the scale and character of twentieth century American economic regulation? The explanation of historians of the Left is that the large firms themselves, seeking certainty and order in an economy plagued by the inherent instability of capitalism, took the lead in creating (and controlling) the regulatory system.[21] Certainly there were corporate leaders who saw tempting possibilities of greater rationality—and more control for themselves—in national regulation. But American regulation both in theory and practice had a number of goals, as varied as the interests involved: those of farmers, shippers, middlemen, merchants, and retailers, as well as manufacturers. Regulation emerged from a system of politics, government, and law responsive not only to the principles of consolidation and efficiency but also to the values of competition, the demands of particular interests, and the political pressure of an ever larger consuming public. The sheer scale and complexity of the inputs involved explain why, as a contemporary observer put it, "in the old world [the trusts'] . . . presence seems to cause little troubling of the waters of politics; in the United States, the problem of the Trusts is recognized as one of the greatest problems of the day."[22]

Railroads, the first big business in the United States, were the first objects of federal regulation. The Interstate Commerce Act of 1887 addressed itself more to interests with particular grievances—farmers, merchants, and middlemen hurt by rate discrimination, a few larger railroads seeking an alternative to state regulation—than to broad regulatory policy. Rate discrimination was the only practice specifically condemned by the act. Its mechanism was no less circumscribed: an Interstate Commerce Commission modeled on decades-old state railroad commissions, whose work would be subject to federal court review. Thomas M. Cooley, the judge and treatise writer who was the first chairman of the ICC, conceived of its work as judicial rather than administrative: "The Commissioners realize that they are a new court, . . . and that they are to lay the foundations of a new body of American law."[23]

The scale of conflicting interests nevertheless led the ICC to take on a growing administrative role. During the first decade of its existence the commission handed down rulings on more than 800 rate controversies. And during the early 1900s, new laws—the Elkins Act of 1903, the Hepburn Act of 1906, the Mann-Elkins Act of 1910, the Railroad Act of 1920—substantially extended the ICC's authority over rates, valuation, and other railroad matters.

But the economic and political power of shippers, hostile public opinion, and the rise of the truck and the automobile were more important than ICC policy in determining the fate of the railroads. ICC rate policy before World War I responded more to shipper than to railroad interests. Insofar as this pioneering venture in national regulation had economic consequences, it appears to have furthered the decline of the railroads.[24]

The British railroad regulation experience around the turn of the century was very like the American case. The 1894 Railway and Canal Traffic Act resembled the Interstate Commerce Act in that it was passed to meet shipper dissatisfaction over rates and created an ICC-like Board of Railway Commissioners to oversee rate policy. As was the case with its American counterpart, the British Board bent before the pressure of the shippers, and denied rate increases during the early twentieth century. British railroads, like the American lines, complained of a consequent shortage of capital; a similar debate ensued over further consolidation of the lines; a comparably complex politics of regulation involved railroads, shippers, unions, and the government. In this most American-like of British regulatory situations, the result was very American: regulation became more the catspaw of contending interests than the expression of broad public policy.[25]

The Sherman Antitrust Act, like the Interstate Commerce Act three years before, was directed at a particular abuse: "every contract, combination in the form of trust or otherwise, or conspiracy, in restraint of trade or commerce among the several States, or with foreign nations." The Justice Department was given an investigatory role similar to that of the ICC. Again, ultimate jurisdiction lay in the federal courts.

The Sherman Act took old common law proscriptions against restraint of trade and encased them in federal legislation. Its operative phrases, said the economist Walton Hamilton, were "remnants from a local society which is gone, . . . the ideas which the people of the eighteen-hundred-and-nineties borrowed from a smalltown culture." The Supreme Court in 1905 set down what it took to be the purpose of the act: "Competition, not combination, should be the law of trade. If there is evil in this, it should be accepted as less than that which may result from the unification of interests, and the power such unification gives."[26]

Yet in the near-century since its passage, the Sherman Act as interpreted by the courts and modified by subsequent legislation has remained the cornerstone of American economic regulation. This fact speaks eloquently of the degree to which traditional values continued to shape public policy in the twentieth century United States.

Industrial regulation in the early 1900s dealt primarily with the structure and practices of the large holding companies that became so conspicuous a part of the American economy around the turn of the century. Between 1897 and 1900, 183 of these corporate giants were formed, embracing a seventh of all American manufacturing capacity and capitalized at over $4 billion, more than four times the value of all industrial combinations from 1860 to 1893.[27]

Not surprisingly there was a substantial public—and hence political, governmental, and legal—response to this development. Fear of "the trusts" was fanned by the disclosures of muckraking journalists, by the rhetoric of politicians, and not least by the practices of the companies. Injured interests—often with considerable political power—added to the force of the antitrust movement. Local oil producers, refiners, and distributors kept alive the long fight against Standard Oil; the American Newspaper Publishers Association, concerned over the price of newsprint, did much to spur the government's suit against the International Paper Company. Federal antitrust actions rapidly increased: eighteen suits in equity were initiated and twenty-five indictments secured under Theodore Roosevelt, forty-six suits and forty-three indictments under William Howard Taft.[28]

Historians have made much of the differing approaches of Roosevelt, Taft, and Woodrow Wilson to trust regulation. Roosevelt had a growing skepticism regarding the effectiveness of the Sherman Act. "The successful prosecution of one device to evade the law immediately develops another device to accomplish the same purpose," he observed. He dwelt increasingly on the distinction between "good" and "bad" trusts, preferring, vigorous chief executive that he was, "continuous administrative action" to "necessarily intermittent lawsuits." Taft shared Roosevelt's disbelief in the economic soundness of the antitrust law, and like TR favored federal incorporation of large enterprises. But, as the quintessential lawyer-judge, he saw no alternative to strict enforcement of the Sherman Act by the courts.[29]

Wilson was closely bound to the antimonopoly, small-is-good tradition of the Democratic party. During his tenure as governor of New Jersey he oversaw the passage of strict new state corporation laws, including a provision—soon repealed—outlawing holding companies. Wilson in 1912, thought an observer, was promising to secure "the destruction of monopoly not by regulation, but by the enactment of specific legislation."[30]

But in fact all three men belonged to a Progressive generation of political leadership and public policy. Their shared social, economic, and governmental beliefs were stronger than their political and personal differences. Throughout the Western world during the early twentieth century, there arose a new stress on efficiency, organization, and the active state as means by which to cure the ills and evils of urban-industrial society. At the same time, older American beliefs—in an economy of small, free competitors, in limited government—continued to influence public policy and action. Early twentieth century American regulatory policy reflected both streams of thought.[31]

That policy unfolded not so much through administrative or legislative fiat as through judicial decisions. The Supreme Court's interpretations of the Sherman Act were the most important determinants of government policy. The contrast with Britain was marked. Eleven of the fifty leading American industrial companies faced government-initiated lawsuits in appellate courts during the early 1900s; none of the fifty leading British firms did.[32]

The initial Supreme Court response to the rise of big business was as traditional as that of Congress. It rested heavily on established legal precepts, and favored competition over cartelization. In its first important antitrust case, the E. C. *Knight* sugar trust decision of 1895, the Court held that commerce in the products of manufacturing came under the Sherman Act, but that corporate consolidation and the production process did not. This followed established precedent that placed the internal affairs of corporations under state law, and the flow of goods from state to state under the national commerce power.[33] Indeed, the early applications of the Sherman Act—the *Trans-Missouri, Joint Traffic,* and *Northern Securities* decisions—involved that most literal instrument of interstate commerce, the railroads.

At the same time, in sharp contrast to German and British law, the Court refused to give legal standing to cartel agreements. Although cartels, especially in the iron and steel products industry, continued to appear, their attempts to control prices and production won no legal sanction. The Court's position on cartels was so pronounced that it was a spur to the turn-of-the-century movement to consolidate firms into holding companies.[34]

The persistence of old legal assumptions in the face of new conditions was evident in the *Northern Securities* decision of 1904. Northern Securities was a holding company designed to end the long rivalry between the Hill and Harriman transcontinental railroad interests. Because the parties were so literally engaged in interstate commerce, their arrangement was doomed. It was appropriate, too, that John Marshall Harlan, the most eloquent Court spokesman for individual freedom, wrote the majority decision. *Northern Securities* may be said to have complemented the *E. C. Knight* case a decade before, in that it reaffirmed the federal regulatory interest in commerce as distinct from production and corporate structure.

Oliver Wendell Holmes's *Northern Securities* dissent was far from a modern, efficiency-minded apologia for big business. He argued that the traditional common law definition of restraint of trade applied to contracts between strangers or third parties, not to "an arrangement by which competition is ended through community of interest." The common law of contract, not restraint of trade, was the key issue. And since in this instance the common law rule did not explicitly disavow the contract, it must not be struck down by the Court.[35]

Still, it was evident that the ambiguities of the law allowed the courts to interpret corporate consolidation either as exercises in freedom of contract and survival of the competitive fittest, or as illegal restraints of trade. From the first, they developed their own definitions of *pro bono publico*. Thus the New Jersey court's acceptance of the Trenton Potteries combination in 1899 and the Illinois court's rejection of a distilleries combine in 1895 appear to have been based not so much on the legal nuances of antitrust as on judgments as to the relative social benefits of the more efficient production of toilets in the one case and of hard liquor in the other.[36]

Not surprisingly, a 1910 review of two decades of judicial interpretation of the Sherman Act concluded that "great uncertainty exists as to its meaning and legal effect." If any discernible policy seemed to be emerging, it was that "under a complex civilization the lawfulness of acts often must be made to depend upon complex considerations and cannot be determined by simple rules that can be applied without the exercise of discretion and in a mechanical manner."[37]

The *Standard Oil* and *American Tobacco* decisions of 1911 exemplify the truth of that observation. Not railroads and the flow of commerce but the structures and practices of complex industrial corporations now were at issue. Northern Securities had been a holding company in the making; Standard Oil and American Tobacco were going concerns. The scale and complexity of the regulatory process also had grown: the government's case against Standard Oil rested on twenty-three volumes of evidence totaling 12,000 pages.

Chief Justice Edward D. White's "rule of reason" dictum in *Standard Oil*—that the prevailing "standard of reason" was the proper measure of whether or not restraint of trade had occurred—was a bald-faced alteration of the Sherman Act's original meaning. As one contemporary said, it "justified those who believed that the logic of facts was stronger than the logic either of theories or even of tolerably well-settled law." Appropriately, Harlan was the only dissenter.[38]

In these cases the Court found a clear intent to monopolize, and called for the dissolution of the two companies. But then complex reality intruded. Standard Oil was not to be enjoined from doing business during the dissolution period, "in view of the possible serious injury to result to the public from an absolute cessation of interstate commerce in petroleum and its products by such vast agencies as are embraced in the combination." Breaking up the American Tobacco combine of sixty-five American and two English companies was complicated by the fact that "every concern made brands owned by some other concern, or had made for it by some one of the other companies a brand or brands which it owned." The interests of American Tobacco bondholders, preferred stockholders, and common stockholders often conflicted with one another, and had to be treated separately. The elaborate dissolution plan was worked out in a series of conferences involving American Tobacco officials, company lawyers, federal circuit court judges, and the attorney general and his staff. Efforts were made to assure the new companies the brand names, factories, distribution facilities, and earning power necessary to compete on reasonable terms. But it was recognized that "the business itself offers insuperable obstacles to the creation of perfect competitive conditions under any method of distribution."[39]

Neither decision resulted in the sort of dissolution that antitrust advocates hoped for. Attorney Samuel Untermyer percipiently predicted that the money men would do as well from the process of divestment as they had from the creation of the companies, and that community of interest and gentlemen's agreements would diminish the effect of the breakup. An antitrust expert summed up the episode: "In the extent of the business affected, in the learning displayed in the decisions and in the lack of results obtained, the Standard Oil and American Tobacco cases are fairly representative and fully convincing of the futility of injunction and dissolution suits. . . ."[40]

The increasing complexity of inputs into the regulatory process is evident in the passage of the Federal Trade Commission and Clayton Acts of 1914. The FTC was supposed to provide an "expert machinery" continually monitoring a variety of business practices. The commission was given considerable administrative flexibility. It would not be required to initiate proceedings regardless of circumstances, but only when it judged them to be in the public interest; it was not confined to the judicial process, but could issue "cease and desist" orders; it was empowered to act as a special master in chancery, carrying out the dissolution orders of the courts.[41]

The Federal Trade Commission embodied the belief of the Progressive generation in efficient government by an administrative state. Both parties, the United States Chamber of Commerce, and almost all trade associations approved its creation. Wilson announced that the FTC "has transformed the government of the United States from being an antagonist of business into being a friend of business."[42]

The Clayton Act tried to define more precisely those activities that came within the purview of the Sherman Act and the FTC. Practices endemic to corporate enterprise—price discrimination, exclusive dealing and tying contracts, intercorporate stockholding, interlocking directorates—were singled out as actions fostering restraint of trade. New political interest groups also were recognized: an attempt was made to exempt labor unions and agricultural associations from the antitrust law on the ground that "the labor of a human being is not a commodity or an article of commerce."

The FTC and Clayton Acts have been described as the response of Congress to the Supreme Court's arrogation of regulatory power through its "rule of reason." In fact, both branches of government were engaged in a larger, common effort to adjust the regulatory system to an increasingly complex economy. The Federal Trade Commission Act modernized the procedural component of antitrust, the Clayton Act its substantive component. By establishing the FTC, said one observer, Congress "recognized ... that the trust problem was not a single problem but a large number of problems." Much the same could be said of the Supreme Court's "rule of reason."[43]

By 1914 it was clear that the rise of large enterprise in America went hand in hand with the rise of a complex system of government regulation. But as the experience of the years between World War I and the Great Depression amply demonstrated, a more elaborate regulatory system was not necessarily a more effective one.

American Regulation and Large Enterprise, 1914–1930

Events in the years after 1914 appeared to be fostering a close relationship between big business and the regulatory infrastructure. American participation in World War I further strengthened large enterprise, and exposed a generation of public officials and corporate leaders to the possibilities of large-scale government intervention in the economy. The probusiness stance of the Republican administrations of the 1920s, the growing acceptance of corporate consolidation by the courts, and Herbert Hoover's well-publicized encouragement of business associationalism lend credence to the view of the 1920s as a time when "corporate liberalism" flourished in the land: a paler American version of the contemporary European effort to preserve stability and order.[44]

But more was afoot in the postwar years than maintenance of the status quo. Significant changes in the American economy undermined the surface continuity with the prewar years. The organizational emphasis in big business was shifting from intercompany consolidation to intracompany control: a change chronicled in Berle and Means's *Modern Corporation and Private Property*. Devices such as no-par stock, convertible bonds, and voting trusts fostered the growth of managerial domination.[45]

This was not a uniquely American development. Walter Rathenau observed of German industry: "The depersonalization of ownership, the objectification of enterprise, the detachment of property from the possessor, leads to a point where the enterprise becomes transformed into an institution which resembles the state in character." But as with the earlier rise of big business itself, managerial control seemed to be most advanced in the United States. State-based American corporation law aided this trend, as it had the earlier rise of holding companies. Not until the Securities Act of 1933 did the national government attempt to regulate securities issues.[46]

The Pluralist State

A change even more important in its regulatory consequences was going on in the economy at large. Before 1914 the major economic development—and regulatory response—was in the realm of capital goods industries: railroads, steel, coal, oil. After the war, industries more directly aimed at massive consumer markets—motor vehicles, packaged foodstuffs, appliances, electric utilities—came into prominence. They posed new problems for a regulatory system designed primarily to deal with entry, competition, and control within a given industry. Now that system was called on to deal as well with issues raised by the marketing of goods and services to a mass consumer public. A 1932 survey concluded that "as an increasing part of urban business life is concerned with what are technically 'services', the state [antitrust] laws become inadequate."[47]

But the net effect of these changes for American economic regulation in the 1920s was a splendid demonstration of Mark Twain's dictum that while history does not repeat itself, it rhymes. The old conflicts—between centralism and localism, uniformity and diversity, efficiency and opportunity, dependence on and hostility to the active state—continued to permeate the regulatory system. Varied goals and pluralistic interests still were its most distinctive features. When the Great Depression of the 1930s came, the only viable model of purposeful economic policy making was the emergency mobilization of World War I.

An observer of the Supreme Court's antitrust decisions in the 1920s concluded that judicial policy towards business consolidation "appears now to have become fairly well crystallized." Judicial acceptance of large enterprise almost without regard for the degree of its sectoral control came to be the norm. The *United States Steel* (1920) and *International Harvester* (1927) decisions sustained combines that dominated more than 60 percent of their markets, but whose behavior was judged not to constitute an abuse of power. Justice Joseph McKenna saw no violation of the antitrust law in the United Shoe Machinery Company's control of over 90 percent of shoe machinery production: "The Company, indeed, has magnitude, but it is at once the result and cause of efficiency, and the charge that it has been oppressively used is not sustained." After the passage of the 1920 Transportation Act, even railroads, whose direct involvement in interstate commerce made them especially vulnerable to antitrust action, fared better in the courts. It appeared to be the case, according to one contemporary expert, that "judicial interpretation of the anti-trust laws has had the effect of legalizing almost any degree of concentration of economic power if certain legal formalities are observed."[48]

A similar state of affairs prevailed in the Justice Department's antitrust division. An estimated 1,268 mergers, absorbing about 7,000 firms, occurred between 1919 and 1928; of these, 60 were questioned by the government and only one was blocked. The department's antitrust expenditure fell from over $270,000 in 1914 to only $81,000 in the inflation-ridden year of 1919. William J. Donovan, who headed the antitrust division from 1925 to 1929, concentrated on questionable proposed mergers rather than on misbehaving existent ones.[49] Consent decrees rather than convictions—few before 1917, 112 by 1932—became the favored antitrust device. Where once the test had been "the existence of power," now it was "the abuse of power." As one observer put it, "We are no longer implicated in a conflict of economic orders, but are considering what we shall do with the one we have."[50]

These changed conditions may be seen with special clarity in the experience of the Federal Trade Commission. The FTC (like the ICC before it) had been expected to create a "new common law" through its rulings. But once again, changing economic conditions and the clash of diverse economic and governmental interests dictated otherwise.

The business of the FTC came to be not with corporate ownership and control but with consumer sales activities. Of the 1,318 FTC complaints issued by mid-1925, 59 percent dealt with deceptive trade practices; by the early 1930s, more than 90 percent were of this nature.[51] By then the sad truth was that the primary role of the FTC was "preventing false and misleading advertising in reference to hair-restorers, anti-fat remedies, etc.—a somewhat inglorious end to a noble experiment." (Even this turned out to be too sanguine a statement. The Supreme Court soon held that ads trumpeting the scientific worth of fat-reducing tablets, to which the FTC took exception, were opinion, not fact, and threatened no substantial injury to competitors or consumers.)[52]

The commission's ineffectiveness was part of the general entropy afflicting the pre–World War I regulatory structure in the 1920s. For years the FTC was housed, with appropriate symbolism, in an uncomfortable wartime building. The appointment of the resolutely probusiness William E. Humphrey to the commission in 1925 contributed to its desuetude. It was weakened, too, by endless conflicts among varied economic interests and their political advocates. A commentator in the early 1930s observed, "It is not uncommon for the Commission to be under fire in the Senate for exercising its powers too gingerly and in the House for daring to use them at all."[53]

Judicial decisions also did much to reduce the effectiveness of the FTC as an administrative agency. The Supreme Court was reluctant to accept a broad definition of the commission's powers. Justice James McReynolds in *FTC* v. *Gratz* (1920) held that, in defining unfair methods of competition, "it is for the courts, not the commission, ultimately to determine as a matter of law what they include." Louis D. Brandeis in dissent sought to justify the FTC's power to issue cease-and-desist orders as a "prophylactic" function, aimed not at "the commission of *acts* of unfair competition, but the pursuit of unfair *methods*." But McReynolds's belief that the FTC was "certainly not intended to fetter free and fair competition as commonly understood and practiced by honorable opponents in trade" prevailed. Traditional views both of judicial supremacy and of economic policy thus persisted.[54]

Even Holmes's more permissive judicial outlook could work against the growth of the administrative state. In *FTC* v. *American Tobacco* (1924), he invoked the Fourth Amendment to strike out at a commission investigation of the company: "The mere facts of carrying on a commerce not confined within state lines and being organized as a corporation does not make men's affairs public as those of a railroad company now may be. . . . [T]here still exists," he noted, "a deep legal chasm between the governmental powers in dealing with public utilities and with so-called private business." Not surprisingly, one FTC commissioner concluded that the Court's rulings "completely devitalized" the commission, "reduced it to terms of a futile gesture." Diverse and clashing branches of government, and a complex and dynamic economy, made effective administrative regulation all but impossible in the 1920s.[55]

These conditions had a comparable impact on attempts at business-government corporatism. During the war federal authorities encouraged intraindustry price and production agreements. From 1921 to 1928 Secretary of Commerce Herbert Hoover, pursuing the goal of an "associative state," fostered trade association activity designed to make the productive process more efficient and to lessen destructive competition.[56]

Trade associations flourished in this benign atmosphere. By 1926 there were about a thousand of them, covering the spectrum of goods and services—indeed, of life—from the National Association of Baby Vehicle Manufacturers to the Casket Manufacturers Association of the United States. Their activities included not only traditional sub rosa price and production agreements, but also responses to the demands imposed by a complex, consumer-oriented economy: arbitration and labor relations machinery; traffic bureaus to deal with freight rates; the encouragement of research and development, product standardization, and the interchange of patent rights; education in cost finding; cooperation in advertising to stimulate consumer demand; information on customers' credit standing; and representation before legislative and administrative bodies.[57]

But this new, state-assisted associationalism made heavy way in a polity suffused with older, opposed economic beliefs. A price-fixing Industrial Board of the Department of Commerce, established in the spring of 1919, lasted only a few months before it fell victim to the hostility of other government agencies such as the Railroad Administration, to the political appeal of antitrust, and to the sheer diversity of interests in the American economy. A similar fate befell the efforts of the United States Chamber of

Commerce and the National Association of Manufacturers to "liberalize" the antitrust laws. Hoover's attempts to make the Commerce Department the base of his "associative state" faced the same problems. And even when he was at the height of his power in the mid-twenties, he was hardly a spokesman for cartelization in the European sense. "Probably the most compelling reason for maintaining proper trade associations," he argued, "lies in the fact that through them small business is given facilities more or less equivalent to those which big business can accommodate for itself." His "corporatism" thus was not only compatible with but positively supportive of equality of opportunity, individual initiative, small enterprise, and open competition.[58]

The Supreme Court only marginally modified its traditional hostility to price and production agreements. During the 1920s the Court continued to strike down blatant price fixing by trade associations: in *American Column & Lumber* (1921), in *American Linseed Oil* (1923), in the *Window Glass* case (1923). As the activities of trade associations expanded, and government approval grew, the Court became more permissive; but it stopped far short of accepting cartelization.

Holmes and Brandeis led the way in their *American Column & Lumber* dissents. Holmes argued that the shared information of the trade association's members made for more rational competition ("I should have thought that the ideal of commerce was an intelligent interchange made with full knowledge of the facts as a basis for a forecast of the future on both sides"), and caustically observed that the government's decree was "surprising in a country of free speech that affects to regard education and knowledge as desirable." Brandeis, too, held on Hoover-like grounds that the shared activities of the hardwood industry were designed "to make rational competition possible. . . . May not these hardwood dealers, frustrated in their attempts to rationalize competition, be left to enter the inviting field of consolidation?"[59]

In its *Maple Flooring* and *Cement Manufacturing* decisions of 1925, the Court sanctioned information sharing so long as its contribution to greater efficiency was evident and its price and production-fixing function not too obvious. Harlan Stone's *Maple Flooring* opinion rested on a rationale very like White's "rule of reason" for corporate consolidation a generation before:

> It is the consensus of opinion of economists and of many of the most important agencies of Government that the public interest is served by the gathering and dissemination, in the widest possible manner, of information with respect to the production and distribution, cost and prices in actual sales, of market commodities, because the making available of such information tends to stabilize trade and industry, to produce fairer price levels and to avoid the waste which inevitably attends the unintelligent conduct of economic enterprises.
>
> . . . Competition does not become less free merely because the conduct of commercial operations becomes less intelligent through the factor of free distribution of knowledge of all the essential factors entering into the commercial transaction.

Just as John Harlan's had been a lone dissenting voice in the 1911 *Standard Oil* and *American Tobacco* decisions, so now did James McReynolds, the author of the *Gratz* decision cutting back the FTC, speak in his *Maple Flooring* dissent in the spirit of a simpler regulatory tradition: "Ordinary knowledge of human nature and of the impelling force of greed ought to permit no serious doubt concerning the ultimate outcome of the arrangements. . . . Pious protestations and smug preambles but intensify distrust when men are found busy with schemes to enrich themselves through circumventions."[60]

But in the *Trenton Potteries* case (1927) it emerged that Stone and McReynolds did not profoundly differ in their economic views. Here trade association price fixing was open and overt. Stone, speaking for the Court, refused to accept so manifest a violation of antitrust law: "Whatever difference of opinion there may be among economists as to the social and economic desirability of an unrestrained competitive system, it cannot be doubted that the Sherman Law and judicial decisions interpreting it are based on the assumption that the public interest is best protected from the evils of monopoly and price control by the maintenance of competition." On into the early years of the Depression, the Court continued to strike down such practices as an attempt by movie producers to require exhibitors to accept a standard contract with a compulsory arbitration clause. It would be fair to say that by 1930 the judicial response to trade associations and cartelization had not markedly changed in forty years.[61]

The experience of agricultural marketing associations, like that of industrial trade associations, showed how difficult it was to get the regulatory system to accept cartelization, even when its economic necessity and political appeal were substantial.

After the great agrarian protest movements of the late nineteenth century, the politics and economics of organized agriculture took on a new character. A shift in emphasis occurred from equity to efficiency, from protest to pressure group politics. The rise of agricultural marketing cooperatives was a part of that transformation—and one replete with irony. The cooperative, the mode of economic organization thought to be most representative of the democratic socialist strand in the Populist movement, now became the preferred instrument of agrarian market capitalism. This instrument of agrarian collectivism was turned into the closest approach to large-scale cartelization in the early twentieth century American economy. And it was fostered, to a point, by a regulatory system supposedly dedicated to preserving competition.[62]

Cooperatives, long a part of American agricultural life, took on added importance after 1900, as concentration and consolidation increased in other sectors of the economy. The Nebraska Farmers Cooperative Grain and Livestock Association, established in 1903, secured the state's first cooperative law in 1911. This act allowed existing grain elevators to become cooperatives without running afoul of Nebraska's antitrust statute. Kentucky and Tennessee burley tobacco growers, forced to deal with one major buyer, the American Tobacco Company, sought "to meet Trust methods in buying with Trust methods in selling." The Burley Tobacco Society and the Planters Protective Association worked for a state law allowing cooperative pooling in the sale of tobacco. But the problem of getting 40,000 burley growers to sign contracts, and the difficulty of enforcing them, encouraged a practice already familiar to the area: an epidemic of "night riding," in which recalcitrants were threatened, beaten, and had their barns burned.[63]

A more functional solution to the problem emerged in California. That state's growers faced special difficulties because of the distance to eastern markets and their dependence on a single railroad, the Central Pacific. Crop pooling attempts were frequent during the late nineteenth and early twentieth centuries, but they ran into the same difficulties that afflicted railroad pools in the 1870s: the temptation (fostered in this case by large packers and distributors) for pool members to break their contracts, and the inability of the pool to enforce its contracts in the courts. A 1910 review of these efforts concluded, "Viewed in the most favorable light, the achievements of co-operation in the marketing of California fruit are still largely prospective."[64]

The Clayton Act's apparent exemption of non-stock agricultural associations from the antitrust laws spurred efforts to add legal and legislative force to marketing cooperative contracts. The office of the State Market Director was created in 1915 to help farmers reduce their marketing costs. Harris Weinstock, the first incumbent, was the half brother and business partner of David Lubin, a prominent advocate of increased cooperation among farmers. Weinstock shared this interest, and served on American commissions studying cooperatives and rural credit in Europe. He used the State Market Commission to encourage the formation of marketing coops in the major lines of agricultural produce.[65]

A model statute designed to exempt these cooperatives from the antitrust laws and make their marketing contracts enforceable in the courts was drafted in part by a young attorney, David Sapiro, who was related by marriage to Lubin and Weinstock and was the Market Bureau's legal counsel. He said of the Cooperative Marketing Act: "Under the stress of economic pressure and legal confusion, it seemed best to try to anticipate and settle most of the legal difficulties by statute and to fix the trend of legislation which would in turn fix the trend of court decisions."[66]

Sapiro wanted farmers to benefit from the same emphasis on efficiency, pooled effort, and rationalization that was occurring in industry. For a while he was successful beyond his boldest imaginings. Major California marketing cooperatives—their membership contracts enforced now by the courts—made Sunkist oranges, Sun-Maid raisins, and Diamond walnuts familiar national brand names. And the postwar collapse of farm prices, particularly in cotton, tobacco, and wheat, gave the California law national appeal. By the mid-1920s, more than forty states had adopted variants of the statute. Sapiro grandly announced that "a new national policy has been proclaimed and has been universally followed. . . . The State has become the encourager of cooperation."[67]

In 1921, with Texas cotton prices abysmally low, a major campaign got under way to bring that state's cotton farmers into an agricultural marketing cooperative. In its fervor the effort resembled the Grange, Alliance, and People's Party crusades of the previous century; in its style and substance it was pure Babbitt boosterism. The Texas economic establishment—the Farm Bureau Federation, the State Bankers Association, the Federal Reserve Bank, local chambers of commerce, retail associations, Rotary and Kiwanis, "practically every organized force which could be counted upon to influence the opinions and actions of the farmer"—supported the campaign. Propaganda methods honed in wartime Liberty Loan and Red Cross drives—signs, posters, auto stickers, buttons, barbecues, rallies—were put to use. And as a final touch, Aaron Sapiro was brought in to inspire the farmers:

> At Abilene nearly twenty-five hundred farmers walked nearly a mile through the streets following Sapiro from place to place in their endeavor to find a meeting place large enough to hold the crowd . . . and when they finally decided to try the First Baptist Church, with a seating capacity of 2500, the big crowd broke into a run several blocks before the church was reached, every man anxious to get a seat so that he could hear Sapiro talk. After he got the crowd in the church, Sapiro held them for three hours while he talked cooperative marketing. At times the crowd was so quiet you could hear a whisper; again Sapiro would evoke thunders of applause and wild cheers when he pictured the plight of the farmer and the solution. It was the same all over Texas. Sapiro "delivered the goods."[68]

Regulation in Perspective

By 1925, 300,000 cotton farmers had signed "ironclad" contracts guaranteeing to deliver more than $100 million worth of cotton to their association. Tobacco farmers in Kentucky and other states, encouraged by state marketing laws modeled on the California act, followed suit. Sapiro helped to organize the Tri-State Tobacco Growers Cooperative Marketing Association in 1920–1921, signing up about half the tobacco farmers of Virginia, North Carolina, and South Carolina. "Night riding" gave way to what in effect was a legislatively and legally enforced cartel. It appeared to the economist Walton Hamilton that "'a new and different unit' for the doing of business has been in process of development." Another commentator concluded that "the corporate entity, that useful legal mechanism, has served once more to effect a practical adjustment between the interests of a group and the habits and customs of society."[69]

National legislation and court decisions fostered this development. In 1921 the War Finance Corporation was authorized to make loans to marketing cooperatives. The Agricultural Credit Act of 1923 established federal credit banks empowered to discount or purchase agricultural paper from cooperatives, and make loans or advances. The 1922 Capper-Volstead Act extended the Clayton antitrust exemption to stock as well as non-stock cooperatives. The 1926 Cooperative Marketing Act exempted coops from paying income taxes, and authorized the secretary of agriculture to establish a Bureau of Cooperative Marketing.[70]

The courts held that entry into a marketing cooperative was equivalent to a contractual obligation. And they upheld the legal remedies provided by the state marketing acts for coops to use against errant members or their tempters: liquidated damages (that is, punitive damages for breach of contract), injunctive relief, and the obligation of specific performance. In the *Liberty Warehouse* case (1928) the Supreme Court upheld the constitutionality of the Kentucky marketing act provision making it a crime for third parties to interfere with contracts between a cooperative and its members.[71]

But for all this, severe practical and legal limits kept the marketing cooperatives from becoming true cartels. American farmers were too numerous and individualistic, wholesalers too assertive, marketing outlets too varied for the coops to get secure control of most crops. Many were mismanaged, and failures mounted. By 1926 only 8 percent of the cotton crop was marketed through cooperatives, and Sapiro's Tri-State Tobacco Association had passed into receivership. The economic vulnerability of farmers led legislatures and courts to give legal muscle to the marketing coop. But that same vulnerability prevented them from having more than a minor impact on American agriculture in the 1920s.[72]

Nor were the cooperatives' legal powers unchallenged. The Supreme Court in the *Frost* decision (1929) struck down an Oklahoma law that allowed coops to enter the cotton-ginning business on terms more favorable than those accorded individuals. This weakened the position of the marketing coop as an agency entitled to special classification and thus to favored legal status. More important, no state dared to empower coops to set pricing and production standards, for it was obvious that the courts would not enforce them. In sum, the agricultural marketing cooperatives were so hedged about with limitations as to reinforce the point that the regulatory system of the 1920s was more committed to the competitive-individualistic past than to a corporative future.[73]

Regulatory policy was obliged to respond as well to another major twentieth century innovation in the provision of goods and services: the rise of massive gas and electric, telephone, and public transit utilities. The classic morality play of antitrust was reenacted with the public utility holding companies of the 1920s. Samuel Insull and others pyramided electric utilities as Rockefeller had done with oil refineries a half century before. The House of Morgan sought through the United Corporation, a super-holding company designed to foster "closer relations among the greater utility systems of the East," to repeat its earlier merger successes in railroads and steel. And once again there were strong public and political reactions. Governors Gifford Pinchot of Pennsylvania and Franklin D. Roosevelt of New York found ample ground for (and political benefit in) an assault on the utility combines. After 1929, when these giants staggered under the weight of their indebtedness and their financial and political improprieties, much state and national legislation was passed, culminating in the Public Utility Holding Company Act of 1935.[74]

The public utility corporation was a peculiarly American creation, a quasi-public firm as indigenous as the holding company. As businesses manifestly affected with the public interest, the utilities soon spawned a new regulatory device: the public service commission. The first commissions were established in Wisconsin and New York in 1907, and soon spread to almost every state. The growing scale and importance of the utilities' services vastly expanded the flow of regulatory activity. It was estimated that by 1933, 21 state public service commissions had handed down more than 142,000 decisions on utility matters.[75]

This field of regulation was plagued by diverse interests, rapid change, and ambivalent policy goals. In the prewar years it seemed that the concept of business affected with a public interest—what the leading expert in the field called the public as distinct from the private callings—would be a fruitful basis for regulation. But Chief Justice Taft, speaking for a unanimous Court in the *Wolff Packing* case of 1923, defined business affected with a public interest in terms vague enough to ensure that the Court, not the legislatures, would decide just what the phrase embraced. In ensuing decisions the Supreme Court declined to place theatre ticket agencies, employment agencies, or gas stations within the penumbra of public interest.[76]

New and difficult problems afflicted utilities rates regulation. Railroads were the obvious analogue; but significant differences intruded. The utilities' primary customers were large numbers of consumers with daily, continuous needs, not the more independent and better organized shippers who provided the bulk of the railroads' business. This fostered a new regulatory environment, in which decisions of the public service commissions were at once more abstract—less keyed to the demands of particular interests—and more exposed to broad popular and political pressure.[77]

Utility rate fixing took on added complexity with the steep rise in the price level during World War I. The prevailing doctrine was that public utility rates should allow for a reasonable return, based on the "fair value" of the property. As with the rule of reason in antitrust law, this was a highly subjective standard. Each of the interests involved—state commissions, tax assessors, the utilities, the investment market, consumers and their spokesmen—had its own method of measurement. The major point of conflict was whether "fair value" should be based on the utility's initial cost or its reproduction cost. The rise in prices led utilities to argue for present reproduction cost; consumer spokesmen held out for initial cost; utilities commissions and the courts, swayed by politics and public opinion, by utilities industry pressure, and/or by the dictates of their economic beliefs, sought more or less to mediate between the two extremes.[78]

This complex, esoteric controversy rested on greatly varying valuation and accounting procedures. In the course of hearings on the New York Telephone Company's rates that stretched through the 1920s, estimates of the company's fair value ranged from $367 to $615 million. It is not surprising that one judge observed that estimates within 10 percent of each other automatically raised a suspicion of collusion.[79]

In *Southwestern Bell* (1922) and *Bluefield Water Works* (1923) a majority of the Supreme Court criticized public service commissions for not taking sufficient account of higher wage and equipment costs in their rate setting, and seemed to be opting for reproduction cost as the preferred standard. But Brandeis argued for a more eclectic measure that he called "prudent investment," and in *Georgia Railway and Power* (1923) his approach—temporarily—prevailed. In truth, by 1930 the question of what constituted a utility rate based on "fair return" was no closer to resolution than the question of what constituted a "reasonable" restraint of trade.[80]

The rapid spread of truck and bus transportation generated its own special regulatory problems. As bus and truck companies multiplied in number, a growing body of municipal and state regulations governed the weight, size, and safety of commercial vehicles. These the courts upheld as valid applications of the states' police power.[81]

Regulation in Perspective

At first there was little control of the bus and truck businesses themselves. But soon the customary stimuli of regulation—the demands of users, of competitors (railroads in particular), of those concerned over what unlimited competition might do to the condition of the streets or to the condition of the business—came into play. By the mid-1920s almost every state defined bus and truck firms doing a general business as common carriers requiring certificates of convenience or necessity. The Supreme Court in the *Duke* (1925) and *Frost* (1926) decisions refused to let the states lump contract carriers (serving particular customers rather than the general public) with common carriers. But by the 1930s it was held that both were properly subject to state regulation. Within fifteen years, regulation went from encouraging entry into a new industry to protecting the established structure of the enterprise.[82]

The courts were ambivalent in defining the relationship of motor transportation to interstate commerce. The ICC was singularly ill-equipped to regulate a multitude of small, diffuse truck and bus companies; and the judiciary was disinclined to disturb the dense web of vehicle regulation spun by the states. Yet these new modes of transportation increasingly crossed state lines, raising questions of inter- and intrastate commerce, of federalism and states' rights, as old as the Constitution.

In *Buck* v. *Kuykendall* (1925) the Supreme Court held that the State of Washington could not restrict competition in motor transportation that crossed its borders. Brandeis argued that a state certificate of convenience and necessity "is not regulation with a view to safety or to conservation of the highways, but the prohibition of competition." But later decisions gave greater weight to state regulation. An observer concluded in 1931 that the concept of the common carrier, like that of the public utility, was "now little more than jargon." Once again, the characteristic American regulatory response to rapid economic change was complex and ambiguous.[83]

The new consumer economy impinged most directly on the regulatory system in the areas of resale price maintenance by manufacturers, and the competition of chain with independent retail stores. But here, as elsewhere, recognition of a problem did not necessarily lead to its resolution.

During the nineteenth and early twentieth centuries, the legality of resale price maintenance contracts rarely was in doubt. The validity of one such contract was questioned in the wake of the Sherman Antitrust Act; but a federal circuit court sustained it in 1892, and the government did not bring a challenge again for twenty-three years. In a number of cases involving the right of firms holding patents on new products to make price maintenance part of their licensing contracts—Edison alone faced more than fifty such suits from 1904 to 1911—the courts consistently upheld its legality. It would appear that in this early stage of mass production for consumer markets, the courts played their classic role of fostering economic growth by favoring the manufacturers.[84]

A similar policy prevailed abroad. A leading British case in 1901 held that price maintenance agreements were not in restraint of trade, and hence were enforceable in the courts. Decisions in the 1920s involving mass consumer products such as Dunlop tires and Palmolive soap drew a similar conclusion. French law went further, holding that price cutting was a form of unfair trading. But these views belonged to the same regulatory mind-set that countenanced cartels.[85] America's was a very different regulatory tradition; and it is not surprising that its courts pioneered in questioning resale price maintenance once large-scale consumer marketing was in place.

The first Supreme Court challenge to price maintenance came in *Miles* v. *Park* (1911). The case involved one of the oldest mass consumer industries, patent medicines. Charles Evans Hughes's majority opinion concluded that in this instance resale price maintenance was contrary to public policy, and insofar as it interfered with interstate commerce violated the Sherman Act. Holmes's dissent (as in *Northern Securities* a few years before) rested on his unwillingness to question the validity of a contract when neither statutory law nor judicial precedent weighed against it. He thought that a fair price might be relied on to emerge from "the competition of conflicting desires" or (in another metaphor) "the equilibrium of social desires," and that "the most enlightened judicial policy is to let people manage their own business in their own way." Brandeis, too, favored resale price maintenance, for his own familiar reasons: because it would help small manufacturers to compete against large integrated firms, and protect them from the coercion of large mail order and chain distributors.[86]

The resale price maintenance issue grew in intensity, as manufacturers and retailers competed for profits and consumer goodwill. The American Fair Trade League was organized in 1913 to support price maintenance, the National Trade Association in 1915 to oppose it. Department, chain, and cut-rate stores—growing powers in retailing—were particularly active in resisting resale price maintenance. Jobbers and manufacturers wishing to protect the market value of brand-name products, and lesser retailers and wholesalers suffering from the competition of the large retail outlets, led the fight for it. By 1916, Massachusetts, North Carolina, and South Dakota laws made price maintenance an illegal restraint of trade. About thirty "fair trade" laws enforcing price maintenance came before Congress between 1913 and 1932, though all failed to pass.[87]

This activity was part of a more general shift of public concern from corporate consolidation to the business practices of a consumer economy. And the judiciary responded. Lower federal courts began to find particular resale price maintenance arrangements illegal. True, the traditionalist McReynolds in the *Colgate* case (1919) held that a manufacturer was free to set prices at which his product might be resold if there was no monopolistic intent. But the *Beech-Nut* decision (1922)—Holmes and Brandeis dissenting—upheld the FTC contention that the manufacturer's resale price schedule violated the antitrust laws. This encouraged the FTC to issue complaints against a number of manufacturers and distributors. In the traditional pattern of regulator's thrust and regulated's parry, large producers then developed their own sales networks, in which retailers acted as their agents while the firm held title to the product: a practice upheld in the *General Electric* case of 1926.[88]

This continuing review of resale price maintenance went hand in hand with a regulatory response to the growth of large-scale retailing. Chain stores in particular were an object of concern to local retailers, who could not match their purchasing and competitive power. Between 1929 and 1931 about eighty anti-chain store laws were introduced in state legislatures; six passed (in Georgia, Indiana, Kentucky, Mississippi, North Carolina, and South Carolina). They either imposed a license tax on each unit in a chain above a specified number, or limited outright the number of retail units that could operate under centralized control.[89]

The courts at first were inclined to strike down these laws as violations of the Fourteenth Amendment's equal protection clause. But it was widely feared that the rise of retailing combines threatened the independent merchant. The coming of the Depression heightened this concern. Its continuity with the antitrust sentiment of the turn of the century was evident to one contemporary: "The feeling aroused by the sight of the rapid expropriation of the field of merchandising by the chain store is of the same type, psychologically, as the fear of the growing power of the corporation and the consequent discouragement of individual initiative, so common fifty or seventy-five years ago."[90]

In 1930 the North Carolina Supreme Court reversed a 1929 decision voiding the state's anti-chain store act. Now it accepted a revised law reducing the number of chain stores that would be subject to special taxation, on the ground that this was an appropriate means of raising state revenue. The United States Supreme Court in the *Jackson* case (1931) upheld Indiana's anti-chain store law. But in *Liggett* v. *Lee* (1933) the Court struck down a Florida law outlawing chains with stores in more than one county; this, the Court said, was an unacceptable classification. Brandeis in dissent reviewed the history of American corporations—"the Frankenstein monster which States have created by their corporation laws"—and argued that the decision unduly limited the power of the state to control this portentous economic force. By the time of the Great Depression it was clear that the regulation of chain stores was no more satisfactorily resolved than any other sector of the complex and pluralistic American economy.[91]

Regulation in Perspective

The Depression and After

When the Great Depression came, national economic regulation in the United States was more than forty years old. Over that time it was distinguished by two features: a substantial flow of public debate, legislative action, and judicial and administrative decision making; and a persisting ambiguity in policy goals, the product of American economic and political pluralism.

Did the Great Depression significantly change things? Certainly the hard times of the 1930s led to unprecedented questioning of the economic order. And the New Deal brought legislative and administrative changes on a scale not known before. Yet to a striking degree the old issues, the old uncertainties persisted.

In the realm of antitrust, economic conditions during the early 1930s induced the Supreme Court substantially—if temporarily—to modify its traditional hostility to price and production agreements. In the *Nebbia* case (1932) the Court accepted price fixing in the deeply troubled milk business; in *Appalachian Coals* (1933) it refused to strike down a sales agency for 137 bituminous coal producers.[92]

The New Deal's National Recovery Act of 1933 was the boldest attempt yet to institute government-fostered price and production controls. Four hundred and fifty of the 650 codes prepared under the National Recovery Administration sought to fix price and production, and most were shaped by the largest enterprises: a triumph for big business that, ironically, had been denied it during the Hoover years.

The NRA was more than a spur-of-the-moment response to a national crisis. It drew on the associational ideas of the 1920s, on Depression-born schemes such as General Electric head Gerard Swope's plan for a national network of compulsory trade associations supervised by the FTC, and most of all on the government's World War I economic controls. It was justified on the ground that the Depression, like the War, was a national emergency. The procedure by which industries drew up trade agreements and submitted them to the government for approval was similar to the one provided for in the 1916 Shipping Act.[93]

But for all this, it cannot be said that with NRA a new regulatory era had dawned. The Roosevelt administration denied any intention of superseding the antitrust laws, and the National Recovery Act itself included the proviso that the codes "are not designed to promote monopolies." In short order, a variety of interests similar to those that had stymied previous attempts at economic control—organized labor, small business, advocates of antitrust—rose against this venture in government-sponsored cartelization. And in 1935 the Supreme Court in the *Schechter* case held that the NRA was an improper delegation of legislative powers to the executive and an unconstitutional regulation of intrastate commerce: this last point eerily reminiscent of the argument in the *E. C. Knight* decision of 1895.

It is doubtful whether the NRA would have lasted much longer even without the *Schechter* decision. The scale and complexity of the economy made the codes difficult to enforce; and the divisions within the New Deal among advocates of traditional antitrust, democratic collectivism, and corporative policies were profound and growing. During the mid- and late 1930s there was a recrudescence of antitrust activity by the government—which proved to be no more lasting than the NRA venture into corporatism.[94]

In other ways too the traditional character of American economic regulation remained relatively unaltered by the Depression. Hard times fueled the demands of small retailers for price maintenance and anti-chain store legislation; and the NRA prohibited "predatory price cutting." By 1935, nine states (including New York, Pennsylvania, Illinois, and New Jersey) had copied California's pioneering 1931 "fair trade" law, and fifteen others had imposed some controls on retail pricing. These laws legalized contracts that restrained price cutting and other practices harmful to independent retailers. But old constitutional questions of due process and interference with interstate commerce remained, and when economic recovery began, the courts became less inclined to accept these controls.[95]

An extensive FTC report in 1935 on chain stores and widespread political pressure by retailers induced Congress to pass the Robinson-Patman Act of 1936. This law extended the antitrust provisions of the Clayton Act to chain and other multiple-outlet stores, and empowered the FTC to act against quality discounting, advertising allowances, and other practices that made things difficult for independent retailers. Robinson-Patman sought to prohibit "certain competitive practices because their effectiveness is so great that their continued existence ultimately leads to the negation of competition itself"—precisely the rationale of FTC, Clayton, Sherman, and ICC. And as so often before, administrative implementation and court interpretation of the law came to be thoroughly muddled by the gulf between the policy goal and economic realities, by the sheer complexity and multiplicity of the interests involved.[96]

The historian's proper province is not the present but the past. But he does have the right to utter an occasional "déjà vu."

After some decades of relative quiescence, a large-scale corporate merger movement rose in the 1960s. Since antitrust response follows consolidation challenge as night follows day, there appeared in the late 1970s "a new generation of trustbusters . . . girding for an assault on monopoly far more aggressive than anything attempted by the relaxed antitrust authorities of the Ford and Nixon era." The FTC was reported to be reloading its harquebuses; Naderites ranted and raided; the courts, it was thought, would be sympathetic to the new assault on monopoly. But—the question was, "whether the popular feeling against over-regulation or against big business would prevail."[97]

American regulation today, as over the past century, is determined by the peculiar characteristics of the society: a roiling diversity of interests and authorities; the pressure of economic, technological, and demographic change; the deep national ambivalence towards the private power of corporations and the public power of the state. But this does not necessarily mean that the *ronde* of regulation is without value or meaning. A complex and ever changing economy requires a dense and flexible regulatory system. The antisocial forces that regulation seeks to counter must always be resisted, even if they will always be present. As Justice Holmes once reminded us: "Continuity with the past is only a necessity and not a duty."[98]

Three Facets of Hooverian Associationalism: Lumber, Aviation, and Movies, 1921–1930

ELLIS HAWLEY

University of Iowa

•

I

Writing in 1927 to Edward Eyre Hunt, Herbert Hoover's principal aide and handyman, paper manufacturer Henry S. Dennison deplored both the workings of uncontrolled markets and those of governmental regulation. The public, he conceded, was entitled to industrial efficiency, reasonable prices, and rising standards of living, but the way to secure these was not through the recipes put forth by laissez faire ideologues, archaic antitrusters, or utility-type regulationists. It was through a "scientific regulation" built "from the inside" through structures "controlled by the laws of Scientific Management." And the government needed was not a "political government" operating through antitrust bureaus or regulatory commissions. It was an "economic government" resting on socially responsible economic institutions and processes and operating through enlightened economic councils and authorities.[1]

What Dennison was expressing, although he would not have used the term, was an American variant of the neo-corporatism then appearing in most of the world's advanced industrial societies.[2] Underlying his prescription for meeting public needs was the

95

notion that the disinterested "public man" envisioned in earlier regulationist theory[3] could be found not in a civil service or a political elite but rather in enlightened areas of the private sector, and that, consequently, the essence of good public policy was to fashion a form of regulation that made use of this social resource. For America it was a notion that lost much of its credibility during the 1930s. But in a variety of ways it has continued to influence regulatory policy, and during the years from 1916 to 1934 it was a prime influence, not only on the shape that publicly approved regulation took but on the support that antitrust and utility-type regulationists could muster. It deserves study as a factor shaping a whole era of the nation's regulatory history, one that influenced in particular the histories of those industries that became that era's "national problems." And at a time having striking parallels with this earlier era—a time when concern with market failures is again combined with a turning away from governmental regulation and a search for alternatives that can make use of regulatory resources in the private sector—a fuller knowledge of this historical experience seems especially relevant.[4]

My purpose, then, in what follows is to examine and analyze selected aspects of this earlier search for a corporative as opposed to a governmental form of "regulation." I propose, first of all, to sketch briefly the general nature of this search, noting the context in which it emerged, the forms that it took, and the central role of Herbert Hoover and his associates, especially in the years from 1921 to 1930. Secondly, with this as background, I want to move from generalities to particulars and examine three of the corporative mechanisms created during these years, namely the Central Committee on Lumber Standards and its offshoots and successors as lumber "regulators," the union of Aeronautical Chamber of Commerce and Aeronautics Branch as aviation "regulators," and the Hays Office with its extensions into government as the "regulators" of motion picture production and distribution. Each of these reflects action in an industry whose competitive behavior had made it a "national problem," and each stands as an attempt to realize the sort of regulation envisioned in Dennison's letter. Yet the three also illustrate, I shall argue, differing kinds of industrial situations posing different problems for those who would make use of the private sector's regulatory resources.

II

The immediate roots of what was attempted during the 1920s reach back to the perceptions of a "new associationalism" that became especially prominent in the years from 1910 to 1917. Appearing primarily in the literature that accompanied a massive wave of associational formation, these perceptions drew qualitative distinctions between an older impetus toward organization and the one currently at work. The older impetus, it was argued, had come from the desire to monopolize markets, exploit the unorganized, or protect inefficient and backward industries. It had been a force working against social and economic progress, and it was therefore appropriate that a progressive people should use their government to keep this organizational activity to a minimum. The new organization, on the other hand, came mostly from the progressive and dynamic elements in society, who were seeking better instruments with which to meet modern needs. It could mean greater efficiency, more orderly growth, better social integration, higher degrees of national competitiveness in international markets, more rational rewards for the meritorious—all of the things, in other words, that American intellectual and political leaders were holding up as the ideals for which a progressive people should be striving. Given the change in the nature of organization, so the argument continued, the antitrust system had become outmoded and antiprogressive. It was not only keeping America backward in an organizational sense. It was also forcing the demand for better organization to be met through governmental expansion or through the creation of giant corporate consolidations, both of which involved dangers and evils that could and should be avoided; beyond this, it was weakening America's competitive position in the increasingly important international economy, especially in relation to countries like Germany that did encourage progressive forms of organization.[5]

In this prewar period such perceptions did not lead to an aban-

97

donment of antitrust action, much less to a strong associational network taking over the regulatory function. But public policy did move away from the antitrust ideal. From the Supreme Court came a "rule of reason" narrowing the coverage of the Sherman Act. From Congress came antitrust exemptions and a monetary regulation heavily reliant on enlightened uses of private power. From executive agencies came efforts to build and cooperate with associational partners in the private sector, efforts that succeeded in producing a network of farm bureaus, a variety of resource users' associations, and in 1912 the Chamber of Commerce of the United States.[6] Following the establishment of the Federal Trade Commission in 1914 there was constant pressure to make it a sponsor of associational activities and industrial self-government.[7] Increasingly, as the war approached, the notions of what constituted progressive policy were changing in the direction of organizational promotion rather than suppression.

The second major step toward the policies of the 1920s was, of course, the system used to mobilize national resources for war purposes. For these ends, so it was said and believed, the market system and its regulatory supplements were hopelessly inadequate. The need was for an administrative network with unifying, planning and directive capabilities; in a society lacking well-developed governmental or party bureaucracies this need was met through the creation of a quasi-corporative bureaucracy, part private and part public, yet with its public side substantially distinct from the regular agencies of government. On this public side the characteristic organization was the commodity division, technically a governmental agency but staffed mostly with people who were on temporary leave from positions in the private sector. On the other side the characteristic organization was the industrial authority or war service committee, chosen typically through the industry's associational machinery, yet endowed with allocative and regulatory powers delegated to it by the corresponding commodity division. In this structure such peak associations as the Chamber of Commerce and the American Federation of Labor also assumed governmental duties, primarily as certifiers and coordinators of private governmental units or as representatives of functional blocs in the new war "councils." And moving into another kind of coordinating role, one calling for official generators of the system's information, were a number of technical, scientific, and professional associations.[8]

The system was sometimes referred to as "war socialism." But the more appropriate label was something like "war guildism" or "war corporatism," and out of this organizational experience, both here and abroad, came movements to shift policy-making power from parliamentary institutions and governmental regulators to associational networks and corporative bodies arising out of the private sector. This, so it was said, was the path to a higher and more efficient form of democracy, one that would allow liberal societies to overcome social fragmentation and realize their ideals without undergoing either socialist revolutions or some kind of statist regimentation.[9]

In America this postwar movement produced a variety of designs for regulatory reform, and it was during the debate over these, in 1919 and 1920, that Herbert Hoover first outlined the approach to regulation that he would attempt to implement between 1921 and 1930. Unlike some of the would-be "corporatizers," he insisted that governmental or monopolistic encroachments on economic liberty must be rolled back and held in check. Liberal societies did need firm restraints on the abuse of both public and private power. Yet they also needed, so Hoover insisted, new mechanisms for dealing with social fragmentation, market failures, and economic disorder. And to provide these he envisioned both a new kind of societal "regulation" and a new kind of government. Within society a systematized network of cooperative associations and councils would provide the ordered freedom needed for continued economic and social progress; and government, as Hoover proposed to use it, would function not as a regulator but as an aide in developing and operating these societal mechanisms. It would recognize what the war had demonstrated, namely, that the resources for meeting new regulatory needs were to be found mostly in the private rather than the public sector, and would act accordingly.[10]

It was Hoover and others with similar views, moreover, who

moved into the policy vacuums opened by Warren Harding's willingness to recruit and defer to the nation's "best minds." Of this a number of congressmen were critical, sensing that in effect it meant the generation of public standards by corporative rather than parliamentary institutions. But this criticism was insufficient to prevent a partial replication of what had happened in 1917 and 1918. While there was no war, there were new economic and social difficulties that the market system and its regulatory supplements seemed incapable of resolving. And while there was no grant of emergency power to the president, there were expandable agency charters under which the "best minds" from the private sector could reestablish the parallel structures of the war period, defend them as instruments of a more efficient democracy, and use them to promote a societal regulation allegedly superior to any that could emerge from legislative debate or governmental bureaucracies. This happened especially under Hoover's charter to promote commerce. But there were also operations of a similar sort under charters to promote agriculture, mining, and better resource usage, and by mid-decade there was a new set of federal trade commissioners intent less upon policing trade than upon building a new form of "self-regulation." If the decade was one of meager federal budgets, it was not one of inactive federal administrators or of a return to laissez faire assumptions. Coming into existence, as the means through which national goals were now to be attained, was a new network of nongovernmental or quasi-governmental mechanisms that were supposed to perform regulatory functions.[11]

In part the proclaimed goals were macroeconomic. From the workings of the structure, in theory anyway, would come a "cooperative competition," a more enlightened monetary management, and a new set of counter-cyclical spending mechanisms, all serving to improve the performance of the economy as a whole.[12] But also involved was the notion of industrial "problems" or "market failures" that could not be dealt with through action at the macroeconomic level. The remedy for these was a set of industry-specific "regulators," and public policy, as it developed under the administrative charters of the period, did make a place for such "regulators" and extend something approaching official recognition to a number of them. In this sense, if not in the sense of a national plan, there was an "industrial policy."

Within this category of problem industries the most prominent, or at least the most studied, were those caught between receding demands and productive capacities resistant to downward adjustments. In the terminology of the time, these were the "sick" industries, and much effort was spent in trying to devise organizational machinery to facilitate the needed adjustments.[13] Such industries, however, did not exhaust the "problem" category; nor were all those that remained in it perceived as inherently monopolistic. Included as well were industrial situations where the chief problems were resource depletion, underdevelopment, or the production of socially harmful goods, all situations that in other times and places might have led to governmental regulation or operation. For these, too, there was to be a new kind of societal regulation, making use of the superior regulatory resources that had allegedly developed in the private sector; and it is upon three bits of the resulting experience, bits that constitute parts of a larger regulatory pattern yet also illuminate differing manifestations of it, that I want now to concentrate.

III

Prior to 1921 Herbert Hoover had not concerned himself with the malfunctioning of America's lumber industry, and as secretary of commerce he might have limited this concern to a few export aids and technical services. This was not in keeping, however, with his image of himself as the nation's trouble shooter and organizational engineer, and within months of taking office he had been drawn into a controversy that had its roots in the prewar concern with resource depletion and the high costs of basic raw materials. Lumber, so a variety of people had then argued and were now continuing to argue, was an industry in which unregulated competition could not secure what its defenders claimed that it could. In theory it should have produced an efficient and technically progressive plant making available a renewable resource at constantly decreasing costs. But what had emerged instead, constituting clear evidence of market failure, was an immensely wasteful plant resistant to technological advance and operated in ways that must eventually mean lower rather than higher living standards.[14]

With these perceptions of the industry Hoover found himself in substantial agreement. Too many lumbermen, as he came to see it, were engaged in forest wrecking rather than forestry, and in almost all phases of the industry enormous wastes were keeping productivity low, returns meager, and prices higher than they should be. The public was not getting efficient and responsible management of a basic resource, nor was it getting the cheaper building materials that could help to improve housing conditions and allow more Americans to become homeowners. Yet the poor performance of the industry, in Hoover's eyes, could not be corrected through regulatory legislation or some form of governmental production. The answer, so he was arguing by 1922, was to foster internal mechanisms capable of redirecting the quest for profits into socially constructive channels. What was needed, in particular, was organizational machinery that could break the traditional barriers to technological advance and reduce the kinds of social support that permitted those engaged in destructive forms of profit seeking to remain in business.[15]

In believing that such mechanisms could be developed in the lumber industry, Hoover was engaging in a considerable act of faith. The industry, after all, was a highly fragmented one, made up of thousands of enterprises, torn by regional and product rivalries, and fiercely resistant to the designs of production engineers and scientific rationalizers.[16] Historically, such organization as had appeared at the industry level had been concerned primarily with protecting existing forms of production and profit making rather than with enhancing productivity, and among those engaged in the lumber trade ethical standards had been notoriously low.[17] Yet here, as elsewhere, the war experience was supposed to have left an expanding nucleus of "industrial statesmanship" out of which the new societal regulation could now emerge. From it, in theory anyway, had come a more "public-spirited" and technically progressive leadership, a new capacity for enlightened forms of associational action, and new perceptions of an industrial future that could be both profitable and socially constructive. And all of this, taken in conjunction with changes in public attitudes, had allegedly created institutional or organizational gaps that could be filled with the mechanisms that Hoover had in mind.[18]

It was to create this "internal machinery," then, that Hoover moved into the ongoing debate, aligning himself, in particular, with men who had administered the wartime system and who had been trying, since the end of the war, to reestablish a public-private partnership in which the National Lumber Manufacturers Association and its constituent groups would play a central role. This had been one objective of an American Lumber Congress in 1919, the idea at that time being an associational partnership with sympathetic administrators in the Forest Service. Interest had then turned to the establishment of such a relationship with Hoover's Commerce Department; and following a series of exploratory conversations, particularly between Hoover and Michigan lumberman John W. Blodgett, the secretary had asserted his jurisdiction over the lumber problem and called an organizational conference. Raising productivity in the manufacture and distribution of lumber, so Hoover told Secretary of Agriculture Henry C. Wallace, should be undertaken by the Bureau of Standards rather than the Forest Service; and while Wallace disagreed, the result was a Hoover conference rather than one at Agriculture.[19]

Convened in Washington on May 22, 1922, Hoover's first lumber conference produced a plan for a quasi-public agency, made up of functional representatives from the private sector yet having access to Commerce Department facilities and theoretically engaged in providing a superior substitute for public regulation. Bureaucracy, so Hoover told the conferees, was often incompetent, grabbing, and inefficient. But through public-private cooperation it was possible to develop "internal machinery" that could correct industrial malfunctions. In lumber such "machinery" could establish grades, standards, and guarantees, which, once established, could alter the pattern of demand in ways that would encourage a less wasteful production and a more scientific forestry. It could, in short, meet public needs while rendering governmental policing unnecessary, and it was to this dual task that the new Central Committee on Lumber Standards was officially committed. Worked out in more detail at a subsequent conference in Chicago, it consisted of John W. Blodgett, filling, so it seemed, the dual role of "industry leader" and "public man," plus functional representatives from the manufacturers, whole-salers, retailers, architects, railroads, and wood users.[20]

In operation the CCLS tended to think of itself as an indicative planner, generating, through committee action and consultation with advisory bodies, a design for standardization that would then be implemented through the actions of its constituent associations. It also hoped to establish a private inspection service to ensure that standards agreed to were being observed. But initially the gap between aspiration and achievement remained large. The hardwood manufacturers, in particular, refused to abandon the standards of their association for those to be set by the CCLS. They were joined by other groups in opposing a central inspection service. And when subjected to pressure, primarily through critical statements issued by Hoover aide William Durgin, they reacted with countercharges—"rotten" countercharges, as Hoover saw them—alleging misrepresentation, bureaucratic arrogance and intrusion, and gross misuse of the term "scientific."[21] Not until December of 1923, at another lumber conference in Washington, was a design for standard sizes, terms, and grades adopted; and this came only after decisions to leave hardwoods outside the system, lodge inspection responsibilities at the association level, and establish both a standard and an extra-standard thickness for one-inch lumber.[22]

Still, as the industry entered 1924, Hoover remained highly optimistic about the potentialities of its new "internal machinery." At last, so he told William Durgin, the "stupendous problem of standardization" was being tackled in a constructive fashion; and this, when taken in conjunction with improved statistical exchanges, better export promotion, and informed study of building needs, was pointing the way to a new era in organizational development, a time when regulation would become internal yet would be directed for the "combined interest of the manufacturer, [the] distributor, and the public." If it could be done in an industry "so complex and difficult" as lumber, then this very fact would open the way for its adoption in dealing with other industries that had become "national problems." [23]

Far from being discouraged, then, Hoover now moved to supplement the design for standardization with one prescribing fuller utilization of wood products, not only to make them go further but also to bring existing wastes into productive use and thus allow both a cheapening of building materials and an expansion of timber growing. Action along these lines had been under discussion since early 1923. It had been explored both by a Wood Waste Committee, composed of Hoover aides and trade association officials, and through industrial surveys jointly financed by the CCLS and the Commerce Department. The surveyors had thought it eminently feasible, and it was with these perceptions in mind that Hoover and his lieutenants accepted invitations to attend and address a forest products conference scheduled to meet under the auspices of the Department of Agriculture on November 19, 1924. In calling it, Secretary Wallace had combined a justification for Forest Service action with a plea for interdepartmental cooperation, and in a subsequent letter Chief Forester William B. Greeley had reemphasized the importance of working together to realize common aims. [24]

By the time the conference met, Wallace was dead, [25] and by the time it had adjourned it was clear that wood utilization work, like lumber standardization, would be in Hoover's province rather than that of the Forest Service. Following addresses by Coolidge, Hoover, Greeley, Blodgett, and others, the conferees agreed that governmental aids for private forestry, recently expanded under the Clark-McNary Act, must be coupled with an organized effort to reduce wastage of the forest cut. It was only by working from "both ends" that the ominous gap between consumption of forest products and their renewal could be narrowed and eventually closed. [26] But having agreed on this, the conference then decided that the machinery needed was not an extension of the Forest Service, but rather an expanded version of the CCLS. In the organizational design finally approved, this expanded CCLS, to be renamed the Central Committee on Utilization of Forest Products, was to become not only a standardizer and waste eliminator but the central coordinating agency for all lumber and forestry programs involving public-private cooperation. To the apparent dismay of those who had initially convened the conference, it had become the means for moving new pieces of bureaucratic territory into Hoover's expanding empire.[27]

In the days that followed, to be sure, both Hoover and Blodgett backed away from the conference recommendations. The CCLS, they decided, should not attempt to become a "superorganization." Nor should it get involved in such areas as reforestation, fire prevention, forest insects, timber surveys, or forest laboratories. But in "clearing up the situation," Hoover did secure a presidential letter specifying that all organizations concerned with wood utilization or with the manufacture, transportation, and distribution of lumber should be under the jurisdiction of the Commerce Department. This, as he saw it, cleared the way for constructive action, and the result, by May of 1925, was the formation of a National Committee on Wood Utilization (NCWU) designed to work in tandem with the Central Committee on Lumber Standards.[28]

Brought together again were functional representatives from the private sector, who, in theory, could generate designs for improved utilization and secure their implementation through associational action. Representatives of the paper makers, mining engineers, commercial buyers, contractors, and agricultural users served on the committee, as well as representatives of the groups previously involved in the CCLS.[29] In addition, the committee and its secretariat included several individuals who also held public office. Partly, it seems, because Hoover could not find another Blodgett to serve as both "industrial leader" and "public man," he decided to make himself chairman and William Greeley vice-chairman, to install Edward Eyre Hunt as committee secretary, and to designate the chief of his lumber division, Axel Oxholm, as committee director. As finally constituted, the NCWU reflected both a "corporatization" of the policy-making process and a virtual disappearance of the line between public and private administration. Commingled in its operations were both public and private monies, public and private officials, and public and private facilities.[30]

In its efforts to alter industrial and consumer practice, the NCWU undertook a variety of surveys, issued a series of bulletins, and spun off ancillary organizations concerned with specific lines of action. It concentrated, in particular, on reducing the wastage involved in logging, seasoning, milling, and handling operations; on reducing the raw material needs of the paper and wood chemical industries; and on promoting increased usage and hence a larger demand for sawdust, underutilized woods, and short-length lumber. In addition, it studied and urged changes in carpentry practice, wood preservation techniques, container usage, and waste disposal.[31] But in all of these areas it encountered considerable resistance, and the changes actually taking place seem to have been considerably less than those for which the agency and its sponsors had hoped. In any event, this was the view of critics in the forestry profession, the conservation societies, and dissident economic and political circles. While acknowledging some changes, they noted the general persistence of a shrinking timber stand, destructive logging practices, wasteful production and usage methods, and hidden but high social costs.[32]

Some critics also insisted that it was paradoxical to advocate the conservation of forest products while at the same time seeking to create larger markets for them. Real conservation, so it was said, should have a place for nonuse and nonexport as well as more efficient use, and from those seeking to take advantage of these sentiments came such advertising slogans as "Use Brick and Save the Forest." To Hoover, Oxholm, and Greeley, however, this alleged paradox was not a real one. The national interest, they argued, was best served by encouraging timber growing and reforestation rather than hoarding the timber on hand, and the basic prerequisite for this was an adequate, stable, and properly developed market. In their minds the people most likely to bring on a timber "famine" were not the marketers and users of timber but rather those who would undercut the needed market with substitutes, imports, and constraints.[33]

Such criticism, moreover, did not shake Hoover's faith in the kind of "internal machinery" that he had been able to establish in the lumber industry. For him it was "Exhibit A of government by co-operation," and as such was to be kept "at the head of all other industries in the hope that some of them will come into the path of righteousness that are not now in." There would, so he was predicting by the late 1920s, be no more serious proposals for setting up regulatory commissions and subjecting the industry to the control of statist bureaucracies.[34]

Hoover, of course, was wrong. Whatever the accomplishments of his "machinery" in the 1920s, it could not prevent an industry subjected to severe depression conditions from reverting to the behavior that had initially made it a "national problem." As in other natural resource industries, the struggle for survival meant increased wastage and heightened social costs. While Hoover reacted with the creation of a National Timber Conservation Board, another quasi-corporative body intended to check and reverse these developments,[35] the eventual result would be a general discrediting of the "Hoover idea" and the emergence of attitudes that would open the way to the market controls of the NRA period and, following their failure, to new stabilizing roles for the Forest Service.[36] For a time the idea of moving beyond "monopolistic" and "statist" solutions to a system-conscious "internalism" and "government by cooperation" had seemed promising if problematic. But the failure of Hooverism at the macroeconomic level would prevent the realization of what promise there was.

IV

As an industry, air transportation in the 1920s was markedly different from lumbering. It was an infant industry offering a new service, not a mature one providing a basic raw material, and it had become a "national problem" not because of resource depletion and wastage but because of its "underdevelopment" when measured against perceived national needs and potentialities.[37] America, so the argument ran, was in urgent need of a service essential to economic progress and national defense. It was also potentially capable of supporting this service through private market transactions; the gap between potentiality and actuality, a gap held open by barriers that existing market forces seemed unable to overcome, constituted the problem to be resolved through regulatory intervention.[38] In essence, the perceived market failure was of the kind causing stunted growth in essential infrastructure rather than potential resource famines.

Such differences also made for marked dissimilarities in the detailed concerns of aviation and lumber policy during the 1920s. The kinds of standardization, waste elimination, and economic direction envisioned for lumber were different from those envisioned for aviation, and the technical and political problems encountered were not the same. Yet the two stories, dissimilar as they were in detail, are best seen not as discrete responses to unrelated problems but as variations on a common theme. Both were manifestations of the period's willingness to credit the theorists of a new societal regulation, allegedly more effective, more scientific, and more American than controls imposed through governmental action. Both were parts of a more general effort to transfer the generation of public standards from parliamentary to techno-corporative processes. Both reflected the period's discovery of market irrationalities and technical backwardness as major causes of industrial malfunctioning. And at the core of both, acting as prime movers in making things happen, were similar alliances of industrial and Hooverian "statesmen" working together on mechanisms that would allegedly achieve the ends set forth in federal administrative charters. Perhaps the chief difference in this respect was in aviation's emphasis on broadening existing charters and creating a new body of administrative law.

As with the lumber industry, the aviation story had its origins in the immediate postwar period. Aircraft manufacturers, anxious to find a substitute for military markets, believed that a federal administrative apparatus, modeled on the war system, could help them to develop one. The initial idea, as set forth in the report of an American Aviation Mission in 1919, was to create a new aeronautics department under which the wartime machinery could be reassembled. But this had proved politically unfeasible, and by 1921 the Manufacturers Aircraft Association was urging that a new bureau of civil aviation be established in the Commerce Department. Bills for this, introduced in Congress, had been endorsed by the Aero Club of America and the quasi-public National Advisory Committee on Aeronautics. In the press a campaign was underway stressing the benefits that could flow from navigational aids and safety regulations. With them, so it was being argued, air transportation could become an important "medium of commerce" enhancing both economic development and national security. Without them it would remain stunted and retarded, held back by high accident rates, irresponsible adventurism, and public misperceptions of its potential.[39]

As with lumber, too, Hoover had remained essentially uninvolved prior to his becoming secretary of commerce. A bureau of civil aviation was not something that he had seen as a major national priority, and partly perhaps because the aircraft manufacturers were being investigated for wartime profiteering he continued through the early months of his tenure to keep his distance from them. When asked to call a conference, he suggested that they take their problems directly to Congress.[40] By July of 1921, however, the connection that the manufacturers were seeking had been established. Hoover had proved receptive to the arguments of industry spokesmen, especially those of Lester D. Gardner, publisher of the *Aviation and Aircraft Journal*. He had seemingly been persuaded that at least some of the aircraft manufacturers and the engineering leaders affiliated with them were public-spirited individuals, who would respond to his leadership and help to resolve what an interdepartmental committee and a subsequent presidential message had identified as a "national problem." And the result, on July 18, was a conference to discuss legislative, administrative, and organizational action. Represented were not only the manufacturers but the insurance underwriters, the engineers, and the Aero Club of America—the latter, so it seems, as a proxy for the nation's air-minded public.[41]

In the wake of the conference three lines of action were apparent. One consisted of surveys and data gathering, done mostly by the manufacturers' association but with some aid from the Commerce Department. The second was the organization of an Aeronautical Chamber of Commerce, bringing in other groups besides the manufacturers and claiming therefore to be a fit representative of the "new associationalism" and a suitable instrument for implementing the "Hoover idea."[42] The third was intensive legislative lobbying, which did produce passage of an administrative charter, the Wadsworth bill, in the Senate, but failed to get action in the House of Representatives. There Congressman Samuel Winslow, chairman of the House Commerce Committee, had to be enlisted as a sponsor; and Winslow was not only unsure about a bureau in the Commerce Department but unwilling to ignore the viewpoints of states' righters, defenders of congressional prerogatives, and legal experts in aviation law. Eventually a bill did emerge from consultations between these groups and Hoover's representatives. But it was slow to do so, was not ready for congressional action in 1922, and was less than satisfactory to Hoover's industrial allies.[43]

In 1923 and 1924 legislation also failed to pass. Constantly revised, Winslow's bill became increasingly detailed and increasingly unsatisfactory to those seeking a charter to be implemented by administrators. Technically, it still had Hoover's support. But he seemed to agree with criticisms of its complexity and rigidity. While he continued to make a case for legislative action, arguing that the best system was one that combined the practicality and progressiveness of private initiative with a foundation of constructive regulatory law, he was now putting more emphasis on things that could be done without legislation. Close linkages were established between industrial committees and departmental bureaus, and the result was joint preparation and promulgation of an aeronautical safety code, joint development of standardization agreements, and joint action to demonstrate and publicize the usefulness of air transportation.[44]

In 1925 the only legislation to pass was the Kelly Air Mail Act, authorizing the Post Office to contract with private carriers for airmail delivery. By the end of the year, however, a series of developments had opened the way for the kind of legislation initially envisioned at the 1921 conference. One was the decision of Henry Ford to enter the airline business and bid for an airmail contract, a decision that helped to bring other investors into the field. A second was the highly publicized formation of the National Air Transport Company, with Howard Coffin as president, former postal official Paul Henderson as general manager, and movie "czar" Will Hays as chairman of its public relations committee. A third was a new and larger survey, jointly conducted by the Commerce Department and the American Engineering Council, and finding, as one might have predicted, that the potential for commercial aviation in the United States was greater than anywhere else in the world.[45] And finally, there were General William Mitchell's charges of incompetence and negligence in developing aviation for defense. To investigate these and review national aviation policy, Coolidge appointed a President's Aircraft Board with Dwight Morrow as chairman, Howard Coffin as a leading member, and Herbert Hoover as stage manager and star witness.[46]

By late 1925 it had become clear that the Winslow bill would be shoved aside and its place taken by a more discretionary measure under which regulatory law could emerge from "experience" and from "sincere cooperation" between the public and private sectors. This, so Hoover assured Iowa lawyer Clarence Young, was the intent of the bill being prepared by the Aircraft Board's two congressional members, Senator Hiram Bingham of Connecticut and Congressman James S. Parker of New York.[47] Once completed, with substantial assistance from Commerce Department solicitor Stephen Davis, this bill did move through Congress with relative ease. In May of 1926 it became the Air Commerce Act, creating a new assistant secretary of commerce for aeronautics and authorizing the Commerce Department to promote air commerce, provide aids and facilities for air navigation, establish traffic and safety rules, and license aircraft and airmen.[48]

Under the new charter, hailed in some quarters as the Bill of Rights of the aviation industry, Hoover now proceeded to develop a public-private apparatus resembling the "regulators" that he had helped to create for other problem industries. On the public side this consisted of an aeronautics branch, pulling together all air work whether done by the regular bureaus or specially created divisions.[49] On the private side it consisted of industrial committees and the offices and agencies of the Aeronautical Chamber of Commerce. Linking the two were collaborative committees and a kind of revolving door through which officials passed from the private sector to public work and then back to private positions again. William P. MacCracken, the man finally selected to head the new system, had been a governor of the National Aeronautic Association, a participant in drafting the aviation bills, and legal counsel for the National Air Transport Company. In 1929 he would return to the private sector as a lawyer and lobbyist for the major airlines.[50]

Public policy, moreover, as embodied in rules and allocative decisions, was intended to emerge not from adversary proceedings and judicial-like decrees but from consensus-building conferences and consultations. The major body of air regulations, for example, as promulgated in late 1926, was the work not only of a private law-making apparatus on loan to the government but also of a series of consensus-building conferences, bringing together interested government agencies, aircraft and engine manufacturers, aircraft operators, insurance companies, editors of aircraft publications, and the leaders of the Aeronautical Chamber of Commerce. In all, some eight conferences were convened, and what emerged was law that the leadership of the industry wanted and would use its power and influence to help enforce.[51] In theory, of course, it was law that would help to achieve national goals as well.

In addition to a new body of law, the apparatus also produced a new structure of improved airways, licensed planes and pilots, and local commitments to building and developing airports. By 1928 it had licensed over 2,000 planes and 3,000 pilots, designated and improved 7,500 miles of national airways, helped to open a good portion of the nation's 207 municipal airports, and eliminated, as MacCracken put it, the "competition from patched-up war surplus." In Hoover's mind it had become a "great economic and human agency," attuned to American ideals and conditions and acting to implement a "distinctly American plan" under which constructive cooperation was building a better service than the Europeans had developed with their statism and direct subsidies.[52]

What the apparatus did not produce, however, was clear foresight concerning market conditions. Great expectations brought an investment boom in 1927 and 1928. But in 1929 it became clear that the expected demand for air transportation services was not materializing, and under the impact of the stock market crash the aviation boom turned into an industrial "bust." The mission of the apparatus now became a salvage rather than a developmental one. The industry had to be saved, it was argued, if public investments in its support system were not to be lost.[53] And Congress did respond with the Watres Act of 1930, authorizing the postmaster general to use the airmail contracts as an instrument of industrial rationalization. These could now be awarded or extended on the basis of public interest rather than competitive bidding, and the result was the so-called spoils conferences of 1930, in which administration and industry representatives decided which airlines were to be saved and what routes they were to have. In theory "public men" on both sides of the apparatus were still acting to advance the public interest, and the very persistence of the design adopted suggests that it did have a degree of economic rationality.[54] But with the discrediting of the "Hoover idea," the design would be subjected to a long period of political attack. It would have to weather the cancellation of the contracts, the reopening of the routes to competitive bidding, and a series of hostile congressional investigations before something approaching it would again achieve legitimacy under the Civil Aeronautics Act of 1938.[55]

In aviation, then, the apparatus that Hoover helped to create between 1921 and 1930 proved more enduring than the mechanisms through which he tackled the lumber problem. It was, in the end, less vulnerable to political attack, chiefly perhaps because of the differing structure and function of the industry. But as with lumber, the apparatus rested on an ideological foundation that would subsequently lose much of its credibility, partly because of flawed assumptions but also because of the failure of the design at the macroeconomic level.

V

Still another of the decade's new industrial "regulators," differing from yet also bearing marked resemblances to the "regulators" for lumber and aviation, was the Hays Office, established in 1922 by the Motion Picture Producers and Distributors of America (MPPDA). Technically an executive agency for a trade association, the office actually functioned as a quasi-governmental body, both in the sense that it became America's central mechanism for dealing with a public policy problem and in the sense that some of its branches were also federal administrative units. Unlike the offices of most trade associations, moreover, the organization had machinery that was supposed to integrate functional groupings into a harmonious whole and make it capable of acting in the broader social interest.[56] Its appearance and operation was another reflection of the kind of neocorporatism being hailed during the period as America's answer to creeping statism.

The office's primary developer, of course, was Will H. Hays, not Herbert Hoover. Yet from the agency's beginnings, Hoover viewed its machinery as the kind best equipped to protect social interests while preserving essential liberties. It was the kind that government should encourage, the kind that public agencies should cooperate or merge with, and the kind that he was working to establish in other areas of market failure. It was, in short, recognized and treated as a comrade in industrial Hooverization, and on the industry's side the value of such a connection was early appreciated. There had been some discussion in 1921 of luring Hoover into the position that Hays eventually filled, and in that position Hays took pains to relate his version of societal regulation and government by cooperation to what was being attempted in other problem industries.[57]

From the industry's standpoint the need for a Hays Office

stemmed from two major problems that had brought it to public attention and generated hostile criticism and political attack. One was its inability to contain an ongoing battle over control of exhibition, a battle that was perceived in some quarters as a new attack by would-be monopolists on independent entrepreneurs. The other was its failure to find ways of exploiting the "new morality" without arousing the fear and anger of those determined to uphold and protect the old. This failure, in particular, had produced an array of "reform groups" agitating for censorship boards or regulatory commissions; and it was at the height of this agitation, with the industry's position further weakened by scandals in Hollywood, that the Motion Picture Producers and Distributors of America was formed and the Hays Office created.[58] The latter's power rested in part on the industry's fear of punitive or restrictive legislation. But contributing to it also was the hope that a man of Hays's stature and organizational talents could find acceptable solutions to the industry's two major problems.[59] Outside the industry the Hays Office was able to enlist and maintain support among those who viewed the situation as a national problem requiring remedial action yet were anxious to avoid the evils that they associated with legal censorship and governmental controls.[60]

In operation the Hays Office proceeded to create a variety of new mechanisms and to argue that they constituted the practical, effective, and "American" way of dealing with the situation. There was machinery now for screening extras and getting rid of "immoral" players, machinery that would presumably prevent future scandals. There were organized linkages to community and civic groups, linkages that in theory could identify and build support for pictures that were both profitable to make and "wholesome" in content.[61] There was a Studio Relations Committee, the purpose of which was to weed out unsuitable scripts, review pictures before their release, and limit the showing of those produced outside the system.[62] There was contract standardization with arbitration machinery to resolve disputes, the hope being that this would reduce exhibitor discontent and cut down on expensive litigation. And in a studied effort to avoid antitrust prosecution, there was a kind of conscious parallelism in organizational design. Some of the new agencies were technically independent of the Hays Office, and from 1924 on there were two associations rather than one. Interlocked with the MPPDA but legally separate from it was the Association of Motion Picture Producers, commonly called the California or West Coast Association.[63]

While engaged in the creation of this apparatus, the Hays Office also developed a special branch for dealing with international aspects of the movie problem. This was the "foreign department," which, in Hays's own words, became "almost an adjunct of our State Department." In effect it operated as a quasi-diplomatic agency, making foreign policy through officially supported negotiations with foreign governments and organizations.[64] In addition, with Hoover's support and collaboration, Hays secured legislation under which the Bureau of Foreign and Domestic Commerce created a motion pictures unit staffed with individuals selected by the office and used as a part of its data-gathering and publicity apparatus. Formally established in 1926, the unit proceeded to issue numerous bulletins and reports, conduct a variety of surveys and special studies, monitor through a special trade commissioner any "agitation or legislation" against American films, and put out press releases giving the industry's perspective on foreign disputes.[65] Like the lumber division and the aeronautics branch, it was part of an industrial government whose functioning was supposed to be the best means of achieving national goals, the goals in this case being open markets exploited to give positive impressions of the American people and their character.

As in lumber and aviation, moreover, the creators and operators of the new machinery were not timid about presenting themselves as regulatory pioneers opening the way to a new and higher stage of institutional development. Their mechanisms, they insisted, were true regulatory mechanisms, not merely agencies for altering public images or enhancing group bargaining power. They were serving society through their activities as "harmonizers," "moral engineers," and builders of responsible "home rule." And they were, so Hays kept saying, getting at the fundamental causes of the movie problem, not through prohibitions and crackdowns but through actions that filled institutional gaps through the building of an internal "policyship" to become the basis of a "responsible self-direction, considerate of the public good as well as the box office."[66] Such were the claims being made by the late 1920s, and those making policy for the Coolidge presidency seemed to assume that national ends were indeed being served by the expansion and functioning of the Hays Office. Asked to participate in industry convocations, Hoover appeared with words of encouragement and praise for the contributions being made to the nation's economic progress and "cultural advance."[67]

Hoover's own files, however, indicated that the principal successes of the Hays Office had been in blocking censorship legislation, holding foreign markets, and turning out public relations material. Its efforts to harmonize the decisions produced by moral, artistic, and marketing judgments had not succeeded, and the result in 1928 and 1929 was not only growing friction between the office and uncooperative producers but a resurgent agitation for "reform." On one side were civil and artistic libertarians calling for greater freedom and arguing that internal controls of the Hays type were just as pernicious as police censorship. On the other were the champions of "clean," "wholesome," and "decent" movies, who, for some reason, seemed to feel that Hoover should be supportive of their cause. Even as he continued to work with Hays, he was receiving much of the literature generated by such anti-Hays groups as the International Reform Federation, the Citizens League for Better Pictures, and the Federal Motion Picture Council. They complained that the "real business" of the Hays Office was "whitewashing" rather than regulating the movie makers, that the nation was paying an enormous price for the continuation of their "suggestiveness, indecency, and criminality," and that only a "centralized authority" at the national level could "effectively regulate the centralized motion picture industry."[68]

If "harmonization" had failed on the moral issue, it had also failed on issues dividing the major producers and rebellious groups of exhibitors. Protests about the arbitration system and trade practices, especially block booking, had persisted.[69] Efforts to achieve harmony through a trade practice conference at the

118

Federal Trade Commission had not been successful,[70] and by 1929 a new exhibitors' group, the Allied States Association of Motion Picture Exhibitors, had mobilized considerable support for legislative and antitrust action. Headed by Abram F. Myers, a former federal trade commissioner who had worked with Hoover on trade practice codification, the organization looked upon the Hays Office as camouflage for a sellers' cartel, insisted that what Hays called "bulk selling" was really monopolistic exploitation, and demanded that the voice of the exhibitors be heard in the formation of "industrial policy." It had, moreover, formed a loose alliance with those concerned about "immoral" pictures. If the exhibitors could take only the pictures they wanted, it argued, they could function as protectors of their communities from "filth" and "indecency."[71]

As the decade ended, then, the machinery that was supposed to solve the movie problem was under increasing attack, and in the 1930s the problems inherent in it would intensify. Faced with depression conditions, some movie makers tried to save themselves through additions of "spice" or further exactions from exhibitors. As Hays himself noted, calls for morality and cooperation in the "cataclysm" of 1931 and 1932 were like voices "crying in the wilderness."[72] Nor was such behavior conducive to keeping legislators and antitrust officials quiescent. Regulatory proposals won new support in Congress, and antitrust action, despite Hays's efforts to keep it in "constructive" channels, finally forced an abandonment of the industry's arbitration system. In Hays's view the new antitrust chief, John Lord O'Brian, was "absolutely impossible." He was "doing more harm" than "a dozen Walshes or Brookharts or such," largely, so Hays thought, because he had been "poisoned" by Abram Myers, whose wife was on O'Brian's staff. Protests, however, to Hoover and to Attorney General William Mitchell brought little more than advice on how the industry's "internal machinery" might be revamped. They did not put an end to O'Brian's activities.[73]

Still, in the face of these difficulties, the Hays Office proved remarkably resilient and adaptive. It was eventually successful in saving, strengthening, and putting teeth into its production code.

It emerged at the center of the industry's NRA machinery; and while court decisions would finally force the withdrawal of producers from the exhibition end of the industry, the office itself weathered the political storms of the late 1930s, regained quasi-official status during World War II, and continued, after 1945, to function as America's central mechanism for dealing with the kind of market failures that made motion picture production and distribution a public policy problem.[74] In this respect its post-1930 history more nearly resembled that of the aviation mechanisms than of those developed for lumber.

VI

What, then, can be said about these "industrial policies" of the 1920s and more particularly about the mechanisms entrusted with meeting perceived regulatory needs in three of the period's problem industries? What explains these? In what contexts are they best understood? And of what significance were they? In attempting to answer such questions, one must, of course, be cautious about generalizing from a sample of three. But the regulatory experiences studied here, when taken in conjunction with what is now known about other developments during the period, do suggest the need for rethinking some of the central propositions that have governed previous work on the nation's regulatory and public policy history. They tend, at the very least, to call some of these into question and suggest alternatives that may get us closer to historical reality.

In the first place, the stories reconstructed here suggest that ideas and ideology have been important determinants in shaping national regulatory policy and the mechanisms for supplementing it. In part, of course, these took the form that they did because of the peculiar structure, position, and politics of each industry involved. Nor can one rule out the influence of general prosperity and Republican political dominance. Yet in three widely different industries, each a public policy problem for different reasons, one finds variations on a regulatory model that seems to have been adopted for ideological reasons or because certain ideas had gained credibility and could be used to advance particular interests. Without this ideological dimension it is difficult to explain the mechanisms that emerged or what happened to them later.

Secondly, the stories reconstructed here point up the importance of a set of ideas often assumed to be alien to and largely absent from American political culture. They suggest that the regulatory history of the period is best understood not as a return to laissez faire, a foundation for the regulatory state, or a prelude to democratic pluralism, but rather as an effort to realize or make use of a set of techno-corporate ideals that had gained credence and power as a result of the war experience. At work was an American expression of a larger corporative impulse apparent in most industrial societies, one that had its adherents in both public and private bureaucracies. And it is only by ignoring or misinterpreting these developments of the 1920s that current advocates and critics of corporative formulas can claim to be debating a new American ideology.

Thirdly, the stories reconstructed here suggest that some of the mechanisms developed under the influence of this ideology were able to survive the loss of its credibility, adapt themselves to new conditions, and remain parts of the nation's regulatory system. The lumber mechanisms did not do so, reflecting perhaps their weaknesses in terms of industry support, industry power, and rivalry with the older Forest Service complex. But those in aviation and motion pictures did survive and remain important factors in shaping subsequent regulation in these industries. While subjected to attack and stripped for a time of their status as performers of public or social duties, they had developed in the kind of industries and with the degree of industrial support that enabled them to resist attacks and adapt themselves to new social and political roles. Also significant perhaps was the fact that they had no older rivals comparable to the Forest Service complex in lumber. They had taken shape in new regulatory territory where the claims of other would-be regulators had not yet been established.

As to the workability and effectiveness of this New Era regulation, it is more difficult to come to any definite conclusions. In lumber, changes in the plant and in economic behavior seem to have been far less than were claimed in self-congratulatory statements of the Hooverites and their allies in the lumber associations, whereas in movies and aviation they were more substantial. But in each case they were not changes that brought the kind of markets and development that the "regulators" were trying to engineer. In all three cases, moreover, assessment is complicated by the advent of depression conditions that altered the pattern of regulatory support and concern and tended to turn the mechanisms into instruments of salvage rather than development. Given proper action at the macroeconomic level, it might be argued, such "regulators" could have evolved into more effective tools for changing behavior and realizing the proclaimed goals. In other societies similar tools have been used to improve economic performance.

Still, it should be recognized that such societies have had to find ways of dealing with a series of political problems that seem to be inherent in this form of "regulation." They have had to develop institutional arrangements for bringing in or neutralizing the social constituencies that have idealized small business or consumer sovereignty, for giving industrial labor and its associations a satisfactory role in the apparatus, for dealing with tensions between the bureaucracies at the firm level and those at the industrial level, for bringing law made in other quarters into line with that made through the corporative structure, and for maintaining the competence and reputation of the central core of public and private administrators.[75] Experience suggests that these problems have been very difficult to deal with in societies and cultures resembling those of the United States. And while the machinery of the 1920s seemed to be working toward solutions, one wonders whether continued growth alone would have allowed these to be achieved. The possibility exists that it would have strengthened the critics of the mechanisms and created an environment increasingly hostile to their operation.

Finally, it should also be recognized that solving such problems meant, to some degree at least, a movement away from the institutions that had emerged in the democratic revolutions of the eighteenth and nineteenth centuries. To the extent that they were solved, the chances of realizing the dreams of the Jacksonians, the populists, and the new economic and political pluralists were reduced, an argument perhaps for not seeking to solve them or for being glad that those who were developing the corporative regulation of the 1920s suffered major setbacks in the decade that followed.

Political Choice in Regulatory Administration

SAMUEL P. HAYS

University of Pittsburgh

•

In recounting the history of public regulation historians have usually followed the perspective of the policy analyst. They have been concerned primarily with results: how did the policy work out? The emphasis has been on implementation, the details of administration, and the degree of consistency between statutory objectives on the one hand and regulatory outcomes on the other. Historical interpretation often emphasizes the discrepancy between intent and result, the "efficiency" of the regulatory apparatus, or its distortion by opportunistic political forces which sought to turn administration to their own ends. Much of this regulatory history has been written by those who participated in it, or by more detached observers who adopt the problem-policy perspective of the administrative professional and who often add to that perspective a normative stance of justification or disapproval.[1] The administrative historian has usually transferred into accounts of the past the assumptions, values, and particular substantive concerns of former policy analysts.

Precisely because of this, in administrative and regulatory history the historian has not performed adequately. More genuinely historical insight has been diverted. It would be far more productive to examine long-run change in and for itself so that at any given point in time contemporary policy analysis could be informed by a more detached examination of the evolutionary content. The reconstruction of varied social forces within patterns of social and political structure would be conceptually more productive. Regulation of the economy should be viewed as an opportunity to analyze political choice which, in turn, can be combined with other evidence about choice in many political realms to establish patterns of political structure and change. If one emphasizes only implementation, then one tends to assume that the significant choices have been made in legislation, and that the regulator, like all administrators, merely carries them out in a relatively neutral manner. The main question is the effectiveness with which choices made by legislators are implemented. But this approach seems increasingly anachronistic as it becomes clear that administrative choices are themselves fundamental political choices and must be recognized as a major realm of political give and take.

It is often difficult to accept regulation as a central realm of political option and choice. We are still heavily influenced by the inherited formalism of the past concerning the separation of powers: the legislature makes the laws, the administrative branch executes them, and the courts interpret them. Each has a distinct function; together they constitute an interacting and complementary system of government. Looked at in a different way, the separation of powers involves three arenas of political choice, and hence of political combat. Once the choice is made, the political forces at play in legislation transfer their action to the next stage—the administrative agency—and seek to recoup, defend, or extend what they lost or gained in the legislature. Action does not end there, and soon the same constellation of forces forms around litigation and court decision. The legislature, the administrative agency, the courts are merely different settings in which political controversy and choice are ordered. Much of the drama of our political system arises from the way in which each of these institutions remains open to making its own distinctive contribution to resolving political controversies.

Explorations into the politics of administration by historians have also been limited by their tendency to emphasize the evidence of public debate and ideology far more extensively than the records of administrative controversy. The two are not interchangeable. We obtain one view of controversies over railroad regulation if we look at legislative debates leading up to the Hepburn Act and another if we look at the choices in cases argued before the ICC. We obtain one notion of controversies over antitrust if we focus on the ideological debate in the mass media and another if we observe the internal politics within the business community.[2] Our limited conceptual apparatus and limited forays into the evidence have made us peculiarly sensitive to the political choices surrounding the presidency and the legislature, but far less so to those choices involved in the emerging managerial and technical institutions of public life associated with administration. Regulation of the economy was one of these. We need to observe the actors in that regulatory process more directly and to focus on the people involved in it, their perspectives and choices, the web of public and private institutions surrounding them, and the relationship between administrative choice and the larger public ideology and choice.

In this essay I will examine the regulation of the economy not from the customary "problem-policy" emphasis with a sequence of an emerging problem, action to cope with it, and policy outcomes. Instead, I will emphasize regulatory choices as policy choices and the role of regulation in the larger relationship between society and politics. What I will try to do is to place the history of regulation of the economy within the context of the larger political economy and to explore that relationship in terms of substantive values involved in choices. There is a close connection, one might argue, between the value choices made by administrators, managers, economists, planners and scientists, all closely associated in the regulatory process, and the value choices made by society at large. We cannot make sense out of administration and economic regulation simply by assuming that they are relatively divorced from debates in the larger political setting. On the contrary, they are interlaced with value choices, and our task is to work out the relationship between choices made by regulators and choices determined by legislation or public ideological debate.

I should make one more comment by way of introduction. My own personal research in the field of economic regulation is confined primarily to matters of environmental conservation.[3] And my more recent work has stressed heavily the environmental issues after World War II.[4] While the questions I have dealt with emphasize heavily the subject of administrative policies, what I have to say will undoubtedly be limited by a far less than adequate acquaintance with detailed evidence in other areas of administration and economic regulation. I am especially aware of the possibility that sensitivity to recent issues might well lead to an unjustified search for earlier beginnings. Yet a comparative, if not an evolutionary, perspective can be fruitful; the years from 1870 to 1940 can be examined, at the least, in a comparative way from the vantage point of more recent decades, and hence the task might well be more precisely informed.

The Scope of Analysis: The Politics of Administration

In twentieth century America the politics of administration is the emerging central focus of the entire political system. I have already stressed that each of the three branches of government are more than separate functional entities, but serve as different arenas for similar political controversies. Within this role administration has become the critical, ongoing, permanent focal point of political choice, and hence of converging political forces.[5] On the one side the legislature sets some broad limits of administration; and on the other the courts define those limits more precisely case by case. But these actions are sporadic and temporary. The arena of continuous choice which affects the larger society on a day-to-day basis is administration. And the actors well know it. The stakes are enormous. The way in which a regulatory agency calculates a rate base to determine a "fair return" is critical. Each proposed regulation under the Environmental Protection Agency has implications no less extensive. These choices are central to the entire political system. And their observation through the administrative record is central for effective historical analysis.[6]

How do we look at history in these terms? What is the scope of the historical problem, of the evolution of administrative choice with respect to public regulation of the economy? The initial point of departure is administrative decision making itself, not as a process, but as a setting for substantive choice. At the center are administrators, with their own personal values, professional commitments, and bureaucratic loyalties. Surrounding them are economic analysts, scientific and technical personnel, and planners, each also with personal and professional values which tend to steer them in one direction or another. The particular scientists, economic analysts, and planners chosen by administrators for advice reflect significant substantive choices in the first place; their ongoing contributions to administrative decisions represent ongoing political choices. On many occasions management is closely associated with administration in which resource systems such as rivers, forests and public lands, or welfare and medical delivery are managed as systems, giving rise to more tightly knit administrative arrangements. Here also is a setting for political choice. This administrative context is our initial point of departure; we should focus on the substantive choices made by regulators as political choices and work outward from that beginning.[7]

Surrounding administrators are webs of institutions both public and private which constitute the day-to-day external political context within which administrative decisions are made. Political scientists have described these as clientele groups. But this conjures up a less than accurate picture of quid-pro-quo bargains between administrators and their "special interests." The real-life context is more subtle and powerful than that, one of closely related institutions in which there are shared perceptions of a reality of mutual concern, of problems which action must address, of empirical descriptive categories and measurement techniques, of levels of proof required before action is justified. This institutional world is composed of professional associations, educational institutions, private corporations, trade associations, federal and state agencies, which together constitute the environmental web of administration. These perspectives often interact with those of administrators to generate symbiotic relationships of mutual support. Our sensitivity to regulatory history will often be sharpened to the extent that we can identify and analyze these interacting frameworks of thought and perception.

There is also, as a third context of observation, the wider

ideological and symbolic realm within which administrative choices are made. This realm does not impinge on administration in the form of direct day-to-day institutional realities, but constitutes a context within which legitimacy in thought, ideas, and assumptions is established. Some larger ideological settings impose constraints. Antitrust matters had to be discussed continually in terms of the social value of price competition; in our own day, cost-benefit analysis has come to have a similar ideological power. We have done little to identify these ideological contexts of public regulation, or to trace how they arise and especially how they achieve legitimacy to become the accepted language of discourse and discussion in regulatory matters. The larger public ideologies are often formulated by the mass media, but there is a distinction between that setting on the one hand and the media of the political intelligentsia, often in our own day called "thought leaders," who play a distinctive role in formulating the ideological framework of public life. We are often prone to look upon this as simply an intrusion which distorts "sound" administrative policy. On the contrary, it involves a process whereby the ideological worlds of administrative decision makers and the ideological worlds of those in the wider political setting either come into conflict or fuse.

Let me pursue each of these three aspects of the politics of administration a bit further in order to indicate a direction of thought. A large portion of immediate administrative choice lies in the way in which the reality to be dealt with is described. If one is to establish "fair" railroad rates, then some notion as to the patterns of interregional economic competition which rates influence is required. Such regulatory bench lines as "basing points" and distinctions between class and commodity rates flowed from such conceptions. Or if one is to establish a "fair return" on investment, then some notion as to the "rate base" and how it should be calculated is essential; hence the controversy over original cost and reproduction cost, or in our own day over construction work in progress (CWIP). A host of similar "realities" had to be described by the Environmental Protection Agency or the Occupational Safety and Health Administration in the 1970s. If one were to require that pollution control technology used by the "best" firms be applied to all, one had to have a clear notion of the range of technology in place for existing firms so as to know which would serve as examples for the others. Or if reality concerned ambient air, or ecological or health effects, one had to come to some conclusion as to what they were.[8] Amid all these were choices of enormous consequence for both the regulator and the regulated. Hence choices in the assessment of the nature of the economic, biological and human health worlds were fundamental to regulatory action. To decide such matters was a major element in the politics of administration.

Or consider the institutional context within which the agency worked. For the decision maker, that setting was defined by ongoing, day-to-day experience about who wished to influence the agency's world of reality and choice, and who might, if those choices were displeasing, be able to bring some adverse influence to bear. Communications to an agency from interested parties, whether in terms of inquiries, advice or demands, generated a perception of the world of external institutions which the agency had to consider "relevant" to its choices, and with which it had to establish some working relationship. In our own day the major role of the environmental impact statement has been to serve as a "radar" device by which agencies become more knowledgeable about the world of actors "out there" who might impinge upon their choices. As the context of choice became increasingly technical, those external institutions were increasingly represented by scientific and technical professionals who could make life easier or more difficult for the decision maker; some spoke for corporate institutions, but others represented more general professional opinion and institutions. The tension became especially acute when professional scientific and technical institutions were not able to reconcile differing expert opinions within their own framework and the agency then was placed in a position of having to do so itself.

In the post–World War II world, the focal point of relationships with this institutional setting has been the advisory committee. Advisory committees have become distinctive institutions, playing a crucial role on the legislative side of administrative choice much in the same way that administrative law, as a quasi-judicial operation, does on the appeals side. The personnel of advisory committees usually reflects the agency's own perceptions as to the institutional world within which it works, and the relative weights of segments of that world. At the same time changes in that personnel reflect changes in the relevant external climate. Recent changes in membership of advisory committees in the U.S. Fish and Wildlife Service and the Bureau of Land Management, for example, reflect the broader range of environmental interests which have arisen in the last two decades to which those agencies feel they must respond.[9] We might well pose, as an historical problem, the process by which these external relationships became formalized, the more informal contacts which perhaps existed in earlier years, and steps toward a more consciously designed system of administrative representation.

Thirdly, the politics of administration is set within the context of the nation's larger ideological climate. One has a good sense of the complexities of this setting when one finds contradictions between the directions of ideological debate and of regulatory action. Railroad regulation in the Progressive Era, for example, was debated within the aura of a public uprising against the railroads, but examination of the politics of the more limited regulatory context reveals that the drama lay in interregional competition for economic advantage among a wide range of producers, shippers and buyers, all of whom were vitally interested in the relative cost of transportation.[10] To find patterns in all this, one must sort out the relationships among economic regions amid economic growth. While antitrust ideology often involved concepts of small versus larger business and the consumer versus the "trust," the pulling and hauling in antitrust action most often concerned political relationships within the business community, for example those arising out of the impact of the emerging mass-production, mass-marketing and mass-buying firms in the 1920s —the mail order houses, the Ford Motor Company and governments and public institutions.[11] Historians face these contradictions when they draw conclusions based on ideological evidence only to find that they are challenged by evidence drawn from the record of administrative politics. This is more than just a problem of evidence. It is a broad political phenomenon, a major dual context of regulatory politics.

One might profitably distinguish between the ideological context which emerges from the "political intelligentsia," the opinion makers as some might call them, and the more broadly based "public ideology" which is tapped more recently by attitude surveys. Just as there is a discrepancy between public ideology and administrative practice in political choice, there is also a discrepancy, in the more recent evidence, between public ideology and the ideology of the political intelligentsia. A number of attitude studies in environmental affairs now are designed so as to compare and contrast the opinions of the general public and those of "thought leaders" in business, government and the professions.[12] Significant differences have been found; on occasion it has led researchers to recommend that their corporate clients concentrate their opinion-influencing efforts on "thought leaders," since the views of that group are closer to the views of the business community than are those held by the broader public.[13]

Some will find these emphases on the internal setting of administrative choice, the institutional web of that choice, and the larger ideological context as excessively general. But in order to break out of the more traditional instrumentalist view of public administration, and to extend questions from those pertaining to how statutes were carried out to those pertaining to the political choices made by regulatory agencies, it seems appropriate to start out with some aspects of a larger perspective. Above all, these remarks are an attempt to bring administrative politics to center stage in the historical analysis of political affairs, and to think of the larger realms of society and politics surrounding it as the context in which the continuous, day-to-day exercise of political power is carried out.[14] To lay bare that process is a more difficult task than historians have usually undertaken, but at least for the period since World War II the evidence available to pursue the task is abundant. What remains is to get in hand the conceptual apparatus that will enable us to make sense out of it.

Political Choice in Regulation

The Economic Context of Economic Regulation

Let us now turn to the decades under scrutiny here. Economic regulation was heavily related to the internal evolution of the business community and the demands by one sector of the economy that it be advanced or that another be restrained. There was some broader ideological context to this, as we shall see later, but one can understand regulatory political choice only if one reconstructs the internal politics of economic institutions in the first place. Our initial task is to sort out those internal relationships as patterns of economic structure and change which provided the institutional environment for the practice of economic regulation. Three changes seem important.

The first is the increasing scale of organization and the tension between those evolving systems of larger scale and the subordinated and relatively declining systems of smaller scale.[15] It is important to identify these patterns of change in both the public and the private economy. Larger manufacturing firms absorbed smaller ones to give rise to ever larger units of organization and management; all this is quite familiar. But it is equally important to emphasize the growth of larger scale in the public economy, for example, in highway building as larger units organized by state road commissions replaced smaller ones which had been under the direction of township trustees. Throughout these seven decades one can identify a great number of centralizing processes in both the private and public economies. They provided opportunities for those promoting larger-scale and more centrally directed systems to seek out the assistance of government in their ventures, and those of smaller-scale units, in turn, to seek protection from restriction, destruction or absorption by larger systems.

Some of the most significant examples of these processes of change which bear directly on economic regulation are most often missed amid the rather limited preoccupation with the manufacturing corporation. The most pervasive changes in the realm of scale of organization, in fact, took place in distribution.[16] Formerly organized on a highly decentralized and segmented basis, distribution now underwent intense centralization under the aegis of the manufacturing corporation that wished to direct the flow and terms of sale. Innumerable smaller-scale units such as grocers or farm equipment dealers found themselves under pressures from manufacturers to modify their practices in line with the objectives of mass marketing. Some were disciplined; others were absorbed. All up and down the scale of organization demands were made upon government for aid. Mail order institutions sought to expand the use of the postal system to penetrate markets formerly controlled by country stores and urban mom-and-pop shops. Smaller units sought antitrust action against the larger as violators of the Sherman Act, or to impose restrictive taxes, such as those on chain stores. While the media kept manufacturing before the public eye, and hence the later historian's eye as well, the most significant changes, in terms of evolving patterns in the economy, were in distribution.

Banking and insurance provide an equally significant context for the evolution of public regulation of the economy.[17] Both underwent rapid centralization and, in both, larger firms had the political clout to argue that bigger was better, that is, more secure. Many a growing insurance company or banking firm argued that smaller units in the towns and countryside, or in urban neighborhoods, were unsafe places to deposit money. Often the argument hinged on where the local government, or especially the school board, should keep its funds. These local bodies were frequently constrained to use local banks, but failure, embezzlement, and loss of funds would inevitably increase the reputation of larger and supposedly more secure firms. Banking and insurance underwent a rapid increase in state regulation, and often the drive behind that process was the creation in both fields of a larger system considered by the relevant political actors to be more reliable. The deliberate attempt by larger-scale institutions to use the power of the state to undermine the influence and autonomy of those of smaller scale was a rather widespread phenomenon in the politics of modernization, as newer institutions sought to counter the roadblocks of older ones. It provides one of the major contexts of public regulation.

One can separate the private from the public economy only

with great difficulty because the two are often part of the same piece, symbiotic and mutually supportive. This was especially true in the processes of system building. Tendencies toward centralization and away from decentralization and political autonomy in matters of roads and schools in the state and county, or in fire, police, education, streets and general government in the city are one of the most significant contexts of state and urban history.[18] Both involved significant distinctions between those who pushed for centralization and those who fought against it. Those who sought larger and more centrally managed scale in public affairs were often the same people or closely associated with those who sought similar changes in scale in the private economy; similarly, those who defended decentralization and the autonomy of smaller scale in both private and public affairs were also closely related. Hence, in detailing the evolutionary processes of scale of organization as a context of public regulation, we must bring both private and public tendencies into the same analytical context. Here we are identifying broad-ranging processes of social evolution, the central theme of history, which pervade the entire society and shape public regulation as well as private institutions.

The second context of public regulation between 1870 and 1940 is the more familiar and perennial tension between consumer and producer. It seems elementary to point out that in the price-and-market system producers continually seek to raise prices and consumers to lower them; that is the simple dynamics of economic politics. And in doing so they frequently call upon government to assist. The tariff is a case in point. Tariff politics has long been a maze of delicately balanced compromises between producers who wished to protect themselves against imports and consumers who wished to take advantage of their lower prices. We certainly no longer accept the myth that controversies over the tariff were just matters of manufacturers versus farmers, for we well know that manufacturers wanted lower tariffs on what they purchased and farmers wanted higher ones on commodities that might compete with what they sold. The New England woolen manufacturers' demands for freer imports on raw wool and the midwestern cattlemen's demands for restrictions on imports of Canadian beef are classic cases in point. And we also certainly no longer accept the myth that labor, in some fashion, opposed higher tariffs; there is ample evidence of their close support for their employers on this score, no matter whether it is a case of late nineteenth century coal, iron, steel or pottery, or twentieth century automobiles.

Even more important was the evolution of consumer-producer relationships within the business community itself. Often in this analysis we juxtapose the manufacturer as producer against the general public as consumer. The case of railroad rate regulation again requires some reordering of images. We now know that the manufacturer as shipper and consumer of railroad services was one of the major forces behind the drive for railroad rate regulation, joining farmers and merchants in a common demand for change. We also know that similar manufacturers as consumers of electricity, gas, and communications services have long been a major force behind the regulation of public utilities.[19] This type of evidence leads directly to John Galbraith's more general observation about the role of "countervailing" power.[20] Whether or not we accept his argument about the results of consumer leverage within the business community, its political role seems to have been active in many a field of economic regulation.

Consider antitrust cases in the 1920s.[21] The economy was generating new economic institutions geared to the mass market. These were "consumer" industries—distributors such as mail order houses, and manufacturers such as producers of automobiles and other consumer durables, all engaged in mass selling. In their search for lower prices these economic sectors sought to maintain an open and competitive market and to utilize the antitrust laws in doing so. Manufacturers from whom they bought their batteries and tires, their washing machines and refrigerators, equally sought to control prices through joint action. While to the media observer and the historian who relied on generalized ideological evidence antitrust debates pitted the public as consumer against the manufacturing trust, the real world of continuous antitrust politics lay within the business community between those who bought and those who sold. Joining the consumer-oriented mass producers were mass buyers in public agencies, in hospitals and schools, wherever mass purchasing prompted one to seek a lower price and better terms. All this spilled over into the New Deal when much of the debate over the NRA brought forth these tensions, once again obscured by the larger context of ideological conflict between the "people" and the "interests."

Finally, much of the drama of public regulation of the economy lay in the struggle among traditional functional segments—business, labor, and agriculture.[22] One of the most significant developments of these years was the organization of these three groups of producers into highly effective political units, in business the trade association, in labor the trade union, and in agriculture the farm cooperative. All three grew out of attempts in each realm of economic life to organize collectively for joint action where individual action was not capable of achieving results. They involved both efforts to lower costs of commonly shared activities such as advertising, purchasing, shipping, insurance, accounting, and market analysis, and attempts to control prices directly by exercising influence over the flow of supply in commodities, labor, or manufactured goods. While some of these efforts could be and were carried on through cooperative private action alone, few remained solely in that realm and most led to demands that both federal and state government provide assistance.

We are all familiar with these developments, but perhaps it would be useful to point out several less obvious general patterns. There was, for example, the sequence of stages of evolution. Functional organizations first sought governmental assistance in collective efforts to make their operations more efficient; the Departments of Agriculture and Commerce provided many a service to cooperatives and trade associations along that line. Then they sought protection against those who attacked them for interfering with the market and engaging in unfair competition. The right of farm cooperatives to operate without external legal restraint, of trade associations to "share prices" and engage in "fair competition" through the open price system, of trade unions to bargain collectively, all were challenged by their opponents in the economy. Each functional group initiated these practices as collective efforts, but each was opposed and obtained from government different degrees of immunity from such challenges. Finally, there was the stage in which collective action required coercion of recalcitrant members from within their own ranks, which then led to legal arrangements for publicly supervised elections, especially in labor and agriculture, so that collective bargaining agreements for wages and prices would be required of all if approved by a given percentage of those affected.

By the end of the 1930s each of the three functional groups had achieved considerable firm and mutually supportive bonds with particular segments of government. We can observe this in the evolution of the Departments of Agriculture, Commerce, and Labor in both federal and state governments. Functional organization in government paralleled that in the private economy. In the span of time between 1890 and 1946, especially, these demands upon government were formulated, the programs established, and the symbiotic relationships firmly reinforced. As a process of evolution, this unit of history cannot intelligently be broken by World War I or the Depression of 1929, but must be understood as a persistent development over five decades. By 1946 the phenomenon of functional group politics had been fully shaped. The years after the war were marked more by its further elaboration and its exercise than by innovation.

There is another implication in observing all this as a continuous, five-decade process: the New Deal and the 1930s were the end rather than the beginning of an era. Many stages in this evolution were not reached until the 1930s, such as the public supervision of farm marketing and labor-management collective bargaining agreements. True, the receptiveness of the Roosevelt administration to both the Wagner Act and the demands of the Farm Bureau for price supports and marketing agreements were new. But looking at these developments from a bit more distance, we can relate them to a pattern of long-run change in the relationship between the private and public economies which had been in motion for some decades. This is especially the case if we focus on institutional development rather than ideology, which is often detached from ongoing human activities. It is even more clear if we zero in on the politics of administration and the agencies themselves. These decades witnessed the peculiar elaboration of the relevant federal departments—Agriculture, Commerce, and Labor—as contrasted with departments formed in earlier eras such as War, Navy, Treasury, and State, or those formed after World War II, such as HEW, Transportation, HUD, Energy or the de facto department of EPA.

We could, of course, identify other contexts of economic development within which the practice of public regulation evolved. There were, for example, the relationships between sub-sectors of these functional groups, such as farmers who produced grain and wanted higher prices and farmers who purchased grain for converted dairy, beef and poultry products who wanted lower prices; or the relationships between southern textile manufacturers who emphasized cheaper, coarse cloth, and northern who had shifted to fine and luxury products; or northern coal operators whose labor force was organized and those in the South where it was not. Such varied relationships as these came into play at every point in the interaction between the public and private economies. We can observe many of them within the National Recovery Administration when the codes forced firms to enter into a single framework of decision making and thus to put on record for the historian the different views of many different sectors of the economy. Often the most critical point was the debate over the method of making collective decisions in the code agreements: one firm, one vote, or voting in proportion to production or sales? This only underlines the elaborateness of functional group organization and the need to grasp it fully in order to analyze the history of public regulation.

The Regulators and Their Technical World

Let us now turn from the social and economic context to the regulators. This is more difficult to reconstruct, for historians have spent more time examining political impulses in the society at large than those within the more confined realm of administration. There are, of course, the administrators themselves and their related managers of public resources, such as those who managed the railroads during World War I or the Tennessee Valley Authority. But there also are professionals in economics, science, and planning on the one hand, and engineers on the other, upon whom administrators and managers came to rely heavily.[23] We could well observe the particular values, perceptions of reality, and preferences as to choice of action reflected in each of these sets of skills separately and collectively. And we could especially observe the way in which these impulses merged in regulation with those from the larger society.

Analysis of administration has long been inhibited by the aura of detachment, of scientific and technical objectivity, of universal rationality which has surrounded it. These were thought of as professional activities in which the task of discovery and application of knowledge should be granted independence from external political influence. Historians have been prone to observe the accumulation of knowledge and discovery as a relatively autonomous political force and, in governmental affairs, to concentrate especially on the willingness of the various branches to use technical professionals in decision making and to permit them to operate free from external "political" influence. The selective use of the term "political" to describe forces interfering with professionals but not professionals themselves, conveys the notion that the administrator or the regulator was more associated with disinterested inquiry and application than with the demands of the wider political order. We then write history in terms of the tension between the two.

In writing about conservation leaders in the federal government some years ago I became convinced that they advocated particular and not universal objectives, that their role could not be understood outside of an emphasis on their particular choices which were as much a part of the world of politics as were the choices of people in the wider society. More recently I have been examining the far more extensive and complex context of environmental politics since 1960, in which administration and regulation are the centers of political choice to a much greater degree than in earlier years, and the use of scientists, economists, planners, and engineers is far more extensive. In each of these fields the growth and elaboration of a profession have led to intense specialization, and particular rather than universal views have given rise to internal controversies which often parallel those in the wider society. In this manner science and technology become intimately associated with wider political forces rather than detached from them.[24] One feels much more compelled to take up the political analysis of science and technology for this more recent period than one might be tempted to pursue for the late nineteenth and early twentieth centuries.

In those decades the rapid evolution of the empirical professions came about amid an ideological climate of the emergence of a new "tool" to ameliorate society's ills and to carry it on to a greater and more abundant future. One had not yet experienced the intense controversies within the empirical professions that we have today, or the participation by the public in those disputes. There were some, of course. But overarching all of it was an ideological context of more universal human impulse and universal human achievement which the excitement of empirical discovery seemed to convey. Yet examination of the political sociology of administrators and technical professionals in more recent years has made me wonder if this was actually the case. Is it not just a matter of not having probed far enough? Certainly we do not have much to go on in describing the political sociology of the empirical professions and their relation to administration in the decades between 1870 and 1940. For the years since 1960 I think I can analyze conflicts internal to environmental science associated with administration more fully. But the earlier scene is more nebulous.

The central empirical focus of economic regulation was economic analysis; hence a key point of departure is to examine the evolution of economic description as an activity—not so much its academic side but its broader practice. Perhaps we should think of it as the history of economic accounting. A first look at regulation in banking, railroads, tariffs, and antitrust programs makes clear that they all involved a considerable amount of economic empirical measurement. Each regulator found that the job required a more detailed look at the particular facet of economic life with which a particular type of regulation dealt. One had to describe transportation, both in more limited segments and as a system, before one knew how to tackle large problems such as "fair" and "unfair" competition. One had to sort out the various segments of the banking system and especially the different roles of local, regional, and national banks and their relationships to each other in the flow of money and credit before one could think about the normative question of how it should function as a system. Simple economic description was central.

We can put this in the context of related activities in the history of economic description. Publications of the American Statistical Association in the late nineteenth century reflect a veritable explosion in this task.[25] There were papers on transportation, urbanization, public works, banking, almost every subject for which quantitative data was available. These reflected a new excitement in observing an unfolding economy, a task of which economic description associated with regulatory activity was a part. A few decades later during World War I, the search for more systematic and reliable data about the workings of the economy gave rise to even more extensive description.[26] Agencies were formed simply to gather data and describe the nation's production capabilities; they drew into public affairs professionals from the nation's recently established business schools and economics departments. Some of them went on to expand greatly the nation's capacity for economic description in the 1920s.

It is one thing to emphasize the growth of economic accounting as a professional task; it is another to define the type of perception which it fostered and which it brought to public administration and regulatory affairs. Each empirical profession generated its own conception of reality which arose from the particular piece of the world which it examined. Crucial in that perspective were the categories in which data was ordered. Those categories did not develop from universal and timeless sources, but from certain ways of looking at the world which were absorbed into the process of professional training and practice. When those perspectives were translated into action, such as in public regulation, they defined the values peculiar to that profession. Whether it be forestry or wildlife management, the health sciences or ecology, chemical or civil engineering, economics or planning, the political values of an empirical profession can be identified most effectively through its particular categories of empirical description. Hence the history of the development of such categories is a crucial focus for historical analysis. Recent research has emphasized, for example, the way in which U.S. Census categories of occupational description shifted in the early twentieth century from a functional classification—agriculture, commerce and industry—to a vertical and hierarchical one which is common today.[27] That shift in perspective came about slowly and not without debate. I think we could understand much more about the professional and technical context of regulation if we could work out the historical evolution of categories of economic accounting.

The empirical professions as a whole tend to adopt more universal rather than more limited perspectives, seeking to describe larger rather than smaller contexts. Economics is no exception. To focus on a given locality or even a state was considered to be somewhat parochial; knowledge was universal, not bounded by limited time and space. Economic description, therefore, veered quickly into systems analysis in which, over the years, one facet after another of the national economy came to be brought into the totality of description. When one spoke of the economic system, one meant the national system. There was some description of individual firms, of course, and in the years after World War II regional economics came to be emphasized because of the growing focus on cities and "depressed areas" as objects of federal action. But for professional economic analysis as a whole, tendencies toward a universal framework of thought were in the mainstream.

This movement toward universalism in economic description had several consequences in public regulation. One is that it generated a rather close relationship between those in the empirical professions whose perspectives were universal, those in federal regulatory agencies who thought of the object of action to be a national system, and those in the economy who were forming institutions of increasingly larger scope. All these reinforced each other in interactive fashion. Together they generated an aura of a "national" or "public" interest in contrast with a more limited "partial" or "special" interest. These tendencies shaped the ideological self-images of the emerging empirical professions. Their contribution, so they thought, was to define the "public interest" because as the instrument of universal empirical knowledge they represented those larger tendencies. This self-image is often at stake today when political debate lays bare the particular rather than the universal values in scientific and technical choice.

The emerging profession of economic accounting was also reformist. As was the case with most empirical professions, while retaining an aura of detachment and objectivity, it could not remain detached. To apply knowledge was a major element of the outlook of the new professions. It was not enough to discover; the purpose of discovery was application. Hence the economist, like the public health expert, the educator, the political scientist, and many another empirical professional, was a staunch advocate of the reformism of applied science. This thrust the economist squarely into the context of regulatory action in the agencies which emerged prior to World War I and in those during the war as well. Economic analysis became a major instrument of reform action carried out under the auspices of government, moving to center stage and occupying a position from which it has rarely since been dislodged.[28]

These tendencies within economics—toward systematic description through particular categories and techniques, toward universal system analysis, and toward reform—all played a major role in the evolution of the regulatory state in the twentieth century. The economist's major task was to serve as mediator between the regulator and the regulated. The major choices in economic regulation came to be choices in economic description. Conflicts between the regulators and the regulated often revolved around a portrayal of economic reality, and the coming together of the two sides often involved a practical resolution of those different views about what the economy was and how it functioned. In this resolution the economist played a highly influential role. One might argue that the common ground was defined more frequently by the regulated than the regulators. But the contribution of the economist, as descriptive mediator, was essential. The world of economic reality which the professional economist offered, such as the capital value of a railroad or an industry, was crucial in the history of the regulatory economy.

I have emphasized economists because they appear to have been the major technical professionals associated with economic regulation in these years. After World War II other technical problems came to the fore. Environmental scientists who assessed health and ecological effects of pollution played a role similar to that of planners and engineers. These professionals, along with economists, became key figures in defining the "real world" that management and administration sought to shape. Legislation often left the regulatory agency with considerable choice which was often markedly affected by the initial assessment of the situation with which it dealt. Hence, for example, the intense political controversy over the assessment of effects of air and water pollution which appear in the form of "criteria documents."[29]

The most significant challenge in understanding the technical context of regulation is to sort out the values implicit in the choices. These are often obscured by the overlay of technical detail, a fact which plays an important role in the ability of outsiders to understand how decisions are made. The mass of detail constitutes a barrier to ferreting out the choices and frustrates a wide range of interested parties, including legislators, judges, other administrators, professionals, and the general public.[30] It also creates a barrier for the historian, who is tempted not to go very far beyond the external evidence. The technical context of economic regulation, therefore, presents for the historian a special task of laying bare those choices and options, the particular personal values and professional perceptions which led to one choice rather than another. This, I think, means that we must examine the history of the empirical professions associated with economic regulation with far more care than we have.

As a set of guidelines let me describe briefly the format which I have come to use in analyzing the technical context of more recent environmental regulation. First is the notion that scientific and technical choice can be related in origin to three major factors: the institution for which one does technical work and whose stake in the outcome leads to choices in the design and interpretation of the research itself; the profession to which one has established personal ties and commitments and which through training and experience has shaped a particular perception of the world; and personal preference and disposition, which often sorts out those who demand high levels of proof from those who feel comfortable with more indeterminate evidence. A second set of considerations identifies the context of choice: the problems that should be studied in the first place;[31] the research design which involves choices of variables to be related and their possible direction of causality; the categories into which empirical data are ordered and which define the way in which the discipline, in turn, orders the world for observation and interpretation; and the techniques of measurement such as, for example, animal experiments or epidemiology. These two sets of questions I have found useful in analyzing technical and scientific choices in a host of environmental issues ranging from lead and asbestos, ionizing radiation and PCB's to clearcutting and off-road vehicles, acid rain and alternative sources of energy. Perhaps they could be equally useful in analyzing similar technical choices in earlier years.

Public Regulation and the Public

I have emphasized thus far the institutional context of public regulation and the professional and technical world within which it took place. Now for a third context which pertains to the wider public. One is struck by the marked contrast between the relatively high degree of demand for direct public involvement in administrative decision making after 1950 and the similarly low degree in the decades prior to that time. In the late nineteenth and early twentieth centuries the public played little if any direct role in the regulatory system. The broader context of public ideology did not include direct participation. The interested parties who did take part were producers, organized as functional groups; by contrast, there were few consumer or other public interest representatives. It is useful, I think, to look back from the present with respect to this contrast in public involvement and see if it might lead to new insight into the earlier years.

Political Choice in Regulation

One set of explorations might focus on those few ways in which consumer action did play some role within the earlier regulatory state. There were the instances where settlement house leaders during World War I, on behalf of the poor, objected to attempts by farmers to maintain price levels through milk marketing agreements. There were the efforts early in the New Deal to restrain farm price increases by establishing a consumers' counsel in the Department of Agriculture to watchdog the AAA and the marketing agreements program, and also in the NRA by appointing consumer representatives to each code authority. These initiatives had little impact; they were bitterly resisted by producers, effectively neutralized and abolished. The post–World War II efforts were far more successful. While a Department of Consumer Affairs fell by the wayside, a number of initiatives arose within federal agencies during the Carter administration. Far more significant were environmental thrusts which represented a new type of consumer interest concerned with more intangible "quality of life" services. Much of the drive of the environmental movement was directed at administrative decision making and led to a demand for opportunities to become active participants along with producers. This gave rise to a broader base of representation on agency advisory committees, the use of the environmental impact statement for citizen review, extensive programs to disseminate information to the public, and greater involvement of environmental representatives in hearings and informal pre-hearing conferences.[32] The absence of such practices in earlier years helps to identify the regulatory process then as more confined to producer functional groups, a stage in history shaped peculiarly by those forces.

If we cannot find much in the way of historical antecedents in public involvement, we can identify the evolution of those aspects of regulatory action with which the later consumer and environmental forces came into conflict. Regulation gave rise to an ever increasing technical detail in decision making and an upward shift in power and authority. Technical detail made decisions more obscure and less accessible to the vast majority of people who were not continually privy to it. That detail was not especially difficult to comprehend, but there was so much of it that it was difficult to follow and hence to absorb in the decision process.[33] Power and authority had shifted toward that relatively narrow circle of public agencies and their allied producer representatives and away from others. To centralize administrative authority in a technical context sorted out those who were a party to making decisions from those who were not.

The consumer-environmental demands of the years after World War II were a reaction against this earlier narrowing of power and authority. It is important to examine more precisely how this change came about. To what extent was the centralization of decision making a conscious effort to exclude political actors? It appears to have been fostered to facilitate change, a major element of which included strategies to overcome resistance to it. While many sectors of the public accepted the mass benefits of system-atization, others objected because innovation affected them adversely; their resistance created roadblocks for those who sought more rapid change. I have written about some aspects of this process elsewhere, such as the centralization of representation in municipal government, of control over the development of state highways, and the shift in the control of schools from ward and township to citywide and countywide school boards and super-intendents.[34] Throughout the entire society, as administrative centralization took place, political power shifted upward. The elements of this change that were inherent in the spirit of public administration generally have to be sorted out, along with the specific substantive issues over which choices were made to centralize power and authority.

Shifts in power that appear to be externally similar took place in recent environmental affairs in a series of extremely dramatic challenges by higher levels of authority and power to those at lower ones. These are known as "preemption" issues, in which attempts are made to grant a higher level of government an exclusive power to establish higher environmental standards. Such was the question of whether or not federal law prohibited states from establishing standards of radioactive releases from atomic power plants more restrictive than federal, or the more recent case of the proposed Energy Mobilization Board with its authority to override state opposition to energy projects. These were typical of a host of federal preemptions. But an even more active scene for the evolution of such override authority came at the state level, where many a state environmental law prohibited local governments from exercising authority within their jurisdiction that would challenge state regulations with respect to air quality, surface mining, wetlands, forest practices, or pesticides. And the power to use local zoning ordinances to control industrial or waste disposal siting is often preempted by the state.[35]

In their historical role these cases, however, differed somewhat from those associated with earlier upward shifts in power. The older ones centralized systems of production and replaced those of smaller with those of larger scale. The newer cases asserted new consumer values associated with rapid change in an advanced industrial society. These, in turn, clashed with further elaborations of scale in organization. Hence a contest between two evolutionary tendencies emerged, each one bringing about change, each one reaching out to use science and technology in its behalf, each one attempting to shape sources of political power and authority to facilitate its objectives. Since many of the new environmental objectives were site specific, emphasizing environmental quality in a particular place of home, community, recreation or leisure, they were often expressed through attempts to enhance local authority and, taken as a whole, constituted a challenge to higher levels. These higher levels, in turn, were actively sought as sources of power by those who centralized decision making. Within these broad trends were many opportunistic variations, as different political forces would pick and choose the level of power most conducive to their immediate objectives.

In order to understand inequality in the ability to influence administrative decisions, this analysis of the upward shift in power is crucial. Against this historical background came the later search for involvement by environmental and consumer groups. The range of actors considered to be legitimate participants in decision making had been narrowed; consumer and environmental drives attempted to reverse that by procedural innovations for "input" at various stages of formal decision making. Earlier centralizing tendencies in regulation were bound up with production and commodity development. More recent demands were associated with newer values of an information-consumer society in which work and production were challenged by consumption, recreation and leisure.

The public context of public regulation also involves the larger ideology of political debate. During the late nineteenth and early twentieth centuries there was considerable overlay of antitrust ideology in which political issues discussed in the media were thought of as a conflict between the "trusts" and the "people." We know enough about this now not to translate it directly into our own analytical framework, but to examine its own sociology as firmly as we examine the sociology of broader political forces and of administration, science and economics. But how to undertake the analysis is another matter. The major problem in the historical analysis of ideology is one of systematic description, of identifying the range of ideological formulations in the society at large, the explanatory roles which particular ideologies play for particular segments of the population, and how those explanatory frameworks changed over time. Most frequently we assume that varied sources of historical evidence reflect a relatively uniform underlying pattern of ideas. Yet there is as much variation in how people perceive the world and what they think about it as there is in demographic data. Hence our task is to root each source of evidence in a particular thrust of perception, values and objectives. We should not go for central tendencies in ideologies in the first place, but establish variation and pattern within which later central tendencies can be informed.

The range of contemporary evidence makes this task far more feasible for more recent decades than for earlier ones. There are attitude studies in the form of public opinion polls, industry-sponsored market research, and focused sociological work.[36] Some of these disaggregate data which display considerable variation in underlying ideas. Far more evidence of this kind than in the past is produced by participation in the political process: by environmental and consumer organizations to appeal to their member publics; by professionals, business, labor, and agricultural leaders to communicate with others like them; by governmental officials to secure more information about the views of relevant publics who might challenge their decisions. The final environmental impact statements, for example, put on record the views of a vast range of actors about a host of specific policies and projects, an historical record which makes the researcher trying to ferret out the same range of views in the early twentieth century deeply envious.[37] And there are the specialized media sources which communicate among selected publics. All this evidence enables one to reconstruct a far more elaborate set of patterns of human ideas and perspectives, even to establish continua in ideas, a task which seems to be far less possible for earlier years.

One distinction, already indicated, which comes out of this more recent evidence sorts out the broader public ideology from the ideas of the "political intelligentsia." An increasing number of attitude surveys include both a national sample and a group of "opinion leaders." Some pertaining to forest management and chemical regulation, for example, have found that the attitudes of these two "idea groups" differ considerably about such questions as risk in modern society and appropriate conceptions of economic analysis.[38] The ideological evidence we rely upon for the Progressive Era is usually drawn from the journals of opinion, which probably reflected the ideas of a relatively small group rather than of the public at large and define roughly the perspectives of the political intelligentsia of that day. The current equivalent would be the cluster of newspapers and periodicals such as the *New York Times*, the *Washington Post*, the *National Journal*, the *Wall Street Journal* and *Business Week*.

For recent decades considerable change can be identified in the attitude of the political intelligentsia toward environmental affairs, political life, and economic regulation between the mid-1960s and 1981. That group of idea makers had a considerable range of influence; its views set the pattern for many others in formulating their ideas about how the world worked. The intelligentsia established a public context of explanation of events which had considerable weight beyond its boundaries and which fused or clashed with explanatory notions coming from other quarters.

151

It was influential in providing a climate favorable or hostile to public regulation of the economy by formulating explanations of current and past events or making predictions of the future.[39] It is especially useful to sort out those competing explanations in which the media sector was hard on the evidence and those in which it was easy and tolerant.

In the Progressive Era I have been struck by the way in which ideology and practice varied considerably. The language of anti-trust, for example, was utilized heavily by business groups to form trade associations to promote the open-price system, the major aim of which was to restrict competition. While the ideology conveyed a sense of competition in academic economic terms, to those involved in trade the word meant simply that they wished to survive as institutions in the midst of larger firms. Hence price maintenance in whatever form on the part of smaller business could well be explained as an antitrust action. The antitrust ideology which underlay a considerable amount of public regulation of the economy in the late nineteenth and early twentieth centuries must not be thought of in terms of the logical implications of economic theory, but of competing institutions amid rapid reorganization of the economy.[40] Centralization, in both private and public forms, led to adverse impacts on a wide range of smaller institutions, both private and public, for whom an antitrust ideology provided an explanation that made sense. Hence they expounded it freely.

In contrasting public regulation of the economy prior to the 1940s with later years, it seems important to stress the overall ideology of material growth and production in earlier years with the later competing ideology of quality of life involving health and well-being on the one hand and quality of environment on the other. We are likely to take the first for granted unless the historical evolution of later years is emphasized. Economic growth, under either private or public auspices, was often described not just as desirable but as the "natural order" of events, and the role of government was to facilitate that natural order. In this case both private and public action took common ideological ground to sustain an acceptable regulatory framework. In more recent years this ideology has been challenged by new consumption ideologies which seek to attain legitimacy. It may well be that sensitivity to this competing set of ideas in more recent years might lead to new insight about ideologies in earlier years as well. It might, for example, lead us to probe the history of consumption as fully as we have the history of production and by doing so secure a different view of the American past.

Some Implications

What, finally, shall we emphasize in these remarks about the history of economic regulation? First, the years from 1870 to 1940 emphasized competition among producers as the source of regulatory action, while after World War II organized consumer groups began to challenge that overwhelming producer setting. The role of consumers began to change from one of passive choosers in the marketplace to collective action in the political arena. We should not overemphasize this; consumer political institutions have not reached nearly the degree of evolution of those fashioned by producers. But even at this early stage in the evolution of consumer politics we can profitably contrast the two periods of history. A new stage of functional group organization after World War II, for example, involved formation of specialized consumer groups not around earlier consumption emphases on necessities and conveniences, but around the newer ones associated with recreation and leisure. Common avocational interests gave rise to organization and influence in the political economy much akin to the way in which functional organization of producers did earlier.

Second is the elaboration of science and technology as a context of regulatory choice—choice in perspectives, values, and action and hence of political choice—and not simply as a phase in the universal historical impulse of unfolding knowledge and the perfection of "scientific administration." We have an opportunity especially to examine science and technology as instruments of integrating perspectives between private and public sectors, to observe the choices which scientists and engineers, managers and economists made in deciding the particular private and public sectors to which they would relate and the particular integrating perspectives they sought to foster. We can look upon individuals, professional organizations, and overarching scientific institutions such as the National Academy of Sciences as linkage influences and hence crucial integrating forces in the symbiotic relationships between government and the private economy.

Finally, we could do well to take up a more perceptive description and analysis of the ideological context of regulation, to distinguish for example between the generalized public ideology of the mass media, the specialized ideologies of specialized media, and the overarching ideology of the political "thought leaders." These represented competing alternatives in the world of public perception, description and explanation. Often, for example, the search for simplified explanations as fostered by the mass media served as instruments of influence, of first one and then another of the parties in contention in economic regulation, to bolster regulatory action on the one hand or to inhibit it on the other. At one time it served as an instrument to advance regulation in the spirit of "speculative augmentation" as one political analyst has termed it, or at another it constituted a protective ideological covering to obscure the practice of political power and choice.[41]

All this I would offer as a strategy for frontier inquiry that seems to be called for in the history of public regulation of the economy. We are ripe for new directions of investigation, but our inquiries must be informed by new ways of looking at old phenomena, new questions which will inevitably result in searching out new evidence and lead to unconventional observations. The enterprise is justified fully by the overarching role of administration and the regulatory state in twentieth century society and politics. Highly productive frontiers in political history lie in inquiries into the evolution of the administrative state, through a focus on political power and choice. Administration has become the major arena in the American political system for the exercise of political power and choice, and historians have an opportunity to provide an evolutionary understanding of that phenomenon. It is that opportunity to which this foray into the history of economic regulation has been addressed.

The "New" Social Regulation in Historical and Comparative Perspective

DAVID VOGEL

School of Business Administration
University of California, Berkeley

•

I

The purpose of this essay is to illuminate both recurrent and distinctive features of the federal government's efforts to regulate more closely the impact of corporations in the areas of environmental and consumer protection over the last two decades. More generally, it offers an analysis of the dynamics of the contemporary public controversy surrounding the "new wave" of government regulations of business.[1] While there exists a substantial literature on the economics, politics, and administration of contemporary consumer and environmental protection policies, no effort has yet been made to examine them in terms of the evolution of business-government relations either in the United States or abroad.[2]

Between 1900 and 1980, the United States experienced three sustained political efforts to transform the structure and dynamics of business-government relations. The first two of these periods are familiar to historians as the Progressive Era and the New Deal; the third—which still lacks a convenient label—is rooted in the consumer, civil rights, and antiwar movements that emerged during the sixties. This reform effort maintained considerable momentum throughout much of the seventies with the growth of public concern over the impact of the large corporation on American foreign policy, the physical environment, the safety and health of workers, employment opportunities for women and minorities, the integrity of the political process, the availability of energy, and the stability of the American economy. By the late seventies, the coalition of public interest groups and liberal trade unions that had spearheaded the drive for increased federal controls over the private sector began to meet with more effective political resistance from business. As the public became increasingly concerned with the decline of American industry's economic competitiveness, the proponents of additional government intervention in the economy found themselves on the defensive. By the late 1970s, business had regained much of the political initiative that it had lost during the previous two decades.[3]

To begin with a brief historical overview, the Progressive Era roughly spans the years between 1902 and 1914.[4] Its emergence is marked by Theodore Roosevelt's succession to the presidency in the fall of 1901 and the appearance of the first muckraking magazine in January of 1903. By 1914, its national political momentum had come to a halt, and two years later it was on the defensive at the state level. In a brief resurgence of Progressivism in 1916, Woodrow Wilson appointed Louis D. Brandeis to the Supreme Court; Congress approved a rural credit bill and adopted a model workman's compensation measure for federal employees and a law restricting child labor. These proved to have little lasting political significance; both the campaign of 1916 and Wilson's second term were largely dominated by foreign policy issues.

The New Deal is easier to date. It begins with the inauguration of Franklin Roosevelt in the spring of 1933 and was effectively concluded by 1938, the midpoint of FDR's second term.[5] Indeed, Congress approved only three important reform measures during that entire term: the Wagner Housing Act, the Fair Labor Standards Act, and the 1938 Food, Drug, and Cosmetic Act. Each was substantially watered down in the face of opposition from business and conservative congressmen. Moreover, the administration lost three major political fights—the battle for Court reform, the effort to reorganize the federal bureaucracy, and the attempted purge of anti–New Deal Democrats—the result of which significantly weakened the political strength of liberal forces. By the late thirties, Roosevelt, like Wilson two decades earlier, was increasingly turning his attention to foreign policy concerns.

The boundaries of the most recent wave of governmental intervention in the economy are more difficult to determine. Unlike the two previous periods, this one does not correspond to sudden shifts in focus of any particular presidential administration, but spans four administrations of widely disparate character. Although lack of an adequate historical perspective makes any assessment hazardous, the years 1964 through 1977 appear to be reasonable boundary dates.

While public interest in consumer, environmental, and civil rights issues reemerged in the early sixties, it was during the Great Society that the amount of social spending and the scope of government regulation began a steady increase that was to persist through the late seventies. Within a few years, what had begun as an effort to utilize more effectively the incentives and resources of the profit system to ameliorate the urban crisis had developed into an explicit challenge to the purposes and prerogatives of the modern corporation.[6] As public confidence in business began to decline after 1966, pressures for increased social responsibility became transformed into demands for greater corporate accountability.[7] The former was predicated on the possibility of improved cooperation between business and government, while the latter assumed the need for a significant increase in public controls over corporate behavior. The regulatory laws enacted throughout most of the sixties only marginally restricted business decision making. During the late sixties and early seventies, however, the federal government approved a number of major regulatory initiatives in the areas of environmental and consumer protection and occupational health and safety that affected the entire business community. After the 1974–1975 recession many business executives felt increasingly uneasy with the new regulatory statutes as well as the vigor with which they were being enforced by the executive and judicial branches of government; social goals whose achievement had previously appeared well within the reach of an evergrowing economy suddenly were perceived as threatening the ability of the nation's corporations to compete internationally.[8] Business began to mobilize its political resources to reduce the costs imposed by these new social regulations.

Ironically, it was only following the election of a Democratic president in 1976 that the pro-regulation constituencies began to lose their political momentum. In 1977, the two most important legislative goals of the trade union and consumer movements—labor law reform and the establishment of the Consumer Protection Agency—were defeated in Congress as a result of intense business lobbying. A year later a tax law was enacted that went directly contrary to the professed goals of tax reformers, while the Carter administration's conduct of fiscal and monetary policy became strikingly more conservative. A number of new environmental laws were enacted between 1977 and 1980, including the Surface Mining Control and Reclamation Act, the Clean Air Act Amendments of 1977, the Toxic Substance Control Act, and a bill to establish a superfund for handling toxic wastes. But representatives of the affected industries were far more actively involved in drafting these laws than they had been with regulations approved in the late sixties and early seventies. The successful election campaign of President Reagan in 1980—in part based on his promise to reduce the amount of government controls over business conduct—marks an appropriate epitaph for the left-liberal politics of the 1960s and 1970s.

The argument of this essay is that the government controls over the social conduct of corporations enacted between the early sixties and late seventies in the United States are distinctive from those initiated during both the Progressive Era and the New Deal in three critical respects. First, the degree of political conflict and debate over social regulatory policies in general and environmental and consumer protection regulations in particular was significantly greater during the recent period of business-government conflict. Secondly, there was a quantitative and qualitative increase in the scope and intrusiveness of federal controls over corporate social performance. Finally, and most critically, in sharp contrast to both the Progressive Era and the New Deal, government social regulatory policy became far more politicized.

II

Since the emergence of a national market economy during the last third of the nineteenth century, the social abuses of companies conducting business over state lines have been a recurrent theme of public debate. This concern has been particularly visible during periods when the overall pattern of business-government relations was undergoing some significant change. At first glance, the most recent period of business-government conflict would appear to represent a continuation of this pattern. Ralph Nader has been accurately described as a modern muckraker: the publication of his book, *Unsafe at Any Speed,* in 1966 evoked a public response strikingly similar to the success of *100,000,000 Guinea Pigs,* which went through eleven printings within four months of its publication in 1933, or that of *The Jungle,* which became a best seller shortly after it was published in 1906.[9] The articles on patent medicine fraud featured in the *Ladies' Home Journal* and *Collier's* during the Progressive Era are similar in both tone and content to columns published half a century later by Morton Mintz in the *Washington Post.*[10] Many of the nation's contemporary environmental conflicts seem to resemble those waged three-quarters of a century ago. Access of private companies to public lands, the appropriate scope of public land ownership, the desirability of new construction by the Army Corps of Engineers—these issues were the focus of considerable public controversy during both the nation's first and seventh decades.

Yet these similarities are in fact deceptive. In the public debate over business-government relations during the 1960s and 1970s, the importance of corporate social performance has been unprecedented, not only in the United States, but in any industrial democracy. The exposés of the muckrakers, like the accusations of corporate malfeasance that surfaced during the thirties, focused heavily on corporate abuses that affected the economic welfare of consumers, workers, investors, and taxpayers. The prime corporate villains for the Progressives were the trusts that victimized both consumers and small businessmen, while supporters of the New Deal aimed most of their antibusiness rhetoric at manipulations by the financial community.[11]

In sharp contrast, the accusations of corporate misconduct that so preoccupied public opinion during the 1960s and 1970s concentrated on dangers to the health and safety of the citizenry. The following is a partial list of those corporate products that, during the sixties and seventies, were alleged to cause irreparable harm to the public: DDT, cigarettes, the Corvair, flammable children's pajamas, phosphates, poisonous household cleaners, Firestone radial tires, Kepone, DCP, DES, Tris, leaded gasoline, vinyl chloride, the Pinto, aerosol spray cans, asbestos, tampons, cyclamates, saccharin, Dalkon Shields, and the DC-10. And to this list, which could be expanded almost indefinitely, should be added the environmental hazards associated with the nuclear power plant at Three Mile Island and the toxic chemical wastes dumped at Love Canal, as well as the more generalized threats to public health reportedly caused by the presence of various chemicals and particles in the nation's air and water. In short, we are dealing with a level of public consciousness about environmental, consumer, and occupational hazards that appears to be of a different order of magnitude from public outrage over such issues during both the Progressive Era and the New Deal.[12]

During the New Deal, consumer and environmental protection were on the periphery of the political agenda, while during the Progressive Era, they shared the spotlight with such issues as industrial concentration, tariff policy, banking reform, and the rights of workers. But during the last two decades, while other issues directly involving the relationship between business and government, such as the urban crisis, Watergate, overseas payments, and unemployment, have come and gone, battles over consumer and environmental protection have persisted with extraordinary regularity. Legislation in the areas of environmental and consumer protection was debated and acted upon by every session of Congress from the beginning of the sixties through the end of the seventies. Moreover, growing public concern with the economy's poor performance throughout the seventies did not succeed in pushing social regulatory issues off the political agenda; on the contrary, their relative costs and benefits underlay a significant portion of the public debate over energy shortages, inflation, declining productivity, and reindustrialization. An acceptable history of business-government relations during the sixties and seventies could focus exclusively on issues of corporate social performance. Such an effort would clearly be impossible for either the Progressive Era or the New Deal.

III

In addition to their relative political saliency, the controls over corporate social conduct enacted during the 1960s and 1970s differ in number and impact from those initiated during both the Progressive Era and the New Deal.[13] Prior to the 1960s, social regulatory programs were administered almost exclusively by state and local governments. From 1900 through 1965, only one regulatory agency was established at the federal level whose primary responsibility was to protect either consumers, employees, or the public from physical harm due to corporate activities: the Food and Drug Administration, established in 1931. Between 1964 and 1977, ten federal regulatory agencies were created with this as their mandate: the Equal Employment Opportunity Commission (1964), the National Transportation Safety Board (1966), the Council on Environmental Quality (1969), the Environmental Protection Agency (1970), the National Highway Traffic Safety Administration (1970), the Occupational Safety and Health Administration (1970), the Consumer Product Safety Commission (1972), the Mining Enforcement and Safety Administration (1973), the Materials Transportation Bureau (1975), and the Office of Strip Mining Regulation and Enforcement (1977).[14]

Equally striking is the comparative increase in each period in the number of laws restricting corporate social conduct. In the broad area of consumer safety and health, five new laws were enacted by the federal government during the Progressive Era, eleven during the New Deal, and a total of sixty-two between 1964 and 1979. Job safety and other working conditions were the focus of a total of five pieces of national legislation during both the Progressive Era and the New Deal; from 1960 through 1978, twenty-one laws were approved in this area. Two statutes regulating energy and the environment were enacted by the federal government during the Progressive Era, five during the New Deal, and thirty-two during the most recent period of increased government intervention.

Even more significant is the relative impact of the newer regulatory statutes. Government regulations enacted prior to the sixties generally tended to affect either one or a handful of related industries. Additional such laws were enacted during the sixties and seventies, including the Traffic Safety Act, the Child Protection and Toy Safety Act, the Coal Mine Safety Amendments, the Lead Based Paint Elimination Act, the Wholesale Poultry Products Act, and the Toxic Substances Control Act. What is novel about the social regulatory laws of the sixties and seventies is that a significant portion of them cut across industry lines: this is true of all the air and water pollution control statutes, the numerous laws regulating corporate personnel policies, as well as both the Occupational Safety and Health Act and the Consumer Product Safety Act. By vastly expanding the scope of federal social regulation, these laws have succeeded in undermining much of the historic distinction between regulated and unregulated industries.

The result of the increased number of new regulatory laws and agencies, with their expanded scope, was an increase in the intrusion of the federal government into an array of what formerly were private corporate decisions. Regulatory officials began routinely to shape and influence virtually every important decision made by virtually every firm. A huge number of corporate functions and departments developed their counterparts in the regulatory bureaucracy: routine as well as critical decisions made by corporate officials with respect to marketing, personnel administration, plant location, research and development, and production became circumscribed by legal requirements. As a *Fortune* article noted in 1975,

> through streams of legislation, spending, and minutely detailed regulations, frequent application of moral persuasion, and various other means, the government is now present—either in person, or somewhat like Banquo's ghost, in disturbing spirit—at every major business meeting.[15]

Costs of the new social regulations are a final measure of their significance. These consist primarily of three elements: the costs of enforcement by government agencies, and the direct and indirect costs of compliance by business. Direct expenditures include the installation of pollution control equipment or the managing of product recalls, while indirect expenses cover the time spent filling out government forms or delays in the approval of new products or production facilities. The only item that presents no problem of measurement is that of governmental expenditures. These have increased significantly. Between 1970 and 1980, annual government expenditures on the enforcement of social regulations increased from $539 million to $5,036 million, while the number of personnel staffing these agencies increased from 9,707 in 1970 to 63,574 in 1979.[16] We lack comparable figures for the noneconomic regulatory agencies established or expanded during the Progressive Era and the New Deal, but clearly they would be significantly less.

The direct and indirect costs of compliance by business are more difficult to determine. Some regulations may force companies to make expenditures they would have made anyway, while in other cases the costs may be passed on to consumers. Nor do regulations affect all companies or industries equally: the costs of compliance, in the area of environmental protection, the single most expensive category of regulations, disproportionately affect four industries—utilities, paper, chemicals, and steel—while other companies have managed to carve out a profitable market selling pollution control equipment to companies in those industries. Moreover the debate over the costs of regulation has become highly polarized with supporters of regulation prone to minimize them and critics of regulation likely to exaggerate them. Nevertheless, the overall costs of corporate compliance with the regulations affecting health, safety, and environmental protection that were enacted during the sixties and seventies totaled in the tens of billions of dollars by 1980.[17] According to one reliable study, environmental and worker health and safety programs cut conventionally measured productivity by 1.4 percent between 1970 and 1975.[18]

In sum, we are dealing with an increase in government intervention in the economy at least proportionately as great as that which occurred during the Progressive Era and the New Deal; the difference is that in the sixties and seventies, this expansion primarily took the form of increased regulation of corporate social conduct.

IV

The third distinct difference between the contemporary pattern of social controls over business and those enacted during the Progressive Era and the New Deal is that the former have critically affected the balance of power between business and nonbusiness constituencies. During all three periods the pattern of government intervention significantly influenced the distribution of political power among various interest groups. In the Progressive Era, these shifts largely occurred within the business sector: the conflicts over antitrust policy, federal regulation of the railroad and banking industries, and tariff rates pitted particular segments of the business community against other profit-sector enterprises, both large and small. The New Deal broadened the scope of political participation in the shaping of corporate decisions, largely by enlarging the role of the public sector in the distribution and allocation of income and investment and providing legal protection for workers to organize themselves into independent unions. As a result, both the power and autonomy of industrial corporations were reduced, and those of the federal bureaucracy and corporate employees were strengthened.

The "New" Social Regulation

Both these patterns of conflict were repeated during the 1960s and 1970s. The conflicts over the economic regulation and deregulation of the securities, oil, banking, trucking, railroads, utilities, communications, and airlines industries directly affected the balance of power within those particular sectors as well as among their corporate suppliers and customers. Similarly, the recent battles over social welfare expenditures, monetary policy, and deficit spending can be seen as an extension of the disputes over the increases in government spending and taxation that took place during the 1930s. But what is novel about the politics of business-government relations during the last fifteen years is that conflicts over the scope of social regulation have affected directly the power and wealth of the private sector vis-à-vis nonbusiness interest groups. In essence, during the seventies, the controversy over the social regulation of business became the focus of class conflict: it pitted the interests of business as a whole against the public interest movement as well as much of organized labor. The nature of the conflict over regulation became analogous to the struggle over the adoption of the welfare state and the recognition of unions that defined class conflict during the 1930s.

This perspective makes sense out of an episode that at first appears puzzling: the extraordinary mobilization of business political resources during the mid-seventies to defeat the proposal to create a Consumer Protection Agency.[19] A coalition of more than 450 separate organizations and institutions was organized to defeat the CPA—even though the agency itself would have no enforcement powers against business and was certainly among the more innocuous of the newer social regulatory agencies that had been proposed since the early sixties. Only the labor reform bill—a traditional focus of class conflict—stimulated as much corporate coalition building. The explanation is that by 1977 business had come to see regulation as a class issue: executives became concerned not simply with the impact of particular regulatory policies on their companies' balance sheets, but with the broader principle of government regulation itself. CPA became for business a symbol of its struggle to preserve the prerogatives of its class vis-à-vis public interest activists and regulatory administrators. How had this come about?

Prior to the mid-1960s, the business community itself was the most important participant in shaping government controls over its social performance. While the publication of Upton Sinclair's *The Jungle* certainly played a key role in making a political issue of the need for legislation strengthening federal meat inspection, the 1906 Meat Inspection Act was actually initiated and strongly supported by significant segments of the packing industry. The battle over its enactment centered not on the principle of additional federal meat inspection, but on whether the government or the industry should pay for the costs of additional inspection—a contest which the industry won. On this issue, the larger packers favored stricter regulation, both to "assure the public that only sound and wholesome meat and meat food products may be offered for sale" and to strengthen their competitive position in the export trade.[20] While middle-class consumers of canned meat as well as the immigrants who worked in the Chicago packing houses benefited somewhat from the 1906 legislation, neither group played an important role in its formulation. Sinclair himself did not even regard the Meat Inspection Act as a political victory, since he had had other motives in writing *The Jungle*. As he concluded, "I aimed at the public's heart, and by accident I hit it in the stomach."[21]

The 1906 Pure Food and Drug Act, the other major regulation affecting consumer health and safety in the Progressive Era, reflected only a slightly different pattern of political participation and influence. In his efforts to promote a pure food and drug law, Dr. Harvey Wiley, chief chemist for the United States Department of Agriculture, was supported by the Federated Women's Clubs of America, the Consumers League of America, and the American Medical Association. At the time of its enactment, the Pure Food and Drug Act was not even considered by industry to be consumer legislation; its real purpose was to abolish unfair competition in trade. The driving forces behind passage of the law were various farm and industry groups that wanted protection from adulterators and debasers. The drive for federal regulation was supported by the Creamery Butter Makers Association, the Brewers Association, the Confectioners Association, the Wholesale Grocers Association, the Retail Grocers Association, as well as the National Association of Manufacturers. Only the patent drug and whiskey industries and a handful of grocers were opposed to the proposal.

The key conservation measures of the Progressive Era were enacted in a roughly similar political context; while particular firms and industries disagreed over specific policies and decisions, their underlying thrust was to use the authority of the federal government to promote more rational use of scarce natural resources.[22] Conservative policy during the Progressive Era was dominated by notions of rational planning and economic efficiency. Important business interests were to be found on both sides of the major controversies that surfaced during the Roosevelt and Taft administrations.

As in the case of consumer protection, a number of middle-class or citizen organizations and associations played a role in the shaping of conservation policy during the Progressive Era. Among the more important were the General Federation of Women's Clubs, the Daughters of the American Revolution, and the American Civic Association. And within organizations such as the National Conservation League and the Progressive Party, frequent conflicts arose between those who shared a relatively enlightened corporate perspective and those who viewed any business influence as corrupting. As a representative of a women's organization told a meeting of the National Conservation Congress: "We feel that it is for us, who are not wholly absorbed in business, to preserve ideals that are higher than business."[23] From a broader perspective, nevertheless, the middle-class consumer and conservation organizations, like the Progressive movement in general, were either heavily influenced by business interests or shared an orientation compatible with the objectives of major corporate producers. On balance, non-business constituencies were either unable or unwilling to develop an independent political base capable of challenging effectively the business community on those issues on which industry was united. Even public officials such as

Gifford Pinchot and Dr. Wiley, whose influence was essential in the initiation and implementation of social regulations, did not view government social controls over business as a zero-sum game; the ideology of efficiency and expertise that was so critical to the Progressive vision assumed a basic compatibility of private and public purposes.

While the New Deal was characterized by numerous instances of severe tension between business and government, these only infrequently involved disputes over environmental or consumer protection. New Deal conservation measures conflicted with business only as a side effect of the issue of power generation. Moreover, many of the New Deal's most important initiatives in the area of conservation—the establishment of the Civilian Conservation Corps and the Tennessee Valley Authority, the construction of dams by the federal government, and efforts to encourage soil conservation—like those enacted a generation earlier, had as their purpose to enhance either the immediate or long-term economic well-being of agricultural and commercial interests. They did not threaten nor were they opposed by any organizations representing business interests save that of the utility industry, and they were only peripherally related to the politics of conservation.

The New Deal's focus on economic recovery meant that consumer protection had a low place on its agenda.[24] Consumer representatives were appointed to the boards of a number of New Deal agencies, including the National Recovery Administration, the Agricultural Adjustment Administration, and the National Bituminous Coal Commission. But they lacked a political constituency and thus had little impact on these agencies' policies. An effort to mobilize grass-roots consumer pressure on the NRA was unsuccessful, and the most important conflicts in that agency focused on issues of labor representation.

The effort to reform the Pure Food and Drug Act did provoke considerable political conflict.[25] Unlike legislation enacted during the Progressive Era, the 1938 amendments were initiated not by business but by FDA regulators, who by the early 1930s had come to define their role as representing the interests of consumers. Moreover, an organized consumer movement, again in the form

168

of a number of national women's organizations, played a crucial role in countervailing business opposition to stricter federal regulation. Yet the passage of the Food, Drug and Cosmetic Act in 1938 hardly constituted a major setback for business. As Charles Jackson concludes in his history of the law,

> it seems quite fair to suggest that without the increasing body of trade interests brought into the consensus after 1935, no federal food and drug measure would have been passed into law before the opening of World War II.[26]

The passage of the 1938 law was made possible by two factors: a significant watering down of many of its key provisions, and various conflicts of interest among the affected industries. By the late thirties, only the manufacturers of patent medicines were unequivocally opposed to additional regulation. The more professional elements of the pharmaceutical industry supported the need for changes—if only to differentiate themselves from the more disreputable manufacturers of patent medicines. By 1937, following a scandal over the legal sale of elixir sulfanilamide that proved to be toxic, even the trade journal of the drug and cosmetic industry called for additional legislation to counter reduced public confidence in the industry.

The contrast with the contemporary politics of social regulation is marked. The most obvious difference is the enormous increase in the number, sophistication, and importance of political organizations committed to challenging business influence over the shaping of social regulatory policy. The real historical analogue to the contemporary "public interest movement" is not the consumer and environmental organizations that were active during the first half of the twentieth century. Prior to the 1960s, the Prohibition movement represented the only comparable effort in this century to organize successfully large numbers of individuals around the pursuit of what are essentially "public goods." Like the Anti-Saloon League of the early 1900s, contemporary public interest groups have been able, through their use of the media, sophisticated lobbying techniques, and grass-roots organizing, to exert an influence on public policy out of proportion to their actual numerical base in the population.[27]

Regulation in Perspective

Contemporary citizen activists share neither the Progressive faith in "public-spirited men" nor the New Deal passion for administrative autonomy; they have become full and enthusiastic participants in the interest group process. The first major national gathering of "public interest advocates," held in 1976 in Washington, D.C., under the auspices of Public Citizen, Inc. (a Nader-sponsored organization), included representatives of more than 100 citizen organizations—most of which had either been established or significantly revitalized since the mid-sixties.[28] That same year the Foundation for Public Affairs, a business-sponsored research organization, identified 150 public interest organizations that have had a significant impact on national politics affecting business and were enjoying a stable or growing base of support.[29] Congressman Abner J. Mikva called the emergence of public interest groups "the biggest change I've seen in Congress since I first came here in 1968." He added, "These groups have really come into their own. Instead of anti-establishment groups handing out leaflets on a street corner we have people working very effectively in the halls of Congress."[30]

Their legal arm, which includes seventy-five public interest law centers, has also made extensive and effective use of the courts to tighten enforcement of regulatory legislation.[31] After the election of President Carter in 1976, the public interest movement began to make its presence felt in the executive branch of government as well. *Fortune* reported in 1977 that Carter had appointed a total of fifty-nine former activists in the public interest movement to various posts in his administration.[32]

The actual membership base of consumer and environmental organizations dramatically expanded. Between 1970 and 1971, membership in the five largest environmental organizations increased by 400,000, a 33 percent increase in one year.[33] While both the Sierra Club and the Audubon Society were founded around the turn of the century, neither became mass membership organizations until the 1970s; by the mid-seventies, their combined membership was more than half a million.[34] The upsurge in public interest in environmental issues during the late sixties was also reflected in the establishment of new environmental organizations. The most important of these included Friends of the Earth, the League of Conservation Voters, Environmental Action, the Environmental Defense Fund, and the National Resources Defense Council. Unlike the more established and traditional environmental organizations, whose interest in shaping public policy was largely an outgrowth of the various aesthetic or recreational pursuits of their members, these new organizations functioned primarily as political or legal lobbies.

The consumer movement has also become both better organized and more politicized. In 1967 a group of activists from a number of organizations, including the President's Consumer Advisory Council, established the Consumer Federation of America, an umbrella organization that currently includes approximately 150 member organizations. A highly visible and influential spokesman for the political interests of consumers emerged during the sixties in the person of Ralph Nader.[35] By the early seventies, "Mr. Consumer" had established a large and relatively well-funded network of lobbyists and litigators based in Washington, with 100,000 Americans annually supporting his political efforts by sending checks to "Public Citizen." Finally, the impact of consumer groups and activists became appreciably strengthened by the alliance they were able to develop with organized labor. While particular trade unions have at times differed with the positions taken by environmental groups, organized labor has been an extremely active and effective part of the consumer coalition.[36] By contrast, organized labor did not exist as an important national political force during the Progresssive Era and was preoccupied with fighting—successfully, to be sure—for its very existence during the New Deal.

Equally important has been the public interest movement's ability to reshape the arenas in which regulatory policy was decided. Prior to the 1960s, the processes by which regulatory policy was formulated and implemented tended to be removed from interest group pressures. Congress passed broad and general enabling statutes, and the actual process for formulating detailed regulations was left to an administrative agency—often created in such a way as to make it as independent as possible from the rest of the executive branch. These agencies conducted their business with a relatively large degree of discretion and tended to rely heavily on the advice of experts in making their decisions.[37] To the extent that the judiciary intervened in this process at all, it was mainly at the initiative of property owners arguing that the agency's officials had interpreted the intent of Congress too broadly. After the mid-1930s, even these interventions became less frequent.

Critical to the movement's political impact on policy during the late sixties and seventies was its success in increasing the role played by nonindustry constituencies in all three arenas.[38] Fearful that the agency officials entrusted with interpreting congressional statutes would be "captured" by industry or experts sympathetic to industry, public interest lobbyists sought to reduce the amount of discretion given to the administrative agencies. Only two independent regulatory agencies were established during the most recent wave of increased government intervention in the economy, namely, the Consumers Product Safety Commission and the Equal Employment Opportunity Commission. More importantly, a number of key regulatory statutes—the Clean Air Acts of 1970 and 1977 are the most notable examples—contained extremely detailed provisions, even to the extent of specifying precise numerical goals. This served two purposes. First, it inflated tremendously the role of Congress in shaping regulatory policy, giving the legislative lobbying efforts of public interest groups increased importance. In addition, it provided a broader basis for the courts to challenge agency decisions on the grounds that they were inconsistent with congressional intentions.

The second critical arena to which the public interest movement succeeded in gaining access was the courts.[39] Beginning in the mid-sixties, the Supreme Court began steadily to broaden its rules governing standing, granting a large number of consumer, environmental and ad hoc citizens' groups the right to file suits on behalf of a broad range of "public interests." This enabled proregulation constituencies to challenge a wide array of governmental decisions which they regarded as too responsive to "private" (i.e., corporate) rather than "public" (i.e., proregulation) interests. The liberalization of standing requirements, on occasion, even enabled public interest groups to magnify their limited legislative gains. One student of this process has concluded that

> recent changes in the law of standing have been important in fundamentally transforming the relationship to the public of private interests, in particular corporate business, causing the environmental and consumer damages complained of—a transformation through adjudication analogous to the changed relationship between business and labor brought about by Section 7 of the Wagner Act.[40]

Equally important, a number of regulatory statutes enacted during the 1970s contained provisions explicitly authorizing private citizens to sue to secure their enforcement.

The third arena to become a battleground between business and political forces favoring additional regulation was the administrative agencies themselves. Through a combination of congressional statutes, Court decisions, and the actions of their own officials, the newer social regulatory agencies have become far more open to participation by nonindustry groups.[41] Rather than justifying their decisions in terms of their independence or expertise, these agencies have attempted to legitimate their actions by providing the public with the opportunity to participate in their deliberations. During the seventies, nearly every social regulatory agency developed a nonindustry "shadow," capable of effectively monitoring and challenging each of its decisions.[42] And just as public interest plaintiffs were frequently able to receive compensation for their legal fees, so too have some regulatory agencies actually subsidized the costs of representation by public interest groups.

As a result of the emergence of both independent consumer and environmental organizations and their increased access to the policy process, business was less able to influence the shaping of social regulatory policies during the 1960s and 1970s than it was during the Progressive Era or the New Deal. None of the major policy departures in the areas of consumer and environmental protection, occupational health and safety, or personnel policy were initiated by corporate interests. On some of the most far-reaching regulatory initiatives, such as the Civil Rights Act, the National Environmental Policy Act, the Clean Air Act of 1970, and the Occupational Safety and Health Act, business was not even a particularly important political participant. On legislation affecting particular industries, companies tended to be more politically involved, but on many occasions the policies that emerged only marginally reflected their input.

Corporations certainly played an active role in the deliberations of the numerous new regulatory agencies created during the sixties and seventies, but on balance, business tended to be more displeased with the decisions of these agencies than were the nonindustry groups that had struggled for their establishment. The overall relationship between the regulated and the regulators became highly strained. Indeed, in the case of several agencies, such as the Environmental Protection Administration, the National Highway Traffic Safety Administration, the Occupational Safety and Health Administration, and the Equal Employment Opportunity Commission, a kind of symbiotic relationship developed between the staff of the agencies and various nonindustry constituencies quite similar to that described by the traditional "capture" theory of regulation. Moreover, judicial oversight during the sixties and through most of the seventies, in contrast to both the Progressive Era and the New Deal, tended to strengthen rather than weaken the stringency of agency rule making.

Intraindustry conflicts have certainly played an important role in the contemporary politics of government regulation.[43] Specific regulatory policies affected individual companies differently, particularly in the area of environmental protection, and, on several occasions, particular segments of business employed the conflict over social regulatory policies either to maintain or strengthen their competitive positions.[44] The important difference, however, is that contemporary intrabusiness conflicts occurred primarily as an indirect and unintended consequence of increases in federal regulatory activity; the disputes among business interests took place within a political framework that business itself did not create. Whatever the ultimate costs and benefits of the new social regulations to society as a whole, their costs do fall disproportionately on producers; regardless of their benefits, it would be difficult to contend that, overall, private sector managers and investors are better off because of them.

The "New" Social Regulation

In sum, it is thus only during the last fifteen years that social regulation emerged as the focal point of conflict between political forces committed to restricting corporate prerogatives and those intent on preserving them. A desire to curb corporate power—to ameliorate the various abuses associated with big business and high finance—was an important part of the political vision of both the Progressives and the supporters of the New Deal. What distinguishes the reform movement that emerged over the last two decades is that it has largely identified the abuse of corporate power with the impact of companies on the health and safety of consumers, employees, and the public. In the numerous proposals that critics of business developed throughout the seventies to restrict the rights of management—ranging from increased disclosure to the protection of the rights of whistle-blowers, from increased penalties for white-collar criminals to changes in the composition of the corporate board—the important underlying motive has been to curb the kinds of corporate behavior that clearly fall under the rubric of social conduct.[45]

V

Just as public interest groups and their allies during the last two decades have largely focused their efforts on corporate social abuses, so too has the business community come to perceive increases in social regulation as the most important contemporary threat to its wealth and power. If executives were asked, at any time throughout the seventies, to cite the changes in business-government relations that had most disturbed them, the newer social regulations would probably be near the top of the list.[46] By the early seventies, executives had begun to resent both the arrogance and ignorance of regulatory officials. Business executives and those sympathetic to them publicly blamed government regulation for a wide variety of ills ranging from increasing the price of consumer products to reducing the incentive for innovation and risk taking, from impairing productivity to retarding the rate of investment in new plants and facilities.[47] Companies, business associations and conservative foundations began to invest considerable sums in the preparation and dissemination of articles, books, studies and reports documenting the problems created by the federal government's efforts to better protect consumers, employees, and the environment.[48]

More abstractly, the social regulations that proliferated in recent years became viewed by some supporters of the business community as the cutting edge of the efforts of a "new class" of middle-class professionals to substitute decisions made by bureaucrats and lawyers for those made by consumers and investors.[49] Much of the focus of corporate public relations programs during the seventies was directed at convincing the educated middle class that increasing the government's power over business was not in fact in "the public interest." These programs included placing advocacy advertising in the nation's print media, sponsorship of various cultural programs on public television, and the endowment of Chairs of Free Enterprise at colleges and universities.[50]

The stakes involved in the conflict over the new wave of social regulations enacted during the sixties and seventies can be further documented by examining the substantial changes in corporate political participation that occurred in the seventies. These can be roughly divided into three categories: lobbying, corporate public affairs efforts, and grass-roots organizing.

Between 1968 and 1978, the number of corporations with public affairs offices in Washington increased from 100 to more than 500.[51] Their size also became larger: the typical Washington corporate office in 1978 contained six or seven individuals, as contrasted with one or two in 1974. For example, the Washington office of General Motors consisted of three persons in 1968; ten years later it had increased to twenty-eight. Trade associations also increased their Washington presence. While in 1970, 21 percent of all national associations were based in Washington, by 1978, 27 percent had Washington as their headquarters. In 1977, an average of one association a week relocated its main office to the nation's capital, bringing the total number of trade associations headquartered in Washington to 2,000. And in 1973, the National Association of Manufacturers moved its headquarters to Washington, D.C., as part of its effort to upgrade its lobbying activities.

The "New" Social Regulation

The growing corporate physical presence in Washington has been accompanied by equally sizable increases in the numbers of lawyers and accountants. The Washington, D.C., bar increased from 16,000 in 1972 to 26,000 in 1978—in large measure because of more corporate demands for legal representation. Not only have Washington law firms grown in both size and number, but a significant number of major law firms throughout the United States now have Washington offices. Similarly, large numbers of new accounting firms have opened up offices in Washington, while those already in the city have doubled and tripled the size of their professional staffs. All told, there are currently 450 law firms and 234 accounting firms in Washington—largely serving corporate clients. And far more corporate public relations efforts now take place in Washington.

The increasing attention of business to government relations is also reflected within the firm itself. A 1979 Conference Board study reported:

> Ninety-two percent of the government relations executives polled said that over the last three years, their companies' concern with and involvement in federal government relations had gone up. Of these respondents, 61 percent said that this increase has been extremely strong. Among the companies [responding to the Board's survey], 28 percent of the [governmental affairs] departments in operation today did not exist three years ago.[52]

Moreover, government relations gained greater status within the corporate organization as its practitioners became more directly involved in corporate decision making and increased their own rank within the management hierarchy; in a number of corporations, the senior public affairs officer became a member of the corporate board. Corporations also began to devote considerably more resources to the monitoring and managing of "emerging issues"—at the federal level. Alerting firms to changes in the public's expectations of business became a prominent feature of management consulting.

Another index of the shift in corporate priorities was the greater personal involvement of chief executive officers in external relations during the seventies. A 1976 study reported that 93 percent of the CEOs polled indicated they were spending more time on external relations than they had been in 1973 or 1970, while a 1978 survey revealed that the chief executive officers of the Fortune 1000 devoted approximately 40 percent of their time to "public issues"—in contrast to 20 percent only two years earlier.[53] More recent estimates place this number as high as 50 percent for "the top people in most large companies."[54] As John de Butts, the former chairman of AT&T, recently remarked,

> So vital . . . is the relationship of government and business that to my mind the chief executive officer who is content to delegate responsibility for the relationship to his public affairs experts may be neglecting one of the most crucial aspects of his own responsibility.[55]

The formation of the Business Roundtable in 1972 is a striking symbol of this heightened commitment: the Roundtable is the first business lobbying organization to be based on the principle of the personal participation of the corporate CEO.

Finally, beginning in the mid-seventies, a number of firms made extensive efforts to mobilize their "natural constituencies," namely, their stockholders and present and former employees. These individuals were encouraged to make political contributions through corporate political action committees as well as to correspond with their congressmen on issues affecting the company. A quarter of the firms polled by the Conference Board had recently developed a stockholder program; it is estimated that by the late seventies corporations were spending between $850 and $900 million per year on these efforts. The company in the vanguard of this effort was Atlantic Richfield, which in 1975 began organizing 53,000 of its individual shareholders, 6,000 of its employees, and 2,000 retirees into 45 regional committees. These committees were encouraged to take stands on public policy issues paralleling those of ARCO's management and to become politically active in their communities; the company spends $750,000 per year on these efforts. The dramatic change in the number of political action committees—from 89 in 1976 to 433 in 1977—testifies less to stepped-up campaign spending by business than to a broadening of the number of individuals personally solicited on behalf of the corporations.[56]

The "New" Social Regulation

No comparable increase in corporate political activity at the federal level took place during either the Progressive Era or the New Deal, though both periods witnessed major increases in government intervention in the economy.[57] Moreover, the threat the New Deal posed to corporate prerogatives was certainly as great as that which took place during the 1960s and 1970s, and yet corporate political pressures on Washington increased only marginally during the 1930s. Why?

The decline in the importance of political parties in the early seventies, the increased access of interest groups to the media, and the weakened power of congressional party leaders and committee chairmen all contributed to the need for companies to develop new mechanisms for influencing federal politics. But at least equally important have been changes in the visibility, importance, and political significance of the social controls over business that took place in the late sixties and early seventies.

Their cumulative result has been to increase enormously the private sector's vulnerability to decisions made in Washington. Unlike fiscal and social welfare policies that only indirectly affect business decision making or economic regulations that vitally affect particular segments of business, or even labor laws that only surface on the political agenda from time to time, social regulatory policies directly interfere with day-to-day business decisions, affect all companies, and are in a continual state of flux. In this they are analogous to the controls over American business enacted during World War II, with one important difference: public interest groups in their adversary role have contributed significantly to business uncertainty over the direction of public policy. Not surprisingly, when asked to what they attribute the increasing involvement of their companies in governmental relations, 71 percent of those corporate executives working in public affairs cited as the most important factor "the impact of recent government regulations and legislation."[58] As GM's Washington lobbyist noted, "More and more decisions are being made in Washington that used to be made in the marketplace. As that happens, it becomes increasingly important for business to keep track of government."[59]

Regulation in Perspective

The distinctiveness of the contemporary pattern of federal controls over corporate social performance can also be appreciated by comparing the American experience with those of other capitalist democracies.

At first glance the similarities are most apparent. Throughout the sixties and seventies, public interest in consumer and environmental issues increased dramatically in both Western Europe and Japan.[60] There were a number of widely publicized cases of abuses of the physical environment as a result of industrial activity. These included a major oil spill after the *Torrey Canyon* was wrecked off the coasts of France and Great Britain in 1967, the accidental pollution of the Rhine River in 1969 by a pesticide discharge that killed four million fish, the washing ashore of eighty drums of dangerous chemicals in southwestern England in 1972, and an outbreak of Minamata disease as a result of mercury poisoning in the mid-sixties in Japan. Moreover, several European cities and industrial centers experienced widely publicized problems with air pollution during the sixties.

The growth of public interest in environmental and consumer issues was reflected in the establishment of a number of new political organizations in both Western Europe and Japan.[61] Between 1966 and 1973, four new environmental groups were established in the United Kingdom: the Conservation Society, the Committee for Environmental Conservation, Friends of the Earth, and the Socialist Environmental Resources Association, an affiliate of the Labour Party. A number of local and regionally based environmental organizations were established in France in the early seventies in order to challenge specific plans for industrial development and in 1974 an ecology candidate ran for president of the Republic; in 1977 ecologists stood for election in thirty-three French departments.

In the Federal Republic of Germany, a loose coalition of anti-nuclear groups formed a new political party in 1980 named "The Greens" in order to compete in both federal and state elections.

Women's associations in Japan, with a total of 15 million members, became increasingly active in consumer politics during the seventies. In 1970 and 1971, a number of these groups organized a successful boycott of television set manufacturers to protest the high profit margins. During the 1970s, *Which,* the English equivalent of *Consumer Reports,* became considerably more concerned with public policy issues, while a number of other private consumer organizations grew in number and strength. A loose coalition of consumer groups, some of which were tied to the trade union movement, also emerged in France during the 1970s.

The multiplicity of government controls over corporate social conduct that arose in Western Europe and Japan roughly paralleled developments in the United States.[62] While several European states have a history of environmental controls dating back more than a century, since 1960 every major industrial nation has approved important new laws designed to protect the environment. Water pollution control statutes were enacted in Great Britain in 1961, France in 1964, Sweden in 1969, Japan in 1970, and the Federal Republic of Germany in 1976; legislation regulating air pollution was approved by Japan in 1962, by Sweden in 1969, and by France and the Federal Republic of Germany in 1974. Moreover, France, the Federal Republic of Germany, and Sweden also began to require environmental impact statements. And between 1968 and 1972, Great Britain, Sweden, and the Federal Republic of Germany passed new consumer protection legislation.

The European Economic Community also became active in both environmental and consumer regulation.[63] In 1970, EEC adopted a directive on motor vehicle air pollution as part of its industrial action program, and three years later the Council of Ministers endorsed the general principles of a community environmental action program. Subsequently, directives have been issued covering a wide variety of environmental hazards, including the dumping of toxic wastes, the sulfur content of gas and oil, and noise pollution. In 1973, the Council of Europe Consultative Assembly adopted a Consumer Protection Charter to encourage its member countries to establish minimum legal standards of consumer protection. The Community itself has issued directives dealing with food standards, labeling and auto safety.

However, issues of corporate social performance have not produced as much tension between business and governmental elites in Western Europe and Japan as they have in the United States. They have produced comparatively few denunciations of government intrusion into private corporate affairs on the part of business spokesmen. While European and Japanese executives have certainly opposed various consumer and environmental regulations, they appear to have invested only a fraction of the resources that their American counterparts allocated to challenging social regulations; no major changes in the political behavior of corporations or business associations in Western Europe and Japan took place during the 1960s and 1970s. In addition, once these new regulations were approved, the businesses have tended to comply with them with a minimum of resistance. Why?

It is not the case that American standards are on the whole stricter: they are in some cases, but not in others.[64] In nations with strong trade unions, occupational safety and health standards tend to be at least as stringent as those in the United States. The recent product liability standards proposed by the European Community are far harsher than anything that currently exists in American law. American air pollution control standards, particularly with respect to mobile source emissions, have tended on the whole to be more severe than those in Western Europe, but the Japanese auto emission standards enacted in 1974 are comparable to those in the United States. The British air and water pollution laws enacted in the early seventies are generally considered to be more effective than those in any other industrial nation. Advertising and marketing are far more restricted in the Scandinavian countries than they are in the United States. This list could be extended. The point is that the overall volume and severity of environmental, consumer, and occupational health and safety standards in Western Europe and Japan are not sufficiently different from those affecting business managers in the United States to account for the uniqueness of the latter's political response.

The "New" Social Regulation

One explanation has to do with the closer ties that have historically existed between business and governmental elites outside the United States. Numerous observers have noted that relations between business and government in Western Europe and Japan are less likely to be characterized by the public hostility and mutual mistrust that are a staple of their relationship in the United States.[65] With a powerful and relatively independent state bureaucracy preceding the emergence of industrial capitalism, the European and Japanese business communities were forced to develop a close working relationship with their governments from the outset. In contrast, the American state played a far less central role in the industrial development of the United States; thus the American business community never needed to learn to cooperate with it as closely. The result is an "adversary relationship" that has persisted for more than a century. Seen from this perspective, the hostility that American executives have displayed toward social regulations is a phenomenon that dates back more than a century.

One consequence of their differing pattern of economic development is that firms in Western Europe and Japan have historically enjoyed considerably less autonomy than those in the United States. Not only are industries more likely to be publicly owned in Western Europe and Japan, but even more importantly, the governments of these nations either control or strongly influence the allocation of a significant share of the capital investment required by industry. They also frequently play an important role in the determination of wage and price levels, and in the direction of industrial development. In addition, trade unions in Western Europe exert a far greater influence in corporate decisions—at both the plant and companywide level—than in the United States. Consequently, increased government controls over corporate decisions affecting consumers, workers, and the environment in Western Europe and Japan since the early sixties represented only a marginal reduction in autonomy for executives in these nations; they took their place beside an already extensive list of constraints over management decisions. Accordingly, the changes in the scope of government intervention associated with social regulations in the United States represented a proportionately far greater increase in the degree of public controls over business than was true outside the United States; they thus tended to meet with proportionately greater resistance.[66]

A second set of factors has to do with the different ways in which social regulations are formulated and administered in the United States and the other industrial nations. While restrictions on corporate social performance in the United States have been associated with a measurable shift in the balance of power between industry and nonindustry interests, this has not been the case in either Western Europe or Japan. In fact the very factors that distinguish the contemporary dynamics of social regulation from that of previous periods in American history also serve to distinguish the contemporary politics of social regulation in the United States from that of other capitalist democracies. The pattern of social regulation in the United States prior to the mid-sixties and that of Western Europe and Japan through the present both included greater participation by industry, in contrast with the contemporary dynamics of social regulation in the United States.

In contrast to the United States, European officials who staff administrative units responsible for enforcing environmental and consumer protection policies are identical in training and social outlook to those who have always staffed the state bureaucracy.[67] Environmental and consumer organizations certainly exist in Europe, but their impact on the shaping of regulatory policy ranges from minimal to nonexistent; they have little formal access to the administrative process and virtually none to the courts.[68] They tend to have very small paid staffs and are often dependent on financial assistance from their governments. Even more importantly, regulatory bureaucrats in Europe and Japan enjoy more discretion in enforcing restrictions on business than most regulatory officials are allowed in the United States.[69] Consequently, the administration of environmental and consumer regulations in Europe is not characterized by the delays and uncertainties that surround their enforcement in the United States. They tend to be implemented through a process of private negotiation between government officials and industry not dissimilar to the way in which most economic as well as social regulations were enforced in the United States prior to the mid-sixties.[70] In the case of water pollution policy in France, Great Britain, and the Federal Republic of Germany, industrial associations actually administer the regulations themselves through a mechanism of pollution fees.[71]

Finally, the politicians and officials responsible for the formulation and enforcement of environmental and consumer regulations in Western Europe and Japan appear to be more sensitive to the economic impact of these rules than their counterparts in the United States. This is most obvious in the case of consumer protection policies in Europe: as in the United States during the Progressive Era, many national regulations have been motivated more by a need to improve the internal competitiveness of the products of a country's own citizenry than by a desire to protect consumers.[72] Even environmental regulations in Western Europe and Japan, however, appear to be designed in such a way as to minimize the hardships they impose on industry. This is true not only of nations that have been dominated by conservative political parties, such as France, but is equally true of Sweden, whose political system was controlled by the Social Democrats up through the mid-seventies.[73] It is noteworthy that the only nation whose private sector pollution-control investment as a percentage of GNP is greater than that of the United States is Japan, which also has by far the strongest economy of any major industrial nation.

Thus the real irony of the contemporary pattern of social regulations among the major capitalist democracies is that they, on balance, seem to be most onerous on business in the United States—traditionally regarded as the most conservative and "pro-business" capitalist polity.

EDITOR'S NOTE

Drafts of the foregoing essays were presented at a Conference on the History of Public Policy sponsored by the Harvard Business School on October 24 and 25, 1980. Several authors substantially revised their papers in response to the conference discussion, and in particular to detailed remarks by the following assigned commentators:

McCraw essay: Louis P. Galambos, Johns Hopkins University
    Barry D. Karl, University of Chicago

Keller essay: David S. Landes, Harvard University
    Richard B. Stewart, Harvard Law School

Hawley essay: Paul W. Glad, University of Oklahoma
    Richard H. K. Vietor, Harvard Business School

Hays and Vogel essays: Robert D. Cuff, York University
    James Q. Wilson, Harvard University

The authors are grateful to these commentators, and to other conference participants as well, for their many valuable suggestions.

Together with extensive critiques of the essays, the conference produced an exceptionally lively and thoughtful series of discussions concerning regulation in general. The concluding essay in this volume—woven from the commentators' written remarks, from other notes, and from tape recordings of the sessions—captures and synthesizes the principal themes of these discussions. The rapporteur, Gerald P. Berk, is a Ph.D. candidate in political science at the Massachusetts Institute of Technology.

Approaches to the History
of Regulation

GERALD P. BERK

•

Regulation and The History of Ideas

The history of antitrust, of public utility regulation, of corporate standard setting and of social regulation is, in large part, a history of how people thought about and debated the nature of the market, economic efficiency, business social responsibility, and acceptable levels of health and environmental risk in industrial society. This means that a substantial part of the historian's task involves searching for the sources of ideas that form the premises and logic for institutional and policy prescriptions. Where to look for the sources of ideas about business regulation, however, is not always clear. Nor is it clear what methods of probing the history of ideas are most advantageous or illuminating for reconstructing an accurate account of regulatory policies and politics. Both issues were the subject of debate in the Conference on the History of Public Policy.

Three explanations of the sources and success of ideas about regulation were emphasized in the conference discussion. The first stressed American culture; the second, the evolution of professional attitudes and commitments; and the third, politics.

On the first view, deep and persistent ideological tensions between centralization and decentralization, competition and cooperation, and individualism and communalism in American thought have been at the core of every debate over the proper role of government in regulating market relations. So, despite historical discontinuity in the issues and the groups involved in regulation,

187

underlying ideological concerns have remained very much the same. These unresolved fundamentals in American political culture, according to Morton Keller and other conference participants, have resulted in the persistence of nineteenth century values amid the growth of the administrative state in the twentieth century. Although the instruments of public authority and the range of interests have grown, the old tensions have been preserved. One must recognize, for example, that antitrust attitudes persisted during the 1920s alongside the corporatist structures and ideology that Ellis Hawley describes in his paper in this volume; although the courts accepted big business in the 1920s, they remained hostile to price and production controls.

Cultural tensions set not only the parameters for public opinion and debate over regulatory structures and policy, but also the context of intellectual discourse within and among the legal, economics, political science and scientific professions. As James Q. Wilson argued, "Within the 'political intelligentsia' there is steadily at war, one with the other, a commitment to individualism and to personal self-expression, which has its origins clearly in the democratic ideology of the revolutionary period, on the one hand; and on the other hand, a desire for communalism, harmony, rationalization, and moralization of society, which perhaps has roots in our Puritan heritage. These two sets of views—the individualistic, rights-oriented view and the communal harmony, rationalized society view—are in constant tension with one another."

The contrast between law and economics was cited as an expression of this tension. The commitment to private rights, individualism, and judicial review, which form the foundations of American law, has resulted in a uniquely American propensity to solve market disputes through case by case adversarial litigation. By contrast, a more comprehensive policy and planning approach, peculiar to economists and public administrators, has historically been the basis for institutional solutions to market disputes.

Although the cultural argument can explain the sources and continuity of fundamental tensions in the history of thought about regulation (and thereby symbols underlying debate during particular periods), it cannot explain why public and elite opinion shift over time along the continuum of individualism and communalism. That is, it cannot explain changes in public opinion or professional attitudes toward business regulation, nor can it explain why some ideas are influential at certain times and not at others.

In discussing Ellis Hawley's work on associationalism in the 1920s, for example, Richard Vietor and other conference participants agreed that Hawley's criteria for corporatism were unique neither to the 1920s nor to his illustrative industries. State-sanctioned private standard setting, agricultural marketing cooperatives, and the structure of shared public and private disciplinary power in securities regulation were cited as examples fulfilling Hawley's criteria. What was unique about the 1920s, Louis Galambos argued, was that the beliefs held by a small coalition of businessmen, politicians, and professionals were made formal and legitimate in the public eye. Similarly, during the Progressive period the cultural tension between competition and cooperation was manifest in the debate over antitrust between corporate lawyers and progressives like Brandeis. Yet American society chose to celebrate not only Brandeis himself but also the Progressive interpretation of structural changes in the economy and the antitrust solution to these changes.

There was no dearth of examples, moreover, of significant changes in elite and professional attitudes toward regulation. Despite the tension between law and economics cited above, in both professions dominant attitudes toward the use of administrative agencies to solve economic, political, and environmental problems have fluctuated over time—at times embracing the ideas of communalism and rationalization and at other times those of individualism and private rights.

The evolution of administrative law in the twentieth century is such an example. Richard Stewart pointed out that in American jurisprudence the tension between individual rights and communitarian rationalization is embodied in the formal, eighteenth century distinction between public and private law. In public law it is assumed that electoral representation—the will of the community—will legitimate policy outcomes, while in private law legitimacy is derived from the substance of private agreements, that is, contracts. In the absence of formal voting procedures, any amount of administrative discretion in policy formation or rulemaking is subject to the possibility of exclusive interest representation, and the distinction between public and private legitimation tends to break down. Therefore, how the legal profession has assimilated the administrative agency to the public-private distinction is central to the evolution of American legal doctrine and institutional disputes over regulation.

Stewart defined four periods in the evolution of twentieth century administrative law, each distinguished by its position on the public-private continuum. In the earliest years of positive regulation, legal doctrine denied the rightful exercise of administrative discretion. Adhering to a "narrow delegation of legislative authority" doctrine, the courts held that legislatures could not simply hand over power to regulatory agencies in blocks, but should provide clear directions for the exercise of regulatory authority through statutory commands. Judicial review would serve as a procedural safeguard to assure private parties that a particular exercise of regulatory authority was in fact consistent with the statute in question. This "traditional model" of administrative law served as a legitimator of administrative regulation by asserting that each time a regulator acted against a private firm, his action must be consistent with a statutorily defined public norm.

After the First World War and in the wake of state management of the railroads, the traditional model was relaxed. During the 1920s the courts began to perceive the need for forms of harmonization or planning in the market that could not be captured through explicit statutory commands. Yet early New Deal legislation brought the traditional model and the 1920s doctrine into conflict. And, in the 1935 *Schechter* case, the Supreme Court reasserted the public-private distinction by striking down NRA code agreements as an unlawful use of governmental power to achieve private ends. Reversion to the traditional model, however, did not survive the Depression. In later New Deal decisions the courts once again saw the need for a positive role for the state in industrial planning and rationalization and deferred to administrative discretion.

With the revival of the economy, legal opinion turned to a compromise. In the Administrative Procedures Act of 1946, Congress steered a middle course between the very tight restriction of administrative power in the traditional model and the extreme discretion permitted in later New Deal decisions. That compromise operated until the mid-sixties, when, for the first time, access to the judicial and administrative systems became extremely open to a wide variety of interest groups and individuals. This third phase was legally justified on public interest grounds, namely, that some groups had been systematically neglected in administrative rulemaking and procedure.

The notion of an objective public interest, however, quickly broke down into an "interest representation model" as a variety of private advocacy groups made claims to substantive outcomes and representation in regulatory decision making. In this third phase, as in the deferential phase, the public-private distinction in administrative law became hopelessly blurred. The traditional separation of powers model, in which Congress was empowered to aggregate competing interests, was bypassed in favor of direct representation in regulatory administration. As a result, regulation became the locus for competing demands on the allocation of private investment capital.

Responding once again to the state of the economy, the courts, in the belief that interest group representation in administrative procedure has exacerbated declining investment, productivity, and economic growth, have attempted to shift the struggle over investment to another political arena. In a recent decision striking down OSHA's standards for industrial exposure to benzene, the Court retreated from the public interest or representational conception of administrative law and returned to the traditional model of narrow delegation of legislative powers, thus restoring the public-private distinction as a premise of legal opinion.

The relationship between changing professional attitudes and institutional evolution is equally germane to the current deregulation movement. In order to explain deregulation, James Q. Wilson observed, one must identify the sources of change in professional perceptions of the market—perceptions which underlie the logic of deregulation. Taking the case of airline regulation, Wilson

191

pointed out that the conventional wisdom holds that the Civil Aeronautics Board was created to foster the development of the industry. Yet, at its inception the board was not considered a potential instrument for price fixing and cartelization, while in retrospect it is seen as nothing but that. This changed perception of the status of the market, in Wilson's view, cannot be explained by changes in technology or the economy, but must be explained by the changing attitudes and commitments of the "political intelligentsia." The current generation of "thought leaders," bureaucrats, and legislative aides, who have been deeply influenced by the capture image of regulatory agencies, have sought to break the unholy alliance between the captured regulatory agency and the business firm. This attitude represents the individualist strand in our political culture—that is, the worries about corporatism in American life. The capture analysis, moreover, forms the intellectual premise for the argument that consumer welfare would be enhanced by releasing the free play of the market.

A second hypothesis suggested by Wilson concerns that segment of the political intelligentsia whose primary concern is not with minimum prices or consumer welfare per se, but with the "quality of life." This position, held by a left-liberal segment of the intellectual community, represents the communitarian strand in American thought. Elevating the quality of life in advanced industrial society, for this group of thought leaders, involves labor representation on corporate boards, reduced environmental, health, and safety risks, and enhanced civil rights for women and minorities.

In the two examples cited above—the evolution of administrative law and the changing status of the market among social scientists—the focus is on intellectual history; and the method, similar to that of the historian of science, is to search for theoretical premises of policy remedies in the evolution of a bounded body of professional thought. Whether or not scientific or legal ideas actually influence regulatory policy, however, is another question—one which a number of conference participants thought could not be assumed.

An opposing view stressed, instead, class or interest group influence on the evolution of statutory and administrative policy. In this view, if professional ideas have been successful it is because they have given formal arguments and a logic of justification to politicians pursuing personal or cliental goals. The legal, adversarial approach to market regulation—antitrust—was attractive in the Progressive era, according to this thesis, because it cushioned the impact of rapid social change for a politically active segment of American society. Similarly, the economist's efficiency paradigm is currently embraced by politicians because of its relevance to such problems as depressed investment, low productivity, and economic stagnation.

A compromise position in the conference debate over the influence of intellectuals was implicit in Paul Glad's commentary on Ellis Hawley's essay. Glad suggested that it was insufficient to explain corporatist regulatory structures during the 1920s as simply the "triumph of an idea." Instead, one must look more closely at the motivations of those who formed the corporatist alliance. Hoover's brand of associationalism allowed him to form a coalition through which he could exercise his ideas. Glad postulated three probable components to that coalition: 1) the idealists—believers in associationalism and scientific efficiency, many of whom were Hoover's disciples; 2) the profit maximizers or the "greedy"—the lumbermen, for instance, who endorsed associational idealism as long as it did not lead to bureaucratic interference with their autonomy; and 3) the diffident—those who feared government regulation and saw associationalism as a way to forestall an encroaching administrative state. Thus, both ideas and interests influenced the rise of corporatist regulatory policy.

Other participants argued that the influence and autonomy of intellectuals cannot be assumed, but rather are historical and empirical questions. Albert Foer* underlined this point by arguing that knowledge of the career patterns of bureaucrats is crucial to explaining the policy orientation of regulatory agencies. Since upper-level bureaucrats have increasingly been drawn from specialized professions and the private sector, they tend to have competing intellectual loyalties. Consequently, their commitment

---

* Federal Trade Commission

to professional modes of reasoning, to bureaucratic goals, or to a combination of the two varies over time from one policy area to another and from agency to agency. Subjective criteria—whether a bureaucrat sees himself or herself as a career public servant or as the representative of a profession—have important implications for an agency's posture and its policies.

The methods reviewed so far through which scholars have explicated regulatory institutions and policy are three in number: inquiries into the intellectual, cultural, and political roots of thought. A fourth method uses current models and ex post facto evidence to evaluate the accuracy and success of past theories and policy prescriptions. Thomas McCraw's essay in this volume uses the current model of industrial dualism to evaluate the economic thought of Louis Brandeis and his generation—its accuracy, and its potential for successful policy formulation. Conference participants agreed that this approach has both risks and benefits.

On the risk side, Louis Galambos argued that by identifying naturally center or peripheral firms, the historian might underemphasize subtle but important problems in business history such as the nature of innovation. Similarly, in the political or cultural realm, Robert Cuff remarked that in applying current models to policy history, historians may understate the influence of moral ideas on theories and models used in the past. Margaret Graham* and Mary Yeager** worried that the application of the dual economy model was deterministic and ahistorical. That is to say, any model derived from economics that stresses the imperatives of efficiency will fail, in its application, to show other historically determined options and the effects of noneconomic factors on seemingly economic institutions and events.

Conceding this danger, several participants asserted that current models applied to historical problems need not result in deterministic history. Instead, they argued, such models can help to

---

* Harvard Business School
** U.C.L.A.

define with greater clarity the range of political possibilities and policy options during the period under historical scrutiny. As Barry Karl pointed out, by counterposing the current model of economic dualism to Brandeis's analysis of industrial consolidation, it is possible to show how many of his ideas were derived analogically from other areas and theories of social policy. Although they might have shed light on inherently political and cultural concerns about the nature of industrial bigness, they also obscured Brandeis's understanding of the motivations and strategies of newly formed, large, and integrated firms. Robert Cuff added that Brandeis's insistence that the illicit motivations and behavior of entrepreneurs and financiers had caused bigness was rooted in his aversion to placing the business corporation in the natural world, that is, as part of the natural order of things, like the laws of physics. Instead, Cuff argued, because he recognized the political power implications of large scale, hierarchical business organization, Brandeis wanted to embed the corporation in culture and mass politics.

In attempting to refine Ellis Hawley's generalizations drawn from three industries during the 1920s, several participants proposed applying the "life cycle" model of organizations to regulated industries in order to gain insight into business-state relations. In particular, it was suggested that fruitful hypotheses about the types of regulatory structures appropriate to or desired by an industry might be generated by looking at the industry's position in its life cycle. In commenting on the corporatist structure of the 1920s, Albro Martin* pointed out that the subjects of Hawley's work—lumber, aviation and movies—were three rather helpless or fledgling industries. Martin inferred from these cases that the structure of shared power indicative of associationalism, which Hoover sought to institutionalize throughout the economy, was most successful in troubled industries "requiring things to be done for them that they could not do for themselves." Hooverian

---

* Editor, *Business History Review*

associationalism was bound to be less successful in the growing and prospering manufacturing sectors of the economy.

Finally, it was argued that an industry's position in its life cycle can shed light on the process and substance of regulatory rule making, on the nature of shared public and private power, and prescriptively (as Albert Foer contended) on the potential effects of regulatory or antitrust policy on the life cycle itself.

The Functions of Regulation

One of the most profitable aspects of historical research on regulation has been to show that overarching theories which attribute single functions to regulatory agencies fail to stand the test of history and policy comparisons. As Thomas McCraw pointed out in a review article published in 1975, "Regulation in America has been a multifunctional pursuit." That is, "regulation is best understood as an institution capable of serving diverse, even contradictory, ends, some economic, some political, some cultural."[1]

In discussing a wide range of topics, conference participants identified a number of functions served by regulatory institutions in American history. Though functional explanations were often only implicit, and though any synthesis of the discussion could be categorized in a number of ways, the functions of regulation discussed below provide analytical categories for further research and for generalizations on the papers in this volume.

1) Policing Functions. The "public interest" image of regulation presumes that under the command of government directive businesses are forced to pursue goals which, left to their own, they would not pursue. Whether regulation historically has served the interest of business or has enforced business behavior consistent with competing social values or other interests is a question at the center of scholarly and public debate over regulation.

In support of the view stressing the policing functions of regulation, Albro Martin suggested that we recast our thinking in

---

[1] "Regulation in America: A Review Article," *Business History Review* 49 (Summer 1975): 180.

terms of the sovereign power of the state. That is, state action in regulation should be understood as either giving powers to business or taking them away. Although giving power is the norm in America, the possibility of preempting that power is always present, and the question scholars of regulation ought to ask is under what conditions this occurs.

Numerous examples of successful preemptive or policing powers exercised by regulatory agencies and the judiciary were mentioned in the conference discussion. Richard Stewart noted that despite the Court's deferential attitude toward bigness resulting from internal growth and merger after the First World War, antitrust doctrine has been consistently hostile to private agreements that create the danger of cartelization or other exercises of power against consumers.

The corporatist model of regulation is typically used to describe the granting of sovereign public powers to private agents. In this bypassing of the regulators' policing function, corporatist regulation serves simply to enforce self-regulation among private parties. But, as Thomas McCraw noted, effective policing has at times functioned precisely through such corporatist structures. Citing his own research on securities regulation, McCraw portrayed regulation of the over-the-counter securities market as meeting Hawley's criteria for corporatism: a high degree of autonomy granted to the private industry association. The National Association of Securities Dealers, Inc., since 1939 has undertaken a major role in policing the trading practices of over-the-counter dealers. Under the constant threat of losing its autonomy to the Securities and Exchange Commission, the association has, by a number of measures, provided effective watchdog functions and disciplinary actions against member firms.

A third area in which regulation has functioned to command business behavior is in environmental, health, and safety regulation. Citing his ongoing research on social regulation, Samuel Hays noted that the role of statutory agencies in assessing and setting acceptable levels of risk in these areas has been to open the process to scientific theories, information, and goals which historically had not entered into private business decision criteria.

Thus, as well as directing business to meet new, often more stringent standards, social regulation has forced business firms and their research divisions to consider outside sources of information in their own decision making.

2) Rationalization Functions. Ellis Hawley's essay in this volume shows that the motive force behind Hoover's notion of industrial regulation was scientific rationalization. The barrier to efficiency for Hoover and his disciples was competition. By replacing market transactions with publicly and privately planned factor procurement and output schedules, business-government associationalism could serve the public interest. The "progressive cartel" could regulate competition, not to maintain exploitative prices, but to serve the ends of efficiency. Hoover conceived a corporative function for state administrators: to provide state resources for research and planning, and to help enforce efficiency criteria within regulated industries.

Under what conditions were associational structures possible or successful? More particularly, can we refine the notion of rationalization as a function of regulation? In the 1930s rationalization of this type served to prop up ailing industries or to promote industries such as aviation that had yet to secure a reliable market.

3) Standard-Setting Functions. Conference participants held unanimously that regardless of who benefits from business regulation, setting standards for products and services is always a central function in the regulatory process. Setting standards increases reliability and certainty in market transactions and in the relations between business and the state. Moreover, since reliable and accessible information is important to consumers, producers, and government regulators, the nature of shared power among these groups in determining standards merits close historical investigation. How and why government has assumed the function of standard setting in specific contexts is a continuing problem for historians of regulation.

Approaches to History of Regulation

Douglas Ginsburg* made a cogent argument that standards will arise spontaneously in any market economy. That is to say, since all market transactions involve contracts (implicit or explicit) and risk, standards will emerge to facilitate confidence between buyers and sellers. As early as the eighteenth century, he argued, standards for grading flax and cotton emerged without government initiative. Only as time passed were these standards supplemented with state sanctioned weights and measures—a standard-setting authority eventually allocated to the state in all industrial market societies.

In addition to increasing the reliability of transactions between buyers and sellers, standards also served competitive and anticompetitive purposes in relations between producers. Louis Galambos suggested that standardization was a precondition for price fixing, since without it firms had no consistent criteria to compare their own product prices with those of competitors; hence, they lost confidence that pricing rules (tacit or otherwise) represented the same commodities, and agreements broke down. On the other hand, as James Q. Wilson pointed out, standard setting could result from shared, rather than competitive, incentives among producers. Unlike voluntary price-setting associations, in which members had an incentive to defect from cooperative agreements, standard-setting associations created market signals that established the honesty and reliability of member firms. For a firm in an industry to fail to comply with industrywide standards, then, was to signal that its product was presumptively defective or the firm itself dishonest.

If standards emerged inherently from private market transactions and were effectively enforced on the basis of private incentives, then how can historians explain the functions that state regulators have assumed in standard setting? First, the state can lend legitimacy to privately set standards—a government stamp of approval, particularly in fledgling or crisis-ridden industries, tended to engender confidence in the minds of consumers. But

---

* Harvard Law School

government standard setting can serve ends other than consumer confidence. In the securities industry, as Thomas McCraw pointed out, financial disclosure was a precondition to any form of effective market regulation (whether to serve investor confidence or the SEC's ability to monitor trading practices). And meaningful disclosure necessarily involved standardized accounting procedures, which, by and large, did not exist prior to the creation of the SEC in the 1930s. Thus, in this case the impetus for standard setting came primarily from government, in alliance with the accounting profession. As a result, power over setting standard accounting procedures ultimately came to be shared between the profession and the commission.

Finally, Samuel Hays noted that standard setting in the area of occupational health and radiation exposure was initiated by industry and professionals, with only marginal government involvement. The National Council of Radiation Protection, for instance, was a nonstatutory body which, unlike OSHA and EPA, had virtually no power to open the standard-setting process to sources of scientific information other than industry. It grew up simply as a device to facilitate communication between industry and professionals, and was replaced by statutory agencies as professionals with new and conflicting sources of information pressed for access into the tightly knit group that was setting exposure standards previously.

4) *Interest Representation Functions.* Possibly the firmest conclusion of the conference was that in the years since the New Deal, politics over the distribution of wealth and investment and the debate over corporate power and discretion have progressively shifted from political parties and Congress to administrative agencies and other public bureaucracies. Administrative regulation has become, more and more, an arena for political struggle over health and safety risk in advanced industrial society, over the location and substance of investment, and over the social responsibility of business in American life.

Approaches to History of Regulation

Riding the crest of the "capture" critique of regulatory agencies during the 1960s, formal intervenors and consumer and professional groups gained representation in traditional areas of public utility regulation, in nuclear energy regulation, and in the newer areas of social regulation. For the historian concerned with how values are formed, debated, and chosen in American politics, recent experience relegates the traditional separation of powers model to normative theory. It is for this reason that Samuel Hays urged that political historians direct more time to detailed studies of administrative process.

A variety of explanations were offered for the dramatic increase in the interest-representation functions assumed by regulatory agencies since the 1960s. The fragmented structure of American political institutions provided one answer: if groups could not secure access through political parties or Congress, they turned to the courts or directly to the point of allocation—administration—for representation. It is precisely this kind of institutional pluralism in the United States, James Q. Wilson argued, that has allowed "a radical redistribution of power since the 1960s, without a redistribution of wealth." Richard Stewart indicated that the courts and a transformation of attitudes in the legal profession were instrumental in realizing functional representation for new and underrepresented groups. Under the public interest mantle, the courts declared that previous administrative practices had systematically underrepresented some groups in American society. As a result, consumer, minority, environmental, and women's groups, backed by the force of law, waged political battles in arenas traditionally limited to access by business alone.

Another explanation emphasized the formation and motivations of new interest groups in American politics. Samuel Hays offered the thesis that leisure and intangible consumption have brought individuals together into recreational organizations and that these voluntary associations have subsequently turned to political activity in order to have their concerns with environmental, quality of life, and health and safety issues represented in the formation of administrative policy.

Other explanations noted the effects of foundation and public money, mass media and mass mailing techniques in lowering the costs of organization for groups seeking access to administrative procedure.

Historical Conjunctures

So far we have considered the conference discussion regarding the role of ideas, culture, the professions, politics and, to some extent, economics in explaining the evolution of regulatory institutions and policy. Some of this discussion can be subsumed by the role that historical conjunctures play in helping to produce certain types of regulatory structures and policies. By conjunctures, we mean a confluence of historical circumstances which produce crises or major transformations in the economy, in politics, or in social structure. Examples of conjunctures important to explaining the history of regulation in America include war, the rise of big business, the rise of mass consumption, economic depression, and stagflation. Conference participants held unanimously that historical conjunctures are important to explaining regulation in America, but were in less agreement over their effects and how historians ought to think about them.

One cannot, of course, consider the origins of positive regulation and antitrust in the United States without considering the rise of big business. But, as Thomas McCraw's essay in this volume shows, this conjuncture can serve as a starting point to investigate the evolution of big business itself, the social response to it, the history of economic and political ideas, or, with the use of economic analysis, the accuracy of theories and explanations from the period. No less ambiguous is the role war played in the evolution of regulatory institutions. In commenting on Ellis Hawley's paper, Paul Glad noted the effects of wartime industrial planning and temporary nationalization of the railroads (wartime corporatism) on associationalism during the 1920s. Yet, having pointed this out, one still wonders what the effects of wartime corporatism were on Hoover and his associates during the twenties. Should the historian merely look at Hoover's experience as head of the

Food Administration as a learning experience, and similarly at the businessmen involved in Hoover's plans? Did the war experience serve to legitimate the later associationalism in the 1920s? And was the wartime experience in industrial planning as positive an experience for everyone involved as it was for Hoover and his disciples?

Conference participants agreed that the rise of mass consumption and, later, of leisure consumption had serious implications for the evolution of regulation in America, but they disagreed over just what the effects were. David Landes argued that there is no apparent economic reason why mass consumption per se should affect the substance of regulation, but also hypothesized that since there are simply many more purchasers of consumption goods than capital goods, mass consumption might have increased the extent of political demands for regulation. Similarly, Morton Keller suggested that although the instruments of public authority and the range and variety of interests involved in regulatory administration have grown in response to mass consumption, the old tensions between individualism and communalism, or, institutionally, between antitrust and corporatism, have continued throughout the twentieth century.

These ideas failed to convince Samuel Hays, who contended that not only the extent of regulation, but its content, had changed with transformations in the history of consumption. For Hays the most significant aspect of post–World War II regulation has been the transformation from a predominantly producer context to a producer-consumer one. Progress in mass consumption from amenities, necessities, and convenience goods to leisure goods, intangibles, and the natural environment has resulted in radical changes in the content of policies considered legitimate within administrative procedure: from price and production policies to policies concerned with the environmental, health and safety, and aesthetic effects of advanced industrialism. Thus, conjunctures in the history of consumption underlie his analysis of the mobilization of new groups seeking representation in regulatory procedure, including scientific controversy over risk assessment in administrative rulemaking.

Regulation in Perspective

A fourth area concerns the effects of market conjunctures on the evolution of regulation in America. There is little doubt that economic depression had profound effects on business strategy and regulatory policy. In comparing America's great merger wave at the turn of the century to the European cartel movement, David Landes noted that the European cartels were formed primarily during protracted periods of recession. Thus, cartelization, when legal, appears to be a typical response to troughs in the business cycle. Indeed, even in the United States, where price and output agreements are clearly unlawful, the courts became more tolerant of cartels during the 1930s depression. This response in antitrust law, moreover, corresponds to Richard Stewart's "deferential phase" in administrative law. On the other hand, Ellis Hawley's paper in this volume argues that the effects of the Depression on associationalism were in some respects devastating. Organized interests and alternative ideologies, which could not be integrated into the corporatist design during the 1920s, reemerged in the 1930s and fueled the antitrust debate over NRA industry codes.

A fifth conjuncture, highlighted in David Vogel's essay, is in the present: declining investment and productivity coupled with high inflation. It is clearly impossible to separate the deregulation movement from the current state of the economy. A central premise of deregulation is based on the critique of the interest representation function assumed by regulatory agencies during the past decade: the high costs of regulation have been fueled by redistributional demands made in administrative procedure. These have promoted a growing budget deficit, have dampened private investment, and have stimulated higher levels of inflation. Congress's recent moves to review the substance of commission rulemaking, and the Court's return to a long abandoned narrow delegation of legislative powers both represent institutional responses to the current conjuncture.

Notes

RETHINKING THE TRUST QUESTION   Thomas K. McCraw

1. Especially helpful in elucidating these issues are Louis Galambos, *Competition & Cooperation: The Emergence of a National Trade Association* (Baltimore: Johns Hopkins Press, 1966); Robert F. Himmelberg, *The Origins of the National Recovery Administration: Business, Government, and the Trade Association Issue, 1921–1933* (New York: Fordham University Press, 1976); Ellis W. Hawley, *The New Deal and the Problem of Monopoly: A Study in Economic Ambivalence* (Princeton: Princeton University Press, 1966); and Richard Hofstadter, "What Happened to the Antitrust Movement?" in Earl F. Cheit, ed., *The Business Establishment* (New York: Wiley, 1964), pp. 113–51. See also Galambos, *The Public Image of Big Business in America, 1880–1940: A Quantitative Study in Social Change* (Baltimore: Johns Hopkins Press, 1975).

2. Arthur S. Link, ed., *The Papers of Woodrow Wilson,* (Princeton: Princeton University Press, 1966–) **25**: 152, 368; Louis D. Brandeis to Woodrow Wilson, September 30, 1912, in Melvin I. Urofsky and David W. Levy, eds., *Letters of Louis D. Brandeis,* 5 vols. (Albany: State University of New York Press, 1971–1978) **2**: 688–94; Urofsky, "Wilson, Brandeis and the Trust Issue, 1912–1914," *Mid-America* **44** (January 1967): 3–28; Richard Hofstadter, *The Age of Reform* (New York: Knopf, 1955), chap. 6; Arthur M. Schlesinger, Jr., *The Crisis of the Old Order* (Boston: Houghton Mifflin, 1957), pp. 17–36.

Theodore Roosevelt's remark about good and bad trusts was not new in the campaign of 1912, but had been identified with the ex-president for several years.

3. *Historical Statistics of the United States: Colonial Times to 1970* (Washington, D.C.: Government Printing Office, 1975) **2**: 731.

4. Paul Uselding, "Manufacturing," in Glenn Porter, ed., *Encyclopedia of American Economic History* (New York: Scribner's, 1980) 409–11. Figures for capital per worker are in constant dollars, and for total capital invested are in current dollars.

5. Ibid.; *Historical Statistics,* **1**: 200–201, 224; John W. Kendrick, "Productivity," in Porter, ed., *Encyclopedia of American Economic History,* pp. 157–66.

6. Smith, *The Wealth of Nations,* Random House Modern Library, (New York, 1937), p. 128.

7. William R. Cornish, "Legal Control over Cartels and Monopolization 1880–1914. A Comparison," pp. 280–303, Leslie Hannah, "Mergers, Cartels, and Concentration: Legal Factors in the U.S. and European Experience," pp.

306–14, and Morton Keller, "Public Policy and Large Enterprise. Comparative Historical Perspectives," pp. 515–31, all in Norbert Horn and Jurgen Köcka, eds., *Law and the Formation of the Big Enterprises in the 19th and Early 20th Centuries* (Göttingen: Vanednhoeck & Ruprecht, 1979).

8. Ibid.; *Historical Statistics* 2: 1103.

9. See the discussion and notes in the two sections of this essay that begin on p. 38, below.

10. A brief discussion of productive efficiency may be found in Robert H. Bork, *The Antitrust Paradox: A Policy at War with Itself* (New York: Basic Books, 1978), pp. 91 and 104–6. See also chap. 11. In Bork's view, "productive efficiency is a simple, indispensable, and thoroughly misunderstood concept. Not one antitrust lawyer in ten has a remotely satisfactory idea on the subject, and the proportion of economists who do, though surely higher, is perhaps not dramatically so. The situation has deteriorated so badly that one can hear it hotly denied that efficiency has anything to do with antitrust" (p. 104).

11. Phillip Areeda, *Antitrust Analysis: Problems, Text, Cases* (Boston: Little, Brown, 1974), pp. 6–9. Maximized allocative efficiency is also called "Pareto optimality."

12. On Henry Ford, see Alfred D. Chandler, Jr., *The Visible Hand: The Managerial Revolution in Modern Business* (Cambridge, Mass.: Harvard University Press, 1977), pp. 280–81; and Allan Nevins and Frank E. Hill, *Ford: The Times, The Man and The Company* (New York: Scribner's, 1954), chap. 18. The "experience curve" has been documented by the Boston Consulting Group in particular, and its refinement may be traced in the publications by that firm and by its head, Bruce Henderson.

13. The seminal article on transaction costs was Ronald H. Coase, "The Nature of the Firm," *Economica*, n.s. 4 (November 1937), pp. 386–405. The fullest attempt to relate the concept to the issues being argued here is Oliver E. Williamson, "Organizational Innovation: The Transaction Cost Approach" (Discussion Paper #83, Center for the Study of Organizational Innovation, University of Pennsylvania, September 1980). See also Williamson, "Transaction Cost Economics: The Governance of Contractual Relations," *Journal of Law and Economics* 22 (October 1979): 233–61.

14. The term "economies of speed" is from Chandler, *The Visible Hand*, pp. 281–83.

15. Virtually all of the huge literature on "trusts," "monopolies," "oligopolies," mergers, consolidations, and so forth applies to horizontal combination. A series of relevant articles and a thorough 29-page bibliography of recent work in the field may be found in Eleanor M. Fox and James T. Halverson, eds., *Industrial Concentration and the Market System: Legal, Economic, Social and Political Perspectives* (American Bar Association Press, 1979). See also Bork, *The Antitrust Paradox,* chaps. 8, 10, and 13; and Chandler, *The Visible Hand,* chap. 10.

16. Harold F. Williamson and Arnold R. Daum, *The American Petroleum Industry: The Age of Illumination, 1859–1899* (Evanston, Ill.: Northwestern University Press, 1959), pp. 474–75 and 483–84; U.S., Bureau of Corporations, *Report of the Commissioner of Corporations on the Tobacco Industry*, pt. 3

(Washington, D.C.: Government Printing Office, 1915), pp. 158–60. Between 1893 and 1899 American Tobacco's costs dropped from $1.74 per thousand to $0.89.

17. The Du Pont executive is quoted in Chandler, *The Visible Hand,* p. 442; and Carnegie in Glenn Porter, *The Rise of Big Business, 1860–1910* (New York: Crowell, 1973), p. 59.

18. The phrases "center firms" and "peripheral firms" are used in Robert T. Averitt, *The Dual Economy: The Dynamics of American Industry Structure* (New York: Norton, 1968). Other authors have invented their own nomenclature, e.g., "the megacorp" in Alfred S. Eichner, *The Megacorp and Oligopoly: Micro Foundations of Macro Dynamics* (New York: Cambridge University Press, 1976) and "the multiunit business enterprise" in Chandler, *The Visible Hand.* John Kenneth Galbraith's "technostructure," used in *The New Industrial State* (Boston: Houghton Mifflin, 1967) is a related concept. In each case the author's purpose is specifically to distinguish the phenomenon from its antecedents, the single-function, owner-managed firm without sufficient resources or power to affect the behavior of other firms. The point I wish to emphasize is that *center firms are peculiar to certain types of industries and are almost never found outside these industries.*

19. See the works cited in note 18 above and the brief bibliography in Averitt, *The Dual Economy,* pp. 202–4. Other sources include Suzanne Berger and Michael J. Piore, *Dualism and Discontinuity in Industrial Societies* (Cambridge: At the University Press, 1980); E. M. Beck, Patrick M. Horan, and Charles M. Tolbert II, "Stratification in a Dual Economy: A Sectoral Model of Earnings Determination," *American Sociological Review* 43 (October 1978): 704–20; Beck, Horan, and Tolbert, "The Structure of Economic Segmentation: A Dual Economy Approach," *American Journal of Sociology* 85 (March 1980): 1095–1116; and Gerry Oster, "A Factor Analytic Test of the Theory of the Dual Economy," *Review of Economics and Statistics* 61 (February 1979): 33–39.

I am not arguing in this essay that every single industry or other economic activity can be characterized decisively as either center or peripheral. These categorizations represent not pure polarities but a continuum whose extremes are clearly differentiated but whose middle ranges are rather more fuzzy. Systematic attempts to measure items in such a continuum quantitatively, including long lists of industries assigned to center ("core") and peripheral status, may be found in each of the two articles by Beck, Horan, and Tolbert cited in this footnote.

20. For elaborations of this problem, together with suggestions for remedying it, see the articles by Oliver E. Williamson cited in note 13 above; and Richard E. Caves, "Industrial Organization, Corporate Strategy and Structure," *Journal of Economic Literature* 18 (March 1980): 64–89. For a pioneering attempt to engage the question, see Alfred S. Eichner, *The Emergence of Oligopoly: Sugar Refining as a Case Study* (Baltimore: Johns Hopkins Press, 1969). Other relevant studies include Burton H. Klein, *Dynamic Economics* (Cambridge, Mass.: Harvard University Press, 1977); and Michael E. Porter, *Competitive Strategy* (New York: Free Press, 1980).

21. *New York Review of Books,* February 8, 1978, p. 36 (emphasis added).

22. These data will appear in Chandler's forthcoming book on the growth of large firms worldwide. I am very grateful to him for permission to use them in this essay. The data show greater divergence in some other industries, e.g., from 20 chemical firms in 1917 to 29 in 1973; 29 primary metals companies in 1917, 19 in 1973; and 5 electrical machinery firms in 1917, 13 in 1973.

I am not suggesting here that the composition of the top 200 companies remained unchanged over this period, only that the configuration of center industries remained stable. One estimate is that only 36 of the largest 100 companies in 1909 remained in the top 100 in 1958. Oliver E. Williamson calls attention to this point in his essay, "Emergence of the Visible Hand: Implications for Industrial Organization," in Alfred D. Chandler and Herman Daems, eds., *Managerial Hierarchies: Comparative Perspectives on the Rise of the Modern Industrial Enterprise* (Cambridge, Mass.: Harvard University Press, 1980), pp. 198 and 202, n. 60.

23. Chandler, *The Visible Hand*, pp. 320–44; Leslie Hannah, "Mergers," in Porter, ed., *Encyclopedia of American Economic History*, pp. 649–50. (Pp. 650–51 of the Hannah essay contain a helpful bibliography on the topic of mergers.)

24. These data will appear in Chandler's forthcoming book on the growth of large firms worldwide.

25. Ibid.

26. The standard works include Alpheus Thomas Mason, *Brandeis: A Free Man's Life* (New York: Viking, 1947); Mason, *Brandeis: Lawyer and Judge in the Modern State* (Princeton: Princeton University Press, 1933); Alfred Lief, *Brandeis: The Personal History of an American Ideal* (New York: Stackpole, 1936); Felix Frankfurter, ed., *Mr. Justice Brandeis* (New Haven: Yale University Press, 1932); Samuel J. Konefsky, *The Legacy of Holmes and Brandeis: A Study in the Influence of Ideas* (New York: Macmillan, 1957); A. L. Todd, *Justice on Trial: The Case of Louis D. Brandeis* (New York: McGraw-Hill, 1964); Melvin I. Urofsky, *A Mind of One Piece: Brandeis and American Reform* (New York: Scribner's, 1971); Urofsky, *Louis D. Brandeis and the Progressive Tradition* (Boston: Little, Brown, 1981); Janice Mark Jacobson, "Mr. Justice Brandeis on Regulation and Competition: An Analysis of His Economic Opinions" (Ph.D. diss., Columbia University, 1973); Allon Gal, *Brandeis of Boston* (Cambridge, Mass.: Harvard University Press, 1980); Richard M. Abrams, "Brandeis and the Ascendancy of Corporate Capitalism," introduction to Abrams, ed., Louis D. Brandeis, *Other People's Money: And How the Bankers Use It* (New York: Harper & Row, 1967), pp. vii–xliv; and Abrams, "Brandeis and the New Haven-Boston & Maine Merger Battle Revisited," *Business History Review* **36** (Winter 1962): 408–30.

27. See the early chapters of Gal, *Brandeis of Boston*; and Melvin I. Urofsky and David W. Levy, eds., *Letters of Louis D. Brandeis*, 5 vols. (Albany: State University of New York Press, 1971–1978) (hereinafter cited as *Brandeis Letters*), vol. 1 (1870–1907).

28. Brandeis testimony before Senate Committee on Interstate Commerce (the "Clapp Committee," after its chairman, Senator Moses Clapp), U.S., Senate, *Report of the Committee on Interstate Commerce, Pursuant to Senate Resolution 98: Hearings on Control of Corporations, Persons, and Firms Engaged in In-*

terstate Commerce, 62nd Cong., 2nd sess. (Washington, D.C.: Government Printing Office, 1912), (hereinafter cited as Brandeis Clapp Committee testimony [1911]), p. 1226. See also Brandeis to Alfred Brandeis, June 18, 1907, *Brandeis Letters,* 1: 584: "I am experiencing a growing conviction that the labor men are the most congenial company. The intense materialism and luxuriousness of most of our other people makes their company quite irksome."

29. Mason, *Brandeis,* pp. 432–35; Gal, *Brandeis of Boston,* chaps. 1–3, passim.

30. Brandeis to Alice Goldmark, December 28, 1980, *Brandeis Letters,* 1: 97.

31. Brandeis to H. W. Ashley, January 31, 1914, *Brandeis Letters,* 3: 239; Brandeis to Felix Frankfurter, September 30, 1922; Brandeis to George Henry Soule, April 22, 1923, *Brandeis Letters,* 5: 70, 92.

32. Brandeis to George Henry Soule, ibid.; Brandeis to Frankfurter, February 12, 1926, *Brandeis Letters,* 5: 207.

33. Brandeis to Edwin Doak Mead, November 9, 1895, *Brandeis Letters,* 1: 121–22.

34. Lecture notes, pp. 320–21, Document 9 of *A Microfilm Edition of The Public Papers of Louis Dembitz Brandeis in the Jacob and Bertha Goldfarb Library of Brandeis University* (Cambridge, Mass.: General Microfilm Co., 1978).

35. Ibid., pp. 321–23.

36. Ibid., pp. 322–24.

37. Ibid.

38. See notes 16 and 17 above, together with the discussion to which they refer.

39. Lecture notes, pp. 323–24.

40. Ibid., p. 334.

41. Ibid., pp. 324–33. The indirect promotion of tight combinations through the prohibition of loose ones is discussed in Chandler, *The Visible Hand,* p. 357, and—with more doubt—in Hans B. Thorelli, *The Federal Antitrust Policy: Organization of an American Tradition* (Baltimore: Johns Hopkins Press, 1955), pp. 604–6.

42. Jesse Markham, "Survey of the Evidence and Findings on Mergers," in *Business Concentration and Price Policy* (Princeton: Princeton University Press, 1955), p. 157. See also Ralph Nelson, *Merger Movements in American Industry, 1895–1956* (Princeton: Princeton University Press, 1959) and William Z. Ripley, *Trusts, Pools, and Corporations* (Cambridge, Mass.: Harvard University Press, 1905).

43. Chandler, *The Visible Hand,* pp. 315–44.

44. Brandeis Clapp Committee testimony (1911), p. 1148.

45. Ibid.

46. Ibid.

47. The Pullman Company was an integrated firm which manufactured and operated the sleeping cars, paying the railroads a fee for hauling them. It enjoyed exclusive servicing contracts, which it performed more efficiently than the railroads themselves could. This was an additional "barrier to entry."

48. Brandeis Clapp Committee testimony (1911), p. 1234.

49. Ibid., p. 1170; Brandeis to Elizabeth Brandeis Raushenbush, November 19, 1933, *Brandeis Letters,* 5: 527.

50. Brandeis Clapp Committee testimony (1911), p. 1167.

51. 221 U.S. 1 (1911). For information on American Tobacco and the other center firms as well, Brandeis relied heavily on the excellent and very detailed studies of these companies by the United States Bureau of Corporations. See the frequent references to the bureau's studies in Brandeis, *Business—A Profession* (Boston: Small, Maynard, 1914), pp. 198–235; Brandeis to William Cox Redfield, May 21, 1913, *Brandeis Letters,* 3: 94–95; and Brandeis to James Walton Carmalt (memorandum), November 13, 1913, ibid., p. 210.

52. 221 U.S. 1 (1911). See also In the Circuit Court of the United States, for the Southern District of New York, *Objections of National Cigar Leaf Tobacco Association . . . [et al.], to the Plan of Disintegration, Filed by the American Tobacco Company and Others, October 16, 1911*; In the Circuit Court of the United States for the Southern District of New York, *Brief in Support of Objections of National Cigar Leaf Tobacco Association . . . and Others,* October 16, 1911, p. 46; Brandeis Clapp Committee testimony (1911), p. 1255.

53. Glenn Porter and Harold C. Livesay, *Merchants and Manufacturers: Studies in the Changing Structure of Nineteenth Century Marketing* (Baltimore: Johns Hopkins Press, 1971), pp. 199–213; Chandler, *The Visible Hand,* pp. 249–50, 290–91, 382–91; Richard Tennant, *The American Cigarette Industry* (New Haven: Yale University Press, 1950); U.S., Bureau of Corporations, *Report of the Commissioner of Corporations on the Tobacco Industry* (Washington, D.C.: Government Printing Office, 1909).

54. Chandler, *The Visible Hand,* pp. 389–90; Tennant, *The American Cigarette Industry,* p. 31; Brandeis, "An Illegal Trust Legalized," *The World Today* **21** (December 1911): 1440–41.

55. Brandeis, "Trusts, Efficiency and the New Party," *Collier's Weekly,* September 14, 1912, pp. 14–15; Brandeis, "Trusts, the Export Trade, and the New Party," *Collier's Weekly,* September 21, 1912, pp. 10–11, 33.

56. Brandeis Clapp Committee testimony (1911), p. 1182; Brandeis, "Trusts, the Export Trade, and the New Party," p. 10.

57. This analysis follows the conventional economic theory of cartels. The question of whether the increased productive efficiency derived from the concentration of production in the most efficient plants would be passed along by the company via price reductions is less certain theoretically but seems borne out by historical experience in many industries. See notes 16 and 17 above.

Actually, the steel industry does not represent the purest example for the argument in this essay, for two reasons. First, U.S. Steel in its early years was managed by legal and financial specialists led by E. H. Gary, in a manner less pleasing to production-oriented executives such as Charles Schwab (who left the company because it was behaving more like a cartel than like an integrated Carnegie-style firm). Second, the German steel cartels were managed in a way designed to promote efficiency and vertical integration, a policy which was carefully coordinated with tariffs and dumping practices and which overall was a more sophisticated and complex system than the usual European or American cartels. See Stephen B. Webb, "Tariffs, Cartels, Technology, and Growth in the

German Steel Industry, 1879 to 1914," *Journal of Economic History* **40** (June 1980): 309–29.

58. This generalization does not apply after the 1960s, by which time the other countries had caught up with and in many instances surpassed the Americans in their organizational innovations. For elaboration of the point, see the essays on four countries in Chandler and Daems, eds., *Managerial Hierarchies: Comparative Perspectives on the Rise of the Modern Industrial Enterprise.*

59. Brandeis, "Trusts, Efficiency, and the New Party" p. 15; see also Brandeis Clapp Committee testimony (1911), p. 1160.

60. Brandeis testimony before the House Committee on Patents, *Oldfield Revision and Codification of the Patent Statutes: Hearings on H.R. 23417,* 62nd Cong., 2nd sess., May 15, 1912 (Washington, D.C.: Government Printing Office, 1912), pp. 24–25.

61. Ibid.

62. U.S., Congress, Senate, Subcommittee of the Committee on the Judiciary, *Hearings on the Nomination of Louis D. Brandeis to be an Associate Justice of the Supreme Court of the United States,* 64th Cong., 1st sess., February–May 1916, Senate Document 409 (Washington, D.C.: Government Printing Office, 1916), pp. 160–68, 217–26, 231–36, 944–56.

63. Brandeis to Clapp, February 24, 1912, printed in Senate Document 409, (1916) p. 217; Brandeis Clapp Committee testimony (1911), pp. 1160, 1178.

64. Brandeis Clapp Committee testimony (1911), pp. 1160, 1178.

65. *Dr. Miles Medical Co. v. John D. Park & Sons Co.,* 220 U.S. 373 (1911).

66. The unpublished Brandeis Papers at the University of Louisville contain voluminous files on this issue. Important letters to Brandeis include those of William H. Ingersoll dated May 22, May 28, June 18, June 19, July 23, September 16, September 23, September 26, October 2, October 25, November 8, November 17, November 24, and December 17, 1913; also February 26 and March 4, 1915; see also Edmond A. Whittier (secretary of the American Fair Trade League) to Brandeis, June 28, 1913; Gilbert H. Montague to Brandeis, January 10, February 18, and March 27, 1914. See also Brandeis to various correspondents during the period 1913–15 in *Brandeis Letters,* 3: 89–90, 93–105, 111–13, 118–22, 125–29, 131–34, 138–39, 146–47, 152, 169–70, 173–74, 216–18, 225–26, 434, 446–48, and 618–19.

67. Other important cases included *Bobbs-Merrill Co. v. Straus,* 210 U.S. 339 (1908), and especially *Bauer & Cie v. O'Donnell,* 229 U.S. 1 (1913); see Brandeis to John Rogers Commons, May 27, 1913; Brandeis to Robert Marion La Follette, May 27, 1913; Brandeis to William Cox Redfield, May 27, 1913; and Brandeis to Henry Robinson Towne, July 25, 1913, all in *Brandeis Letters,* 3: 99–103 and 152.

68. Brandeis testimony May 15, 1912, before the House Committee on Patents, *Oldfield Revision and Codification of the Patent Statutes,* 62nd Cong., 2nd sess. (Washington, D.C.: Government Printing Office, 1912), p. 4.

69. Brandeis to Hapgood, July 7, 1913. *Brandeis Letters,* 3: 125; Edmond A. Whittier to Brandeis, November 24, November 29, 1913; William H. Ingersoll to Brandeis, November 17, 1913; George Eastman to Brandeis, November 14, 1913, all in Brandeis Papers.

Regulation in Perspective

The magazines included *World's Work, McCall's, Delineator, Designer, Good Housekeeping, Everybody's, Harper's Weekly, Woman's Magazine, Christian Herald, Leslie's, Country Life in America, Outlook, Scribner's, Review of Reviews, Garden Magazine, Cosmopolitan, Hearst's, Metropolitan,* and *Butterick Trio*; see Edmond A. Whittier to Brandeis, July 31, 1913, Brandeis Papers. The note introducing the reprints in these journals states: "This article is published by a number of the leading magazines in the belief that by giving wide publicity to the views of so noted a foe to monopoly as Mr. Brandeis the real interests of the enterprising individual manufacturer, the small dealer, and the public will be served."

70. Brandeis, "Cut-throat Prices: The Competition That Kills," *Harper's Weekly,* November 15, 1913, pp. 11–12; see also Brandeis, "On Maintaining Makers' Prices," *Harper's Weekly,* June 14, 1913, p. 6.

71. Brandeis testimony, U.S., Congress, House, Committee on Interstate and Foreign Commerce, *Hearings on Regulation of Prices,* 64th Cong., 1st sess., January 9, 1915 (Washington, D.C.: Government Printing Office, 1915), pp. 39–40.

72. Ibid., pp. 45, 54.

73. Ibid., pp. 29–30.

74. Ibid., p. 53. In his widely distributed *Harper's Weekly* piece, Brandeis characterized the consumer as follows: "Thoughtless or weak, he yields to the temptation of trifling immediate gain; and selling his birthright for a mess of pottage, becomes himself an instrument of monopoly." See "Cut-throat Prices: The Competition That Kills," p. 12.

75. *Hearings on Regulation of Prices,* pp. 55–57 and 63–64.

76. The Miller-Tydings Act of 1937, strengthened by the McGuire Act of 1952, was the basic federal "fair trade" law. Both were repealed by the Consumer Goods Pricing Act of 1975. For details of the 1930s agitation for such legislation, see Federal Trade Commission, *Resale Price Maintenance* (Washington, D.C.: Government Printing Office, 1945) and Ellis W. Hawley, *The New Deal and the Problem of Monopoly: A Study in Economic Ambivalence* (Princeton: Princeton University Press, 1966), pp. 254–58. A thorough exposition of the rise and fall of federal fair trade laws may be found in Earl W. Kintner, ed., *The Legislative History of the Federal Antitrust Laws and Related Statutes* (New York: Chelsea House, 1978), pp. 457–982.

Economists and antitrust lawyers are not unanimous concerning the effects of resale price maintenance. For arguments that to the extent that they are vertical relationships they do not harm consumer welfare, see Robert H. Bork, *The Antitrust Paradox: A Policy at War with Itself* (New York: Basic Books, 1978), pp. 32–33 and 297; and Richard A. Posner, *Antitrust Law: An Economic Perspective* (Chicago: University of Chicago Press, 1976), pp. 147–66. Most scholars, however, would probably subscribe to the following characterization, jointly submitted to Congress in 1952 by a number of prominent economists and lawyers: "Resale price maintenance has no place in a society which depends on the competitive market as a major instrument for determining price and output. . . . The drive for price fixing by law comes from some groups of retailers who obtain their supplies through the older channels of wholesale distribution.

[That is, the restraints are horizontal, not vertical.] They want to sell in their local markets under monopolistic conditions—that is, free of price competition. Not only do they want to eliminate competition with each other. They also typically oppose the growth of chain stores, mail order houses, cooperatives, department stores, and other techniques of distribution which have over two generations greatly increased the degree of competition in, and reduced the costs of the distribution of consumer goods in almost every local market of the United States." The authors of this statement included, among many others, M. A. Adelman, John Kenneth Galbraith, Edward S. Mason, Fritz Machlup, Lloyd G. Reynolds, Carl Fulda, James Tobin, and George W. Stocking. The statement is printed in Kintner, *The Legislative History of the Federal Antitrust Laws and Related Statutes*, p. 850.

77. Brandeis, "Using Other People's Money," *New York American*, November 28, 1911; Brandeis, "Efficiency and the Trusts," address before the Town Criers, Providence, Rhode Island, October 7, 1912, p. 16, Document 142A of *A Microfilm Edition of the Public Papers of Louis Dembitz Brandeis in the Jacob and Bertha Goldfarb Library of Brandeis University*; Brandeis Clapp Committee testimony (1911), p. 1156.

78. See Beck, Horan and Tolbert, "Stratification in a Dual Economy: A Sectoral Model of Earnings Determination," cited in note 19 above.

79. Hartz, *The Liberal Tradition in America: An Interpretation of American Political Thought Since the Revolution* (New York: Harcourt, Brace, 1955), p. 232.

THE PLURALIST STATE Morton Keller

1. Douglass C. North and Robert P. Thomas, *The Rise of the Western World: A New Economic History* (Cambridge: At the University Press, 1973).

2. J. W. Grove, *Government and Industry in Britain* (London: Longmans, 1962), chap. 1; J. B. Brebner, "Laissez Faire and State Intervention in Nineteenth Century Britain," *Journal of Economic History* 8, supp. (1948): 59–73; François Caron, *An Economic History of Modern France* (New York: Columbia University Press, 1979), pp. 40–41; treatise quoted in Charles E. Freedeman, *Joint-Stock Enterprise in France 1807–1867* (Chapel Hill: University of North Carolina Press, 1979), p. 66. See also A. B. Levy, *Private Corporations and their Control* (London: Routledge & Kegan Paul, 1950), vol. 1, pt. 1; Dennis Sherman, "Governmental Policy and Joint-Stock Business Organizations in Mid-Nineteenth Century France," *Journal of European Economic History* 3 (1974): 149–68; Sherman, "Governmental Response to Economic Modernization in Mid-Nineteenth Century France," *Journal of European Economic History* 6 (1977): 717–36; Sherman, "The Meaning of Economic Liberalism in Mid-Nineteenth Century France," *History of Political Economy* 6 (1974): 171–99; R. Boothby et al., *Industry and the State: A Conservative View* (London: Macmillan & Co., 1927).

3. James W. Hurst, *Law and the Conditions of Freedom in the Nineteenth Century United States* (Madison: University of Wisconsin Press, 1954).

4. Alexis de Tocqueville, *Democracy in America* (New York: Knopf, 1945), 2: 329–31.

5. Adolf A. Berle and Gardiner C. Means, *The Modern Corporation and Private Property* (1932; rev. ed., New York: Macmillan, 1968), p. 313.

6. Much of the ensuing discussion is drawn from Morton Keller, "Regulation of Large Enterprise: The United States Experience in Comparative Perspective," in Alfred D. Chandler, Jr., and Herman Daems, eds., *Managerial Hierarchies: Comparative Perspectives on the Rise of the Modern Industrial Enterprise* (Cambridge, Mass.: Harvard University Press, 1980), pp. 162–65. See also Jeremiah W. Jenks, "Industrial Combinations in Europe," *International Monthly* 4 (1901): 648–75; Francis Walker, "The Law Concerning Monopolistic Combinations in Continental Europe," *Political Science Quarterly* 20 (1905): 13–41; Walker, "Policies of Germany, England, Canada and the United States towards Combinations," *Annals of the American Academy of Political and Social Science* (hereinafter cited as *Annals*) 42 (1912): 184–201.

7. Francis Déak, "Contracts and Combinations in Restraint of Trade in French Law. A Comparative Study," *Iowa Law Review* 21 (1935–1936): 402, 417–19; Freedeman, *Joint-Stock Enterprise,* passim.

8. John Wolff, "Business Monopolies: Three European Systems in their Bearing on American Law," *Tulane Law Review* 9 (1935): 333–34. See also Walker, "Monopolistic Combinations," pp. 27–36; Jenks, "Industrial Combinations," pp. 651–52; Caron, *Economic History,* pp. 41, 43–44.

9. Reinhold Wolff, "Social Control through the Device of Defining Unfair Trade Practices. The German Experience," *Iowa Law Review* 21 (1935–1936): 357. See also David S. Landes, *The Unbound Prometheus* (Cambridge: At the University Press, 1969), pp. 197–99.

10. White quoted in Heinrich Kronstein, "The Dynamics of German Cartels and Patents," *University of Chicago Law Review* 9 (1941–1942): 646.

11. Wolff, "Business Monopolies," pp. 328–33; Walker, "Monopolistic Combinations," pp. 14–21; Walker, "Policies," p. 185; Gilbert H. Montague, "German and British Experience with Trusts," *Atlantic Monthly* 107 (1911): 158–59.

12. Montague, "Business and Politics at Home and Abroad," *Annals* 12 (1912): 161. See also Elmer Roberts, "German Good-Will towards Trusts," *Scribner's Magazine* 49 (1911): 298; Rudolf Roesler, "Attitude of German People and Government towards Trusts," *Annals* 42 (1912): 172–82; Archibald H. Stockler, *Regulating an Industry: The Rhenish-Westphalian Coal Syndicate, 1893–1929* (New York: Columbia University Press, 1932), pp. 10ff.

13. Gerald D. Feldman, *Iron and Steel in the German Inflation, 1916–1923* (Princeton: Princeton University Press, 1977), Epilogue, pp. 8–9, 65, 76, 113, 464; Robert Leifman, *Cartels, Concerns and Trusts* (New York: Dutton, 1932), pp. 168–70, and "German Industrial Organization since the World War," *Quarterly Journal of Economics* 40 (1925–1926): 82–110; National Industrial Conference Board, *Rationalization of German Industry* (New York: NICB, 1931), pp. 32–45; William C. Kessler, "German Cartel Regulation under the Decree of 1923," *Quarterly Journal of Economics* 50 (1935–1936): 680–93.

14. *Mogul* v. *McGregor* [1892] AC 25; *Maxim* v. *Nordenfelt* [1894] AC 535.

15. *Mogul v. McGregor,* LR 23 QBD 618; Talcott Williams, "No Combinations Without Regulation," *Annals* **32** (1908): 248.

16. Archibald P. L. Gordon, *The Problem of Trust and Monopoly Control* (London: Routledge, 1928), p. 139; George R. Carter, *The Tendency towards Industrial Combination* (London: Constable, 1913).

17. Sydney Brooks, "The Benefits of Big Business," *Fortnightly Review* **114** (1920): 945–46; Leslie Hanna, *The Rise of the Corporate Economy: The British Experience* (Baltimore: Johns Hopkins University Press, 1976), pp. 29ff; Boothby et al., *Industry and the State,* p. 41; Bishop C. Hunt, "Recent English Company Law Reform," *Harvard Business Review* **8** (1930): 183.

18. British case figures derived from *All England Law Reports Annotated Index and Table of Cases 1895–1935* (London: Butterworth, 1936); company list from Peter L. Payne, "The Emergence of the Large-Scale Company in Great Britain 1870–1914," *Economic History Review* **20** (1967): 526. See also C. Ernest Fayle, "Trade Combinations," *Edinburgh Review* **230** (1919): 110–29; Felix Levy, "A Contrast between the Anti-Trust Laws of Foreign Countries and of the United States," *Annals* **147** (1930): 125–37; Geoffrey Vickers, "Legal Obstacles to Industrial Integration," *Solicitors' Journal* **81** (1937): 817–20; Fritz E. Koch, "Methods of Regulating Unfair Competition in Germany, England, and the United States," *University of Pennsylvania Law Review* **78** (1930): 693–712, 854–78.

19. Robert H. Wiebe, *The Search for Order, 1877–1920* (New York: Hill and Wang, 1967); Daniel Boorstin, *The Americans: The Democratic Experience* (New York: Random House, 1973).

20. James Bryce, "America Revisited: The Changes of a Quarter-Century," *Outlook* **79** (1905): 847.

21. Gabriel Kolko, *The Triumph of Conservatism* (New York: Free Press, 1963).

22. Richard C. Maclaurin, "Presidential Candidates and the Trust Problem in America," *Contemporary Review* **102** (1912): 651.

23. Cooley quoted in Morton Keller, *Affairs of State: Public Life in Late Nineteenth Century America* (Cambridge, Mass.: Harvard University Press, 1977), pp. 428–30.

24. Albro Martin, *Enterprise Denied: Origins of the Decline of American Railroads, 1897–1917* (New York: Columbia University Press, 1971).

25. P. J. Cain, "The British Railway Rates Problem, 1894–1913," *Business History* **20** (1978): 87–99, and "Railway Combination and Government, 1900–1914," *Economic History Review,* 2nd ser. **25** (1972): 623–41.

26. Walton Hamilton, "The Problem of Anti-Trust Reform," *Columbia Law Review* **32** (1932): 177–78; *National Cotton Oil Co. v. Texas,* 197 U.S. 115, 129 (1905).

27. William Z. Ripley, "Industrial Concentration as Shown by the Census," *Quarterly Journal of Economics* **21** (1906–1907): 651–58.

28. Francis Walker, "The Oil Trust and Government," *Political Science Quarterly* **23** (1908): 18–46; on Paper Trust, Morton Keller, *In Defense of Yesterday: James M. Beck and the Politics of Conservatism* (New York: Coward-McCann, 1958), p. 68; Oswald W. Knauth, *The Policy of the United States towards*

Industrial Monopoly (New York: Columbia University, 1914), pp. 86, 92. See also Bruce Bringhurst, *Antitrust and the Oil Monopoly: The Standard Oil Cases, 1890–1911* (Westport, Conn.: Greenwood Press, 1979).

29. Knauth, *Policy of the U.S.*, pp. 78n–79n; Theodore Roosevelt, "The Standard Oil Decision and After," *Outlook* 98 (1911): 240; James C. Geman, Jr., "The Taft Administration and the Sherman Antitrust Act," *Mid-America* 54 (1972): 172–86.

30. Robert R. Reed, "American Democracy and Corporate Reform: The Democratic Anti-Trust Plank," *Atlantic Monthly* 113 (1914): 261.

31. Morton Keller, "Anglo-American Politics, 1900–1930, in Anglo-American Perspective: A Case Study in Comparative History," *Comparative Studies in Society and History* 22 (1980): 458–77. See also Sydney Brooks, "The Politics of American Business," *North American Review* 193 (1911): 717.

32. Sources cited in note 18 above and American Digest System, *First Decennial Digest*, 1897–1906 (St. Paul: West, 1908).

33. Charles W. McCurdy, "The Knight Sugar Decision of 1895 and the Modernization of American Corporation Law, 1869–1903," *Business History Review* 53 (1979): 304–42.

34. Wallace E. Belcher, "Industrial Pooling Agreements," *Quarterly Journal of Economics* 19 (1904–1905): 111–23; Alfred D. Chandler, *The Visible Hand: The Managerial Revolution in American Business* (Cambridge, Mass.: Harvard University Press, 1977).

35. *Northern Securities Co. v. U.S.*, 193 U.S. 197, 405–406 (1904); Robert L. Cutting, "The Northern Securities Company and the Sherman Anti-Trust Law," *North American Review* 174 (1902): 528–35.

36. *Trenton Potteries Co. v. Oliphant,* 58 N.J. Eq. 507 (1899); *Distilling Co. v. People,* 156 Ill. 448 (1895); National Industrial Conference Board, *Mergers and the Law* (New York: NICB, 1929), pp. 21–23.

37. Victor Morawetz, "The Supreme Court and the Anti-Trust Act," *Columbia Law Review* 10 (1910): 687, 698.

38. Bringhurst, *Antitrust,* chaps. 5–7; Robert L. Raymond, "The Standard Oil and Tobacco Cases," *Harvard Law Review* 25 (1911–1912): 31.

39. Henry R. Seager, "The Recent Trust Decisions," *Political Science Quarterly* 26 (1911): 596; Albert C. Muhse, "The Disintegration of the Tobacco Combination," *Political Science Quarterly* 28 (1913): 254, 276.

40. Untermyer quoted in "The Supreme Court Decisions," *North American Review* 194 (1911): 87; Edgar Watkins, "Anti-Trust Laws A Protection to Monopoly," *Central Law Journal* 96 (1923): 189.

41. Myron W. Watkins, "An Appraisal of the Work of the Federal Trade Commission," *Columbia Law Review* 32 (1932): 272–73; E. Dana Durand, "The Trust Legislation of 1914," *Quarterly Journal of Economics* 29 (1914–1915): 94.

42. Douglas W. Jaenicke, "Herbert Croly, Progressive Ideology, and the FTC Act," *Political Science Quarterly* 93 (1978): 471–93; Woodrow Wilson, "Address on the Relation of the United States to the Business of the World," delivered before the Grain Dealers Association, Baltimore, September 25, 1916, in Albert Shaw, ed., *The Messages and Papers of Woodrow Wilson* (New York: Review of Reviews, 1917) 1:331.

43. Gerard C. Henderson, *The Federal Trade Commission: A Study in Administrative Law and Procedure* (New Haven: Yale University Press, 1925), p. 339; Myron W. Watkins, "The Federal Trade Commission: A Critical Survey," *Quarterly Journal of Economics* 40 (1925–1926): 565.

44. For germane overviews, see Charles Maier, *Recasting Bourgeois Europe* (Princeton: Princeton University Press, 1975); Keith Middlemas, *Politics in Industrial Society: The Experience of the British System since 1911* (London: Deutsch, 1979); Keller, "Anglo-American Politics."

45. Gardiner C. Means, "The Separation of Ownership and Control in American Industry," *Quarterly Journal of Economics* 46 (1931–1932): 68–100; A. H. Feller, "The Movement for Corporate Reform: A World-Wide Phenomenon," *American Bar Association Journal* 20 (1934): 347–48.

46. Rathenau quoted in Berle and Means, *Modern Corporation,* p. 309.

47. "A Collection and Survey of State Anti-Trust Laws," *Columbia Law Review* 32 (1932): 365–66. See also Joseph C. Palamountain, Jr., *The Politics of Distribution* (Cambridge, Mass.: Harvard University Press, 1955).

48. Myron Watkins, "The Sherman Act: Its Design and Its Effects," *Quarterly Journal of Economics* 43 (1928–1929): 32; *U.S.* v. *United States Steel Corp.,* 251 U.S. 417 (1920); *U.S.* v. *International Harvester Co.,* 274 U.S. 693 (1927); *U.S.* v. *United Shoe Machinery Co.,* 247 U.S. 32 (1918); on railroads, Martin Tollefson, "Judicial Review of the Decisions of the Interstate Commerce Commission," *George Washington Law Review* 5 (1937): 540ff.; Dexter M. Keezer and Stacy May, *The Public Control of Business* (New York: Harper, 1930), p. 49.

49. Milton Handler, "Industrial Mergers and the Anti-Trust Laws," *Columbia Law Review* 32 (1932): 171, 181, 183, 271; on expenditures, Howard E. Wahrenbrock, "Federal Anti-Trust Law and the National Industrial Recovery Act," *Michigan Law Review* 31 (1932–1933): 1014n; on Donovan, Robert F. Himmelberg, *The Origins of the National Recovery Administration: Business, Government, and the Trade Association Issue, 1921–1933* (New York: Fordham University Press, 1976), p. 55, and Robert Choate, "Donovan Has Charge of That," *Independent* 117 (1926): 8–10.

50. William J. Donovan and Breck P. McAllister, "Consent Decrees in the Enforcement of Federal Anti-Trust Laws," *Harvard Law Review* 46 (1932–1933): 885; George W. Alger, "The Letter Law and the Golden Rule," *Atlantic Monthly* 130 (1922): 299; Paul T. Homan, "Industrial Combination as Surveyed in Recent Literature," *Quarterly Journal of Economics* 44 (1929–1930): 347.

51. Watkins, "Federal Trade Commission: A Critical Survey," pp. 568–69.

52. E. Pendleton Herring, "Politics, Personalities, and the Federal Trade Commission," *American Political Science Review* 28 (1934): 1021; *F.T.C.* v. *Raladam,* 283 U.S. 643 (1931).

53. Herring, "Politics," p. 1021. See also G. Cullom Davis, "The Transformation of the Federal Trade Commission, 1914–1929," *Mississippi Valley Historical Review* 49 (1962): 437–55.

54. *F.T.C.* v. *Gratz,* 253 U.S. 421, 427, 435, 432, 428 (1920). See also V.R., "Federal Trade Commission—Recent Trends in Interpretation of the Federal Trade Commission Act," *Michigan Law Review* 32 (1933–1934): 1142–54; Carl McFarland, *Judicial Control of the Federal Trade Commission and the*

Interstate Commerce Commission, 1920–1930 (Cambridge, Mass.: Harvard University Press, 1933).

55. *F.T.C.* v. *American Tobacco Co.*, 264 U.S. 298 (1924); FTC commissioner quoted in Davis, "Transformation of FTC," pp. 441–42.

56. Ellis W. Hawley, "Herbert Hoover, the Commerce Secretariat, and the Vision of an 'Associative State,' 1921–1928," *Journal of American History* 61 (1974): 116–40. See also Hawley essay in this volume, p. 131. Joan H. Wilson, *Herbert Hoover: Forgotten Progressive* (Boston: Little Brown, 1975), discusses Hoover's "neoguildist American corporatism," pp. 98–101.

57. Herman Oliphant, "Trade Associations and the Law," *Columbia Law Review* 26 (1926): 382ff.

58. Robert F. Himmelberg, "Business, Antitrust Policy, and the Industrial Board of the Department of Commerce, 1919," *Business History Review* 42 (1968): 1–23; Himmelberg, *Origins of NRA,* passim; Hoover quoted in David L. Podell and Benjamin S. Kirsh, "The Problem of Trade Association Law," *St. John's Law Review* 2 (1927): 6n.

59. *American Column & Lumber Co. et al.* v. *U.S.*, 257 U.S. 377, 412–13, 415 (1921).

60. *Maple Flooring Ass'n* v. *U.S.*, 268 U.S. 563, 587 (1925).

61. *U.S.* v. *Trenton Potteries Co.*, 273 U.S. 392, 397 (1927); *Paramount-Famous-Lasky* v. *U.S.*, 282 U.S. 30 (1930); "Does the Sherman Act Prohibit the Adoption of Standard Contracts and Arbitration Agreements by Trade Conferences?" *Yale Law Journal* 40 (1930–1931): 640–46.

62. Grant McConnell, *The Decline of Agrarian Democracy* (New York: Atheneum, 1969); Ralph H. Gabriel, "The Farmer in the Commonwealth," *North American Review* 213 (1921): 577–86; James H. Shideler, *Farm Crisis 1919–1923* (Berkeley and Los Angeles: University of California Press, 1957), chap. 4. For the romanticization of the cooperative, see Lawrence Goodwyn, *Democratic Promise: The Populist Movement in America* (New York: Oxford University Press, 1976).

63. Floyd Rodine, "Legislative and Legal Struggle of the Grain Cooperatives in Nebraska, 1900–1915," *Nebraska History* 56 (1975): 457–70; Anna Youngman, "The Tobacco Pools of Kentucky and Tennessee," *Journal of Political Economy* 18 (1910): 34–49; John L. Mathews, "Agrarian Pooling in Kentucky," *Charities* 20 (1908): 192–96; Mathews, "The Farmers' Union and the Tobacco Pool," *Atlantic Monthly* 102 (1908): 482–91; James A. Everitt, "The New Farmers' Movement," *Independent* 62 (1907): 1197–99; "Kentucky's Anarchists," *Independent* 64 (1908): 646; McConnell, *Decline,* pp. 41–42.

64. Fred W. Powell, "Co-operative Marketing of California Fresh Fruit," *Quarterly Journal of Economics* 24 (1909–1910): 417. See also Gerard C. Henderson, "Cooperative Marketing Associations," *Columbia Law Review* 23 (1923): 91–112; Edwin G. Nourse, *The Legal Status of Agricultural Co-operation* (New York: Macmillan, 1927), chaps. 3, 4.

65. Carl C. Plehn, "The State Market Commission of California," *American Economic Review* 8 (1918): 1–27; Grace Larsen, "A Progressive in Agriculture: Harris Weinstock," *Agricultural History* 32 (1958): 187–93; Nourse, *Legal Status,* chap. 5.

66. Grace H. Larsen and Henry E. Erdman, "Aaron Sapiro: Genius of Farm Co-operative Promotion," *Mississippi Valley Historical Review* 49 (1962): 242–68; Aaron Sapiro, "The Law of Cooperative Marketing Associations," *Kentucky Law Journal* 15 (1926): 5.

67. Sapiro, "Law of Cooperative Marketing," pp. 12, 14. See also Stanley M. Arndt, "The Law of California Co-operative Marketing Associations," *California Law Review* 8 (1919–1920): 281–99, 384–403, and 9 (1920–1921): 44–55; Theodore R. Meyer, "The Law of Co-operative Marketing," *California Law Review* 15 (1927): 85–112.

68. Robert H. Montgomery, *The Cooperative Pattern in Cotton* (New York: Macmillan, 1929), chap. 4, pp. 106–11.

69. Larsen and Erdman, "Aaron Sapiro," p. 265; Walton H. Hamilton, "Judicial Tolerance of Farmers' Cooperatives," *Yale Law Journal* 38 (1928–1929): 951; Henderson, "Cooperative Marketing Associations," p. 112.

70. Nourse, *Legal Status*, chap. 11.

71. *Liberty Warehouse Co.* v. *Burley Tobacco Growers Ass'n*, 276 U.S. 71 (1928); Abe D. Waldauer, "The Tobacco Growers Association Case," *Tennessee Law Review* 5 (1926–1927): 123–32. See also Nourse, *Legal Status*, chaps. 11–15.

72. Larsen and Erdman, "Aaron Sapiro," p. 265.

73. *Frost* v. *Corporation Commission*, 278 U.S. 515 (1929). See also John Hanna, "Cooperative Associations and the Public," *Michigan Law Review* 29 (1930–1931): 148–90; Milton J. Keegan, "Power of Agricultural Co-Operative Associations to Limit Production," *Michigan Law Review* 26 (1927–1928): 648–73; Matthew O. Tobriner, "The Constitutionality of Cooperative Marketing Statutes," *California Law Review* 17 (1928): 20–34.

74. Forrest McDonald, *Insull* (Chicago: University of Chicago Press, 1962); "High Finance in the 'Twenties: The United Corporation," *Columbia Law Review* 37 (1937): 785–816, 936–80, and "High Finance in the 'Thirties: New Deal Legislation," 37 (1937): 1157–1200. See also Ernest O. Eisenberg, "Recent Tendencies in the Regulation of Public Utility Holding Companies," *Marquette Law Review* 17 (1932–1933): 273–91; David E. Lilienthal, "Regulation of Public Utilities During the Depression," *Harvard Law Review* 46 (1933): 745–75; Lilienthal, "The Regulation of Public Utility Holding Companies," *Columbia Law Review* 29 (1929): 404–40. See also Michael E. Parrish, *Securities Regulation and the New Deal* (New Haven: Yale University Press, 1970), chap. 6.

75. Keller, *Affairs of State*, p. 410; William A. Prendergast, *Public Utilities and the People* (New York: Appleton-Century, 1933), pp. 294–95. See also Marshall A. Dimock, "British and American Utilities: A Comparison," *University of Chicago Law Review* 1 (1933–1934): 265–82; Edwin C. Goddard, "The Evolution and Devolution of Public Utilities Law," *Michigan Law Review* 32 (1933–1934): 577–623.

76. Bruce Wyman, "The Law of the Public Callings as a Solution of the Trust Problem," *Harvard Law Review* 17 (1903–1904): 156–73, 217–47; *Wolff Packing Co.* v. *Court of Industrial Relations*, 262 U.S. 522 (1923); *Tyson & Brother* v. *Banton*, 273 U.S. 418 (1927); *Ribnik* v. *McBride*, 277 U.S. 350 (1928); *Williams* v. *Standard Oil Co.*, 278 U.S. 235 (1919). See also Maurice

H. Merrill, "The New Judicial Approach to Due Process and Price Fixing," *Kentucky Law Journal* 18 (1929): 3–17; Gustavus H. Robinson, "The Public Utility Concept in American Law," *Harvard Law Review* 41 (1927–1928): 277–308; Thomas R. Powell, "State Utilities and the Supreme Court, 1922–1930," *Michigan Law Review* 29 (1931): 811–38.

77. Keezer and May, *Public Control of Business,* chaps. 5–7; Ralph E. Heilman, "The Development by Commissions of the Principle of Public Utility Valuation," *Quarterly Journal of Economics* 28 (1913–1914): 269–91; James C. Bonbright, "The Problem of Judicial Valuation," *Columbia Law Review* 27 (1927): 493–522.

78. E.C.G., "Public Utility Valuation—Cost-of-Reproduction Theory and the World War," *Michigan Law Review* 18 (1919–1920): 774–79; Godfrey Goldmark, "The Struggle for Higher Public Utility Rates Because of War Time Costs," *Cornell Law Quarterly* 5 (1920): 227–46; Edwin C. Goddard, "Fair Value of Public Utilities," *Michigan Law Review* 22 (1923–1924): 652–72, 777–97; Donald R. Richberg, "Value—By Judicial Fiat," *Harvard Law Review* 40 (1926–1927): 567–82.

79. Felix Frankfurter, "Public Services and the Public," *Yale Review* 20 (1930–1931): 15; Goddard, "Fair Value," p. 601.

80. *Southwestern Bell Tel. Co. v. Pub. Serv. Comm.,* 262 U.S. 276 (1922); *Bluefield Water Works v. Pub. Serv. Comm.,* 262 U.S. 679 (1923); *Georgia Ry. & Power Co. v. Railroad Comm.,* 262 U.S. 625 (1923).

81. John J. George, "Establishing State Regulation of Motor Carriers," *Southwestern Political and Social Science Quarterly* 10 (1929): 217–29; David E. Lilienthal and Irwin S. Rosenbaum, "Motor Carriers and the State: A Study in Contemporary Public Utility Legislation," *Journal of Land and Public Utility Economics* 2 (1926): 257–75; Lilienthal and Rosenbaum, "Motor Carrier Regulation: Federal, State and Municipal," *Columbia Law Review* 26 (1926): 954–87.

82. J. Byron McCormick, "The Regulation of Motor Transportation," *California Law Review* 22 (1933–1934): 24–77; Ford P. Hall, "Certificates of Convenience and Necessity," *Michigan Law Review* 29 (1929): 107–48, 276–314; *Michigan Pub. Util. Comm. v. Duke,* 266 U.S. 577 (1925); *Frost v. R.R. Comm.,* 271 U.S. 583 (1926); David E. Lilienthal and Irwin S. Rosenbaum, "Motor-Carrier Regulation by Certificates of Necessity and Convenience," *Yale Law Journal* 36 (1926–1927): 163–94.

83. "Constitutional Obstacles to State Regulation of Bus Transportation," *Harvard Law Review* 40 (1926–1927): 882–86; La Rue Brown and Stuart N. Scott, "Regulation and the Contract Motor Carrier under the Constitution," *Harvard Law Review* 44 (1930–1931): 530–71; *Buck v. Kuykendall,* 267 U.S. 307, 315 (1925); Irwin S. Rosenbaum, "The Common Carrier-Public Utility Concept: A Legal-Industrial View," *Journal of Land and Public Utility Economics* 7 (1931): 154.

84. E. R. A. Seligman and Robert A. Love, *Price Cutting and Price Maintenance: A Study in Economics* (New York: Harper, 1932).

85. "Price-Maintenance Agreements," *Law Times* 164 (1927): 263–64; on France, Charles L. Miller, *Legal Status of Maintenance of Uniform Resale Prices,* reprint from *Pennsylvania Law Review* (New York, 1916), p. 22.

86. *Dr. Miles Medical Co.* v. *John D. Park & Sons Co.*, 220 U.S. 373, 411–12 (1911); A. D. Neale, *The Antitrust Laws of the United States of America*, 2nd ed. (Cambridge: At the University Press, 1970), p. 276.

87. Sumner H. Slichter, "The Cream of Wheat Case," *Political Science Quarterly* **31** (1916): 410; "Fair Trade Legislation: The Constitutionality of a State Experiment in Resale Price Maintenance," *Harvard Law Review* **49** (1936): 811–21. See also "Price Maintenance at Common Law and Under Proposed Legislation," (*Harvard Law Review*) **30** (1916–1917): 68–71.

88. *U.S.* v. *Colgate*, 250 U.S. 300 (1919); *F.T.C.* v. *Beech-Nut Packing Co.*, 257 U.S. 441 (1922); *U.S.* v. *General Electric Co.*, 272 U.S. 476 (1926); Seligman and Love, *Price Cutting*, p. 87.

89. "Organizing Retail Trades," *New Republic* **1** (1915): 19–20; J. Ross Harrington, "The Chain Store Era and the Law," *Notre Dame Lawyer* **4** (1929): 491–505; Edward W. Simms, "Chain Stores and the Courts," *Virginia Law Review* **17** (1931): 313–24.

90. Samuel Becker and Robert A. Hess, "The Chain Store License Tax and the Fourteenth Amendment," *North Carolina Law Review* **7** (1928–1929): 127.

91. *A & P.* v. *Maxwell*, 199 N.C. 433 (1930); *State Board of Tax Comm'nrs* v. *Jackson*, 283 U.S. 527 (1931); *Liggett* v. *Lee*, 288 U.S. 517, 567 (1933). See also Juliet Blumenfeld, "Retail Trade Regulations and their Constitutionality," *California Law Review* **22** (1933–1934), 86–105.

92. *Nebbia* v. *N.Y.*, 291 U.S. 502 (1934); *Appalachian Coals Inc.* v. *U.S.*, 288 U.S. 344 (1933).

93. Himmelberg, *Origins of NRA*, chaps. 8–10; Howard E. Wahrenbrock, "Federal Anti-Trust Law and the National Industrial Recovery Act," *Michigan Law Review* **31** (1932–1933): 1030. See also William E. Leuchtenberg, "The New Deal and the Analogue of War," in John Braeman et al., *Change and Continuity in Twentieth Century America* (Columbus: Ohio State University Press, 1964), pp. 81–143.

94. *Schechter Poultry Corp.* v. *U.S.*, 295 U.S. 495 (1935); Ellis W. Hawley, *The New Deal and the Problem of Monopoly: A Study in Economic Ambivalence* (Princeton: Princeton University Press, 1966).

95. Ewald T. Grether, "Experience in California with Fair Trade Legislation Restricting Price Cutting," *California Law Review* **24** (1935–1936): 640–700.

96. Charles D. Evans, "Anti-Price Discrimination Act of 1936," *Virginia Law Review* **23** (1936–1937): 140–77; Hawley, *New Deal*, pp. 249–54. See also Palamountain, *Politics of Distribution*.

97. *The Economist*, January 6, 1979, pp. 43–46.

98. Oliver Wendell Holmes, *Collected Legal Papers* (New York: Harcourt, Brace, 1920), p. 21.

THREE FACETS OF HOOVERIAN ASSOCIATIONALISM   Ellis Hawley

1. Henry S. Dennison to Edward Eyre Hunt, April 14, 1927, with enclosed memorandum, Hunt Papers, Springfield, Ohio, copy made available by Neil Basen.

2. See the essays in the *Revue Recherches,* special issue on "Guerre, Fascisme, et Taylorisme," September 1978. See also Charles S. Maier, *Recasting Bourgeois Europe: Stabilization in France, Germany, and Italy in the Decade After World War I* (Princeton: Princeton University Press, 1975). "Corporatism" as used in this paper is a designation for an ideal socio-political type in which (a) the basic units are functional groupings, (b) institutions recognize and integrate the units into an interdependent whole, (c) there are deep interpenetrations between state and society, (d) the state functions chiefly as midwife and partner rather than director or regulator, and (e) an enlightened social elite identifies social needs and provides leadership for concerted social action. Movement toward this ideal type constitutes "corporatization."

3. For a discussion of this see Robert H. Wiebe, *The Search for Order, 1877–1920* (New York: Hill and Wang, 1967), pp. 159–63.

4. Indicative of this, I would argue, are such works as Bruce L. R. Smith, ed., *The New Political Economy: The Public Use of the Private Sector* (New York: Wiley, 1975); George C. Lodge, *The New American Ideology* (New York: Knopf, 1975); Neil W. Chamberlain, *Remaking American Values: Challenge to a Business Society* (New York: Basic Books, 1977); and Ezra F. Vogel, *Japan as Number One* (Cambridge, Mass.: Harvard University Press, 1979). Smith's argument that the attainment of national goals requires "the partnership effort of industry, universities, not-for-profit laboratories, and government agencies" and that "the kinds of talent needed, and the professional administrative structures required to integrate the effort, have not been available within the formal government hierarchy" is much like the argument of the 1920s.

5. See, for example, Arthur J. Eddy, *The New Competition* (New York: Appleton, 1912); E. H. Gaunt, *Co-operative Competition* (Providence: Stevens Press, 1917); Forrest Crissey, *Teamwork in Trade-Building* (New York: Association Bureau, 1914); Edward Hurley, *The Awakening of Business* (Garden City: Doubleday, Page, 1917); Ida Tarbell, "The Golden Rule in Business," *American Magazine* 78 (1914); and Gilbert H. Montague, "Business and Politics at Home and Abroad," *Annals of the American Academy of Political and Social Science* 42 (July 1912): 156–71. See also the discussion in Burton Kaufman's *Efficiency and Expansion: Foreign Trade Organization in the Wilson Administration, 1913–1921* (Westport, Conn.: Greenwood, 1974), pp. 32–47, and in the introductory sections of David Horowitz's "Visions of Harmonious Abundance: Corporate Ideology in the 1920s" (Ph.D diss., University of Minnesota, 1971).

6. Various aspects of this movement away from the antitrust ideal are discussed in A. Jerome Clifford, *The Independence of the Federal Reserve System* (Philadelphia: University of Pennsylvania Press, 1965); Grant McConnell, *The Decline of Agrarian Democracy* (Berkeley: University of California Press, 1953); Melvin Urofsky, *Big Steel and the Wilson Administration* (Columbus: Ohio State University Press, 1969), pp. 51–83; James Weinstein, *The Corporate Ideal in the Liberal State, 1900–1918* (Boston: Beacon Press, 1968), pp. 82–91; Richard Hume Werking, "Bureaucrats, Businessmen, and Foreign Trade: The Origins of the United States Chamber of Commerce," *Business History Review* 52 (Autumn 1978): 321–41; and Samuel P. Hays, *Conservation and the Gospel of Efficiency* (Cambridge, Mass.: Harvard University Press, 1959), pp. 272–76.

7. Kaufman, *Efficiency and Expansion,* pp. 153–59; Urofsky, *Big Steel,* pp. 73–78.

8. On the war system, see Robert D. Cuff, *The War Industries Board* (Baltimore: Johns Hopkins Press, 1973); Kaufman, *Efficiency and Expansion*; and Frederick Paxson, "American War Government," *American Historical Review* 26 (October 1920): 57–76. See also Murray Rothbard's provocative "War Collectivism in World War I," in Ronald Radosh and Murray N. Rothbard, eds., *A New History of Leviathan* (New York: Dutton, 1972).

9. See again the references in note 2. See also Robert D. Cuff, "Harry Garfield, the Fuel Administration, and the Search for a Cooperative Order during World War I," *American Quarterly* 30 (Spring 1978): 39–53; Kim McQuaid, "Corporate Liberalism in the Business Community," *Business History Review* 52 (Autumn 1978): 342–46; and Haggai Hurvitz, "Ideology and Industrial Conflict: President Wilson's First Industrial Conference of October 1919," *Labor History* 18 (Fall 1977): 509–24.

10. See especially his "engineering speeches," February 17, August 26, November 19, 1920 and February 14, 1921, all in Public Statements file, Hoover Papers, Hoover Presidential Library, West Branch, Iowa (hereinafter cited as Hoover Papers). See also his testimony in U.S., Senate, Select Committee on Reconstruction and Production, *Reconstruction and Production, Hearings Pursuant to S. Res. 350,* 66th Cong., 2nd sess., 1920 (Washington, D.C.: Government Printing Office, 1921), pp. 609–27, and U.S., Senate, Committee on Education and Labor, *Industrial Conference, Hearing on Report of Industrial Conference,* 66th Cong., 2nd sess. (Washington, D.C.: Government Printing Office, 1920), pp. 26–38. Glenn Frank associated Hoover with "a new kind of creative regulation" capable of avoiding both "the sins of an anarchic business freedom and the sins of an ineffective and suicidal political control of business." See Frank, in *Century Magazine* 52 (June 1921): 312. William Allen White saw him as the proponent of an "extra government life, quite apart from the government, somewhat regulated by the government, but upon the whole a distinct institutional life" that could "solve a good many problems." See White to Hoover, October 18, 1920, White folder, Pre-Commerce files, Hoover Papers.

11. On the expansion of these administrative domains, see Donald L. Winters, *Henry Cantwell Wallace as Secretary of Agriculture* (Urbana: University of Illinois Press, 1970); Donald C. Swain, *Federal Conservation Policy, 1921–1933* (Berkeley: University of California Press, 1963); Craig Lloyd, *Aggressive Introvert: Herbert Hoover and Public Relations Management* (Columbus: Ohio State University Press, 1972); and Ellis Hawley, "Herbert Hoover, the Commerce Secretariat, and the Vision of an Associative State," *Journal of American History* 61 (June 1974): 116–40. On the changes in the Federal Trade Commission, see G. Cullom Davis, "The Transformation of the Federal Trade Commission, 1914–1929," *Mississippi Valley Historical Review* 49 (December 1962): 437–55. For Hoover's initial perceptions of what could be done and what would justify his leaving the private sector, see Hoover to Harding, February 23, 1921, Harding file, Pre-Commerce files, Hoover Papers.

12. On this macroeconomic dimension see Evan Metcalf, "Secretary Hoover and the Emergence of Macroeconomic Management," *Business History Review* 59 (Spring 1975): 60–80; Carolyn Grin, "The Unemployment Conference of

1921: An Experiment in Cooperative Planning," *Mid-America* 55 (April 1973): 83–107; and Ellis Hawley, "Herbert Hoover and Economic Stabilization, 1921–22," in Hawley, ed., *Herbert Hoover as Secretary of Commerce: Studies in New Era Thought and Practice* (Iowa City: University of Iowa Press, 1981), pp. 43–79. See also Edward Eyre Hunt, "Recent Economic Changes in the United States" (1929), Hunt Papers, Springfield, Ohio.

13. Two of the "sickest" areas were bituminous coal and agriculture. On the efforts to equip them with adjustment machinery see Ellis Hawley, "Secretary Hoover and the Bituminous Coal Problem," *Business History Review* 42 (Autumn 1968): 253–70, and Joan Hoff Wilson, "Hoover's Agricultural Policies, 1921–1928," *Agricultural History* 51 (April 1977): 335–61.

14. For the postwar concern with the industry's misbehavior and a possible timber "famine," see Lawrence Hamilton, "The Federal Forest Regulation Issue," *Journal of Forest History* 9 (April 1965): 2–11; William Robbins, "Voluntary Cooperation and the Search for Stability: The Lumber Industry in the 1920s," NEH Seminar Papers, Hoover Presidential Library; and George T. Morgan, *William B. Greeley: A Practical Forester* (St. Paul: Forest History Society, 1961), pp. 39–52. Much of the debate revolved around Gifford Pinchot's report to the Society of American Foresters in late 1919. In it he called for a federal commission to make rules for private forestry, the rules to be enforced through a licensing system to be administered by the Forest Service.

15. See Hoover's addresses on the problem, May 22, 1922, December 12, 1923, November 19, 1924, and May 2, 1925, Public Statements file, Hoover Papers. See also Hoover to William Durgin, April 15, 1924, National Lumber Manufacturers Association file, Commerce files, Hoover Papers.

16. The manufacturing census of 1919 counted 35,872 manufacturing firms. In addition, there were approximately 5,000 wholesalers and 30,000 retailers. On the structure of the industry, its technical backwardness, and its labor intensiveness, see Joseph Zarema, *Economics of the American Lumber Industry* (New York: Speller, 1963), pp. 1–18, 45, 218. See also Nelson C. Brown, *The American Lumber Industry* (New York: Wiley, 1923).

17. John Ise, *The United States Forest Policy* (New Haven: Yale University Press, 1920), pp. 338–53; Federal Trade Commission, *Report on Lumber Manufacturers Trade Associations* (Washington, D.C.: Government Printing Office, 1922).

18. Robbins, "Lumber Industry in the 1920s," pp. 4–6; National Lumber Manufacturers Association, *Highlights of a Decade of Achievement* (1929), pp. 8–12; Hoover to Durgin, April 15, 1924, NLMA file, Commerce files, Hoover Papers.

19. Department of Commerce, *Elimination of Waste: Lumber* (1924), p. 2; Hoover to Wallace, February 8, March 7, 1922, Agriculture Dept. file, Commerce files, Hoover Papers; Emmet to William Mullendore, March 23, 1922, Lumber Grading Simplification file, Commerce files, Hoover Papers; Hoover to Walter Drake, June 15, 1923, National Hardwood Lumber Association file, Commerce files, Hoover Papers. In the Forest Service there was the continuing conflict between Pinchot's "regulationism" and William B. Greeley's "cooperationism." Greeley eventually won out, but his program at this stage stressed the

need for cooperative fire protection rather than organization for greater productivity. See Morgan, *Greeley,* pp. 48–56.

20. Department of Commerce, *Elimination of Waste: Lumber,* pp. 2–3; Hoover, Address of May 22, 1922, NLMA file, Commerce files, Hoover Papers; *New York Times,* May 23, 1922 and October 8, 1922; *Public Ledger,* October 4, 1922; "Action of General Lumber Conference, Chicago, July 22," Lumber file, Commerce files, Hoover Papers. The functional representatives on the original committee were John E. Lloyd (retailers), Dwight Hinckley (wholesalers), John H. Kirby and Charles A. Goodman (manufacturers), Emory S. Hall (architects), and W. E. Hawley (railroads). Later added was E. E. Parsonage (wood users). R. G. Merritt became executive secretary. Attached to the Central Committee there was also a consulting committee, made up of 31 members chosen for their positions or expertise.

21. John McClure to National Hardwood Lumber Association members, September 13, 1922; AP Bulletin, Chicago, June 15, 1923; Hoover to Walter Drake, June 15, 1923; Hoover Statement to AP, June 16, 1923; Drake to Hoover, June 18, 1923, all in National Hardwood Lumber Association file, Commerce files, Hoover Papers; Peri Arnold, "Herbert Hoover and the Department of Commerce" (Ph.D. diss., University of Chicago, 1971), pp. 162–71.

22. Department of Commerce, *Elimination of Waste: Lumber,* pp. 3–4; "Minutes of General Standardization Conference on Lumber," December 12–13, 1923, Conferences, Lumber file, Commerce files, Hoover Papers.

23. Hoover to Durgin, April 15, 1924, NLMA file, Commerce files, Hoover Papers. There had also been cooperation with a number of lumber associations in developing and defending statistical programs, studying building codes, and gathering information on foreign markets. See F. T. Miller, "Building Codes," Building and Housing file, Commerce files, Hoover Papers; Wilson Compton to Stephen Davis, January 21, 1924, NLMA file, Commerce files, Hoover Papers; "U.S. Foreign Trade in Lumber for 1924," Lumber file, Commerce files, Hoover Papers.

24. Axel Oxholm to Julius Klein, February 15, 1923, Commerce Dept., BFDC, Lumber Division file, Commerce files, Hoover Papers; Klein to Hoover, March 6, 1923, File 82219/27, Commerce Dept. Records (RG 40), National Archives; J. C. Nellis to John W. Blodgett, October 28, 1924, Lumber file, Commerce files, Hoover Papers; Wallace to Hoover, October 8, 1924; William Greeley to Hoover, October 13, 1924; Hudson to Stokes, October 15, 1924; Greeley to Walter Drake, November 11, 1924, all in Conferences, Wood Utilization file, Commerce files, Hoover papers.

25. Wallace died on October 25, 1924, of complications following an operation to remove his gall bladder and appendix.

26. "National Conference on Utilization of Forest Products," Conferences, Wood Utilization file, Commerce files, Hoover Papers; National Conference on Utilization of Forest Products, *Report* (1925); Remarks by Secretary Hoover, November 19, 1924; Address by President Coolidge, November 19, 1924, both in Conferences, Wood Utilization file, Commerce files, Hoover Papers; *American Lumberman,* November 22, 1924.

27. National Conference on Utilization of Forest Products, *Report,* pp. 69–

72; *American Lumberman,* November 22, 1924. The Clark-McNary Act had provided funds for developing a number of cooperative activities, especially in fire protection, tax studies, forestry experimentation, and timberland surveys.

28. John H. Blodgett to Coolidge, November 22, 1924; Hoover to Howard Gore, November 24, 1924; Hoover to Coolidge, November 28, 1924; Coolidge to Blodgett, December 1, 1924; Hoover to Blodgett, December 4, 1924; Commerce Dept. press release, April 30, 1925, all in Conferences, Wood Utilization file, Commerce files, Hoover Papers.

29. Commerce Department press releases, April 30, May 2, 1925. As initially established, the committee had 21 members representing 12 functional groups. Later, it was expanded to include more specialized groups who desired representation, such groups, for example, as the plywood manufacturers, shipbuilders, cooperage industries, and wood turners. By June of 1926 it had 98 members, but policy making by 1926 had been largely concentrated in an executive committee that subsequently varied from 9 to 14 members. The changing membership and organization can be followed in "Status of the Work of the NCWU, 1926"; Commerce Dept. press release, January, 11, 1927; Oxholm to Hoover, October 17, 1927, all in Conferences, Wood Utilization file, Commerce files, Hoover Papers.

30. Hoover to Blodgett, March 2, 1925; Hoover to Walter Poleman, March 2, 1925; Press release, May 2, 1925; Hoover to James L. Kilpatrick, September 26, 1925; Daily Bulletin, December 4, 1925, all in Conferences, Wood Utilization file, Commerce files, Hoover Papers; Edward Eyre Hunt to Robert Lamont, October 16, 1929, Box 30, Hunt Papers, Hoover Institution Archives, Stanford University, Palo Alto, Calif.

31. "Status of the Work of the National Committee on Wood Utilization," 1926; Axel Oxholm to Hoover, January 6, 1926, January 11, June 16, October 17, 1927; Press release, November 5, 1926, all in Conferences, Wood Utilization file, Commerce files, Hoover Papers; Hunt to Lamont, October 16, 1929, Box 30, Hunt Papers, Hoover Institution; "Accomplishments of the Department of Commerce," Commerce, Accomplishments file, Commerce files, Hoover Papers.

32. Robbins, "Lumber Industry in the 1920s," pp. 25–29; Ward Shepard and John B. Woods, in *Journal of Forestry* 25 (January 1927) and 28 (November 1930). A subsequent study concluded that there were no major advances in productivity during the 1920s, nor for that matter during the whole period between 1899 and 1953. There were some technological advances, but the effect of these was more than offset by such factors as declining tree size, the lower quality of the timber being cut, and the greater distances that lumber had to be transported. Lumber prices kept rising relative to all-commodity prices. See Zaremba, *Economics of the American Lumber Industry,* pp. 1–3, 222. Interestingly, Zaremba, writing in 1963, still saw the establishment and enforcement of standards and grades as the industry's central problem, one whose solution "would revolutionize lumber manufacture, distribution and use." And like Hoover in the 1920s, he saw its solution coming through "strong industry organization and close cooperation of allied groups."

33. Oxholm to Anderson, January 4, 1928; Oxholm to Greeley, January 20, 1928; Greeley to Oxholm, January 25, 1928, all in Conferences, Wood Utili-

zation file, Commerce files, Hoover Papers; *Engineering News-Record,* December 15, 1927, p. 979.

34. National Lumber Manufacturers Association press release, May 10, 1927, Lumber file, Commerce files, Hoover Papers.

35. Leighton H. Peebles to James S. Taylor, November 17, 1931, reporting on a trip to district offices in the lumber areas, Box 92, Frederick Feiker Papers, Records of the Bureau of Foreign and Domestic Commerce (RG 151), National Archives. The National Timber Conservation Board was structured along lines similar to the CCLS and the NCWU. It brought together industrial, public, and governmental representatives, commingled private and public support, and had a mixed secretariat. Its chief concerns were with surplus inventories, over-production, and disorderly marketing. See Ripley Bowman, in *Southern Lumberman,* December 15, 1931; Wilson Compton, in *American Economic Review Supplement* **22** (March 1932): 101–4; and Robert Lamont to Hoover, June 18, 1932, National Timber Conservation Board file, Presidential Subject files, Hoover Papers.

36. On the NRA experience see Peter A. Stone and others, *Economic Problems of the Lumber and Timber Products Industry,* NRA Work Materials #79, 1936, pp. 103–10, and A. C. Dixon and others, "The Lumber Code," NRA Code History #9, Code Histories file, NRA Records, National Archives. On what followed see the relevant sections of Harold K. Steen, *The U.S. Forest Service* (Seattle: University of Washington Press, 1976).

37. For general accounts of the industry during this period, see Henry Ladd Smith, *Airways: The History of Commercial Aviation in the United States* (New York: Knopf, 1942); Elsbeth S. Freudenthal, *The Aviation Business from Kitty Hawk to Wall Street* (New York: Vanguard, 1940); John H. Frederick, *Commercial Air Transportation* (Chicago: Irwin, 1946); Gene R. Simons, ed., *The History of the American Aircraft Industry* (Cambridge, Mass.: MIT Press, 1968); and Thomas W. Walterman, "Airpower and Private Enterprise: Federal-Industrial Relations in the Aeronautics Field, 1918–1926" (Ph.D. diss., Washington University, 1970).

38. For expositions of this view, see "Notes for a Meeting of the Aircraft Men," July 16, 1921; Press release, November 5, 1925; Hoover's Address to the San Francisco Chamber of Commerce, September 2, 1926, all in Aviation file, Commerce files, Hoover Papers; "Memorandum for Hoover on Proposed Bureau of Aeronautics"; Hoover's Statement before the President's Aircraft Board, September 24, 1925; Press release, January 24, 1926, all in Commerce Dept., Bureau of Aeronautics file, Commerce files, Hoover Papers; "Report of the Joint Committee on Civil Aviation" (1926), Aviation file, Commerce files, Hoover Papers.

39. Charles D. Walcott to Hoover, March 23, 1921, Aviation file, Commerce files, Hoover Papers; clippings from *Buffalo News,* July 21, 1921, *Philadelphia Inquirer,* October 12, 1921, and *Philadelphia Inquirer,* September 3, 1921, in Commerce Dept., Bureau of Aeronautics file, Commerce files, Hoover Papers; "Notes for Meeting of the Aircraft Men," July 16, 1921, Aviation file, Commerce files, Hoover Papers.

40. Hoover to L. D. Gardner, June 14, 1921, Aviation file, Commerce files,

Hoover Papers; David D. Lee, "Herbert Hoover and the Development of Commercial Aviation, 1921–1926," NEH Seminar Papers, Hoover Presidential Library.

41. L. D. Gardner to Hoover, June 18, 1921; Hoover to Gardner, June 23, 1921; Luther Bell to Clarence Stetson, July 11, 1921; "Notes for Meeting of the Aircraft Men," July 16, 1921; Hoover to Maurice Cleary, June 25, 1921; "Aviation Conference," July 18, 1921, all in Aviation file, Commerce files, Hoover Papers; Charles T. Menoher to Secretary of War, April 1, 1921, National Advisory Committee for Aeronautics file, Commerce files, Hoover Papers; Robert Murray, *The Harding Era: Warren G. Harding and His Administration* (Minneapolis: University of Minnesota Press, 1969), pp. 410–11.

42. Samuel Bradley to Hoover, April 11, August 24, 1922; Howard Coffin to Hoover, April 18, 1922, all in Commerce Dept., Bureau of Aeronautics file, Commerce Files, Hoover Papers; *New York Times,* September 20, 1921; Lee, "Hoover and Commercial Aviation," pp. 12–14, 23–24; Howard Mingos, in Simons, ed., *Aircraft Industry,* pp. 55–57; *Aviation,* January 2, 1922. As originally established, the Aeronautical Chamber of Commerce included 26 manufacturing and engineering companies, 31 operators and distributors, 29 manufacturers of accessories, 8 trade publications, and the insurance writers association. The Manufacturers Aircraft Association remained in existence and was closely linked with the ACC. They shared offices and facilities, and Samuel Bradley served as general manager of both associations. Also organized in 1922, largely through the efforts of Howard Coffin, was the National Aeronautics Association. It replaced the earlier Aero Club of America.

43. Hoover to Samuel E. Winslow, December 19, 1921; Hoover to James Wadsworth, December 20, 1921; Hoover to William MacCracken, February 15, 1922; Hoover to Theodore Roosevelt, Jr., April 11, 1922; William Lamb to Emmet, April 15, 1922; Hoover to Howard Coffin, April 21, 1922; Julius Klein to Emmet, May 25, 1922; Hoover to Lamb, June 2, 1922; Hoover to Winslow, June 12, 13, 19, 1922; James O'Hara to Emmet, August 7, 1922; Winslow to Hoover, September 15, 1922, all in Commerce Dept., Bureau of Aeronautics file, Commerce files, Hoover Papers.

44. Christian Herter to Julius Klein, September 28, 1923; Earl Osborn to Hoover, January 9, 1925; R. H. Fleet to Hoover, January 10, 1925; Hoover to Hiram Bingham, September 23, 1925; Clarence Young to Hoover, December 7, 1925; Hoover to Young, December 14, 1925, all in Commerce Dept., Bureau of Aeronautics file, Commerce files, Hoover Papers; Hoover interview, in *Boston American,* October 13, 1924; Press release, November 13, 1924, Aviation file, Commerce files, Hoover Papers; Lee, "Hoover and Civil Aviation," pp. 24–25; *Aviation,* February 19, 1923, June 1, 1925.

45. *New York Times,* May 22, 1925; National Air Transport, Inc., "Public Relations Committee," Aviation file, Commerce files, Hoover Papers; Press releases, November 5, 1925, January 24, 1926; "Recommendations and Summarized Findings of the Committee on Civil Aviation," October 21, 1925; E. S. Gregg, "The Development of Civil Aviation," September 19, 1925, all in Commerce Dept., Bureau of Aeronautics file, Commerce files, Hoover Papers; Will H. Hays, *The Memoirs of Will H. Hays* (Garden City: Doubleday, 1955), pp. 312–17; Lee, "Hoover and Civil Aviation," pp. 28–31; Allan Nevins and Frank

Hill, *Ford: Expansion and Challenge* (New York: Scribner's, 1957), pp. 238–45.

46. Lee, "Hoover and Civil Aviation," pp. 31–33; Alfred F. Hurley, *Billy Mitchell: Crusader for Air Power* (Bloomington: Indiana University Press ed., 1975), pp. 100–101; President's Aircraft Board, *Report* (Washington, D.C.: Government Printing Office, 1925); "Statement of Hoover on Civil Aviation," September 24, 1925, Commerce Dept., Bureau of Aeronautics file, Commerce files, Hoover Papers.

47. Clarence Young to Hoover, December 7, 1925; Hoover to Young, December 14, 1925; Wadsworth to Hoover, December 5, 1925; Hoover to Wesley L. Jones, December 9, 1925, all in Commerce Dept., Bureau of Aeronautics file, Commerce files, Hoover Papers. Young would become the first chief of the air regulations division and would subsequently be appointed director of the Aeronautics Branch.

48. Lee, "Hoover and Civil Aviation," pp. 33–35; 44 *U.S. Statutes* 568.

49. As finally established, the Aeronautics Branch consisted of the new assistant secretary's office, a directorship working in conjunction with the office, a division each from the Lighthouse Service and the Bureau of Standards, a section from the Coast and Geodetic Survey, and newly created special divisions for air regulations and air information. See Laurence F. Schmeckebier, *The Aeronautics Branch, Department of Commerce* (Washington, D.C.: Brookings Institution, 1930), pp. 13–14; Lester D. Gardner, "Development of Civil Aeronautics in America," October 1, 1927, Aviation file, Commerce files, Hoover Papers; *Aviation*, July 13, 1929.

50. Hoover to Coolidge, August 3, 1926, with attached statement; Hoover to Hiram Bingham, July 30, 1926; Hoover to George W. Pepper, June 23, 1926, all in Commerce Dept., Bureau of Aeronautics file, Commerce files, Hoover Papers; William MacCracken, "Re Herbert Hoover," August 1, 1968, Hoover Oral History Program file, Box 13, MacCracken Papers, Hoover Presidential Library. MacCracken was not Hoover's first choice. The position was offered to Paul Henderson, the general manager of National Air Transport, and to Hollinshead N. Taylor, a Philadelphia business executive active in the National Aeronautic Association and in Hoover's programs for standardizing building codes. Both declined because of business responsibilities.

51. Gardner, "Development of Civil Aeronautics in America," October 1, 1927, Aviation file, Commerce files, Hoover Papers; testimony of MacCracken and Hoover before U.S. Senate Committee on Appropriations, *Departments of State, Justice, Commerce and Labor Appropriations Bill, 1928: Hearings on H.R. 16576*, 69th Cong., 2nd sess., 1927 (Washington, D.C.: Government Printing Office, 1927), pp. 10–26; Department of Commerce, *Air Commerce Regulations* (Washington, D.C.: Government Printing Office, 1926).

52. Hoover, "Progress in Commercial Aviation," [1928], Aviation file, Commerce files, Hoover Papers; Clarence Young to George Akerson, July 10, 1929, Aeronautics file, Presidential Subject files, Hoover Papers; MacCracken, in Senate Appropriations Committee, *Hearings: Appropriations Bill, 1928*, pp. 19–20.

53. Clippings from *Boston Herald*, October 10, 1929, and *Commerce and Finance*, November 6, 1929; Fairfax Naulty to Hoover, November 18, 1929; William McAdoo to Hoover, November 21, 1929; Clarence Young to Hoover,

August 22, 1930, all in Aeronautics file, Presidential Subject files, Hoover Papers; Walter Brown, Address to the Cleveland Chamber of Commerce, January 14, 1930, Post Office file, Presidential Subject files, Hoover Papers.

54. *U.S. Daily*, February 4, April 3, April 30, May 3, 1930; clipping of an article by David Rotroff [1930], Airmail file, Box 9, MacCracken Papers; U.S., Congress, House, Antitrust Subcommittee of the Committee on the Judiciary, *The Airlines Industry, Report No. 1328 pursuant to H. Res. 107*, 85th Cong., 1st sess., 1957 (Washington, D.C.: Government Printing Office, 1958), pp. 10–12, 19.

55. For the evolution of New Deal policy in regard to aviation, see Ellis Hawley, *The New Deal and the Problem of Monopoly* (Princeton: Princeton University Press, 1966), pp. 240–44, and Francis A. Spencer, *Air Mail Payment and the Government* (Washington, D.C.: Brookings Institution, 1941). See also House Antitrust Subcommittee, *Airlines Industry*, pp. 12–17.

56. See, for example, Will H. Hays, "The Motion Picture Industry," *Review of Reviews* (January 1923), pp. 65–80, and Hays, "Motion Pictures and the Public," April 20, 1925, Hays file, Commerce files, Hoover Papers. The most corporatively organized portions of the apparatus were (1) the machinery for "harmonizing" producer-exhibitor relations and (2) the public relations committee (later department) with its mixture of industrial, consumer, and "public" representatives. For general accounts of the Hays Office, see Raymond Moley, *The Hays Office* (Indianapolis: Bobbs-Merrill, 1945); Ruth A. Inglis, *Freedom of the Movies* (Chicago: University of Chicago Press, 1947); Mae D. Huettig, *Economic Control of the Motion Picture Industry: A Study in Economic Organization* (Philadelphia: University of Pennsylvania Press, 1944); Louis Nizer, *New Courts of Industry* (New York: Longacre, 1935); and "The Hays Office," *Fortune*, December 1938, pp. 68–72.

57. Hoover to Hays, March 7, May 8, 1922; Hoover to Walter S. Tower, June 7, 1923; Emmet to Hays, July 26, 1923; Hoover to Julius Barnes, August 14, 1922, all in Hays file, Commerce files, Hoover Papers; Hoover to Grace Harriman, December 19, 1921; Emmet to Mrs. M. B. Dean, February 10, 1922, both in Motion Pictures file, Commerce files, Hoover Papers; "Hays Office," *Fortune*, December 1938, p. 139; Hays, *Memoirs*, pp. 356, 510. Officially, however, especially in correspondence with groups seeking governmental regulation, Hoover took the position that the movie "question" was not before his department except in connection with export trade.

58. Moley, *Hays Office*, pp. 27–32; Inglis, *Freedom of Movies*, pp. 62–96; Henry F. Pringle, "Will Hays—Supervisor of Morals," *Outlook*, April 11, 1928, pp. 576–78. As Pringle puts it, Hays was "hired—hokum aside—to block additional Government supervision, to tame radical spirits among the producers, to prevent trade practices which cause expensive litigation, to use his influence as an important politician of the party in power." The most notorious of the scandals were those involving the murder of William Desmond Taylor, the trial of Roscoe "Fatty" Arbuckle, and the political activities of William A. Brady of the National Association of the Motion Picture Industry. In view of these the industry was looking for respectability, much as baseball had done following the "Black Sox" scandal of 1919.

59. Hays was noted chiefly for his feats as a political organizer and conductor

of public relations campaigns. Before entering Harding's cabinet as postmaster general, he had for three years headed the Republican National Committee. His approach to administrative and organizational problems was much like Hoover's, and the two had been associated during the war when Hays was chairman of the Indiana State Council of Defense.

60. See Inglis, *Freedom of Movies*, pp. 73–74, 88–90.

61. *Ibid.*, pp. 97–111; Moley, *Hays Office*, pp. 132–39, 213–19; Hays, "Motion Picture Industry," *Review of Reviews*, January 1923, pp. 74–79. The machinery linking the office to community and civic groups was known as the Committee on Public Relations. Set up in 1922 following a conference in New York, it consisted of representatives from about 80 civic, fraternal, welfare, religious, and professional organizations, each serving in theory to bring the thinking of the movie makers and that of groups making up the "public" closer together. At the heart of the apparatus was a group of administrators functioning both as a unit of the Hays Office and as the executive secretariat for the group representatives. In 1925 the committee as such dissolved itself and the apparatus was absorbed into a Department of Public Relations. There were also cooperating organizations set up by the participating groups, and after 1929 there was a staff position held by a "representative in the industry of organized women."

62. Moley, *Hays Office*, pp. 57–64; Inglis, *Freedom of Movies*, pp. 111–16. The machinery here began with informal consultation and evolved through a formula for identifying and securing industry-wide rejection of unsuitable scripts, an advisory system on pictures to be released, and promulgation of a list of "don'ts" and "be carefuls." Not until 1930 was there a formal production code. Movies were made outside the system, and some were even advertised as "banned by Will Hays." But these could not be shown in theatres owned or controlled by MPPDA members.

63. Moley, *Hays Office*, pp. 50–51, 90–97; Hays, *Memoirs*, pp. 338–39, 355–56, 433; Inglis, *Freedom of the Movies*, pp. 90–91; *System*, September 1926, pp. 277–80.

64. Hays, *Memoirs*, pp. 333–34, 505–10; Moley, *Hays Office*, pp. 169–76.

65. Hoover to Julius Klein, March 5, 1925, Commerce Dept., BFDC file, Commerce files, Hoover Papers; "Accomplishments of the Department of Commerce," Commerce, Accomplishments file, Commerce files, Hoover Papers; Bureau of Foreign and Domestic Commerce, *Annual Reports*: 1926, pp. 13, 45–46; 1927, pp. 41–42; 1928, p. 34; 1929, p. 39; C. J. North, "Our Foreign Trade in Motion Pictures," *Annals of the American Academy of Political and Social Science* 128 (November 1926): 100–108.

66. Will H. Hays, "The Motion Picture Industry," *Review of Reviews*, January 1923, pp. 65–80; Hays, "Motion Pictures and the Public," Hays file, Commerce files, Hoover Papers; Hays, *The Motion Picture and the Public* (New York: MPPDA, 1925); C. C. Pettijohn, "How the Motion Picture Industry Governs Itself," *Annals of the American Academy of Political and Social Science* 128 (November 1926): 158–62; Hays, *Memoirs*, pp. 327–31, 377.

67. Hoover, Address at dinner of MPPDA, New York, April 2, 1927; Hoover to Hays, April 20, 1926; George Canty to Motion Picture Section, BFDC, April 2, 1928, all in Hays file, Commerce files, Hoover Papers.

68. Ernest I. Lewis to Hoover, May 16, 1925; International Reform Federa-

tion to Hoover, January 29, 1927; Mrs. R. M. Gibbs to Hoover, with attached article, July 22, 1927, all in Motion Pictures file, Commerce files, Hoover Papers; William S. Chase to Hoover, May 4, 1929, with attached memorandum by William Seabury; Fred Eastman, "The Menace of the Movies" (reprinted from *Christian Century*, 1930), all in Motion Pictures file, Presidential Subject files, Hoover Papers; Grant M. Hudson and Burt New, "Should the Government Control Motion Pictures?" *Congressional Digest* 7 (November 1928): 314–15; Hays, *Memoirs*, pp. 389–96; Moley, *Hays Office*, pp. 61–67. Under the regulatory proposals being debated, the Upshaw and Hudson bills, a federal commission would be established in the Bureau of Education and would be empowered to censor movies being released, license those operating in the industry, supervise production and distribution, and, if necessary, take over and operate the distribution system. An alternative proposal, by 1929, called for a Film Inspection Bureau in the Commerce Department. This was also sponsored by Congressman Grant M. Hudson.

69. Block booking was the practice of requiring an exhibitor to take all or a certain percentage of a group of films, sometimes all of a company's annual production, in order to obtain any film in the group. The producers called it "selling in bulk" and insisted that the security thus provided was essential to the industry's operation. The exhibitors saw it as an effort to make them shoulder an unfair portion of the risks involved in marketing pictures.

70. The conference produced a fifteen-rule trade practice agreement. But the arbitration provisions of this were quickly challenged, and in the courts the producers continued to defend block booking. They were unwilling to accept an FTC order against it. Federal Trade Commission, *Trade Practice Conferences* (Washington: Government Printing Office, 1929), pp. 83–93, 99; Abram F. Myers, "Fair Methods of Competition in the Motion Picture Industry," October 10, 1927, Motion Pictures file, Commerce files, Hoover Papers.

71. Abram F. Myers to Hoover, March 27, June 18, 1929, Motion Pictures file, Presidential Subject files, Hoover Papers; Moley, *Hays Office*, p. 200.

72. Hays, *Memoirs*, p. 438; "Hays Office," *Fortune*, December 1938, p. 140.

73. Memorandum of a phone call from Will Hays, March 17, 1930, Motion Pictures file, Presidential Subject files, Hoover Papers; Moley, *Hays Office*, pp. 199–202; "Activities and Accomplishments of the Antitrust Division during the Hoover Administration," Box 1, Taylor-Gates material, Hoover Presidential Library. Apparently O'Brian's activities stemmed from a 1929 conference between Hays and Hoover, in which it was agreed that the industry would cooperate in an equity suit designed to clear up the legality of its trade practices, get them established in a consent decree, and thus remove any potential embarrassments for the new administration. See Hays to Hoover, August 28, 1929, Antitrust Laws file, Presidential Subject files, Hoover Papers, and Hoover to Richey, March 17, 1930, Motion Pictures file, Presidential Subject files, Hoover Papers.

74. Moley, *Hays Office*, pp. 74–99, 201–12; "Hays Office," *Fortune*, December 1938, pp. 70, 142–44; Hays, *Memoirs*, pp. 444–504, 526–58, 569–72; Hawley, *New Deal and Monopoly*, pp. 365–68, 451–52. Hays retired in 1945, but the basic mechanisms of the office remained. Hays was replaced by Eric Johnston.

75. See, for example, G. Lehmbruch, "Liberal Corporatism and Party Government," *Comparative Political Studies* 10 (1977): 91–126; Frederick Pike and Thomas Stritch, eds., *The New Corporatism* (Notre Dame: University of Notre Dame Press, 1974); Andrew Shonfield, *Modern Capitalism* (New York: Oxford University Press, 1965); and Vogel, *Japan as Number One.*

POLITICAL CHOICE IN REGULATION   Samuel P. Hays

1. Two recent studies of environmental affairs, written by participants from a problem-policy viewpoint, are John Quarles, *Cleaning Up America* (Boston: Houghton Mifflin, 1976) and John C. Whitaker, *Striking a Balance* (Washington, D.C.: American Enterprise Institute, 1976).

2. Two studies of railroad regulation which emphasize administrative politics rather than ideological debate are K. Austin Kerr, *American Railroad Politics, 1914-1920* (Pittsburgh: University of Pittsburgh Press, 1968) and Richard H. K. Vietor, "Businessmen and the Political Economy: The Railroad Rate Controversy of 1905," *Journal of American History* 64 (1977): 47–66.

3. For the author's earlier work, see Samuel P. Hays, *Conservation and the Gospel of Efficiency* (Cambridge, Mass.: Harvard University Press, 1959).

4. Several pertinent items are Samuel P. Hays, "The Limits-to-Growth Issue: An Historical Perspective," in Chester L. Cooper, ed., *Growth in America* (Westport, Conn.: Greenwood Press, 1976); "Clean Air: From the 1970 Act to the 1977 Amendments," *Duquesne Law Review* 17 (1978–1979): 33–66; "Human Choice in the Great Lakes Wildlands," in Susan Flader, ed., *Environmental Change in the Great Lakes Forest* (Minneapolis: University of Minnesota Press, in press); "Value Premises for Planning and Public Policy—the Historical Context," in Richard L. N. Andrews, ed., *Land in America* (Lexington, Mass.: Lexington Books, 1979), pp. 149–66; "The Political Structure of the Environmental Movement since World War II," *Journal of Social History* (forthcoming).

5. A good case study of administrative politics is a recent doctoral dissertation by John Edward Chubb, "Interest Groups and the Bureaucracy: The Politics of Energy" (University of Minnesota, 1979).

6. The rapid expansion of the administrative record has created far more extensive evidence for the historian. Its use, moreover, is facilitated by a host of "aids," such as the weekly reports series published by the Bureau of National Affairs, for example, *Environmental Reporter.*

7. A number of monographs contain useful segments pertaining to administrative choices. See, for example, Joel Primack and Frank von Hippel, *Advice and Dissent: Scientists in the Political Arena* (New York: Basic Books, 1974); Steven Ebbin and Raphael Kasper, *Citizen Groups and the Nuclear Power Controversy* (Cambridge, Mass.: MIT Press, 1974); Robert V. Bartlett, *The Reserve Mining Controversy* (Bloomington: University of Indiana Press, 1980).

8. The most striking case of making choices about the "reality" to be dealt with involve the "effects" analyses in the "criteria documents" required by air and water laws. These compilations formalize assessments of "reality" which were undoubtedly carried out far more informally in earlier economic regulation.

For those pertaining to air quality see Richard J. Tobin, *The Social Gamble* (Lexington, Mass.: Lexington Books, 1979).

9. See recent events surrounding the appointment of the Public Lands Advisory Council and of an advisory committee for a study, "American Attitudes and Behavioral Relations to Wildlife and Natural Habitat," conducted by the U.S. Fish and Wildlife Service, miscellaneous items in author's file.

10. This economic context for railroad regulation, as an example, is well worked out in Vietor, "Businessmen and the Political Economy."

11. The role of mass-buying firms in antitrust affairs is described, although often tangentially, in Robert F. Himmelberg, *The Origins of the National Recovery Administration: Business, Government, and the Trade Association Issue, 1921–1933* (New York: Fordham University Press, 1976).

12. One example of such a twofold attitude study was sponsored by the American Forest Institute and carried out in 1977 by the Opinion Research Corporation. The survey found that 62% of those questioned felt the U.S. Forest Service should "continue to preserve these trees in their natural state" rather than "try to increase the yield and sales of timber from our National Forests." Only 38% of "thought leaders" agreed. See Opinion Research Corporation, "The Public's Participation in Outdoor Activities and Attitudes Toward National Wilderness Areas," Princeton, N.J., September 1977. See also American Forest Institute, "Research Recap" #10, Washington, D.C., December 1977.

13. The Opinion Research Corporation advised the American Forest Institute: "We do not find sufficient latent support among the American people to warrant a mass communications program to increase public support for greater timber harvesting on federal lands. Instead, since this issue is perceived more rationally and with greater expertise among Washington thought leaders, we recommend that your persuasive efforts be directed toward this target audience, among others." Ibid.

14. The continuity of the administrative political context is described by Chubb as follows: "The bureaucracy and its organized clienteles are surely the most durable components of the policy process" (Chubb, "Interest Groups," p. 21).

15. I have elaborated on the evolution of larger-scale systems and their relationship to smaller in several articles, including "The New Organizational Society," in Jerry Israel, ed., *Building the Organizational Society: Essays on Associational Activities in Modern America* (New York: Free Press, 1972), and "Political Parties and the Community-Society Continuum," in William N. Chambers and Walter D. Burnham, eds., *The American Party Systems: Stages of Political Development* (New York: Oxford University Press, 1967).

16. Changes in marketing and distribution are discussed in a variety of contemporary sources. One of the best is a short work by Arch Wilkinson Shaw, *Some Problems in Market Distribution* (Cambridge, Mass.: Harvard University Press, 1915). See also George B. Hotchkiss, *Milestones of Marketing: A Brief History of the Evolution of Market Distribution* (New York: Macmillan, 1938). Shaw edited the magazine *System,* which included much material on economic efficiency, including marketing. See, for example, a speech by Arthur Brisbane before the Sphinx Club, a New York organization of marketing men, in the June

1912 issue, p. 672: "As compared with distribution, production is relatively well organized. . . . Society is beginning to sense the social waste in our unorganized system of distribution and to take the problem in hand." Varied articles deal with specifics of these changes; see, for example, Wayland A. Tonning, "Department Stores in Downstate Illinois, 1889–1943," *Business History Review,* December 1955, pp. 335–49.

17. A good account of the politics of banking, with emphasis on the relationship between smaller-scale and larger-scale institutions is in Lloyd Sponholtz, "Progressivism in Microcosm: An Analysis of the Political Forces at Work in the Ohio Constitutional Convention of 1912" (Ph.D., diss., University of Pittsburgh, 1969).

18. I have worked out the tensions between centralization and decentralization in the city in "Politics of Reform in Municipal Government in the Progressive Era," *Pacific Northwest Quarterly* 55 (October 1964) and "The Changing Political Structure of the City in Industrial America," *Journal of Urban History* 1 (November 1974).

19. Producer-consumer tension within the business community was reflected in many cases. In 1980, for example, General Motors objected to a provision in a permit granted by the Federal Energy Regulatory Commission to construct a coal gasification plant in Beulah, South Dakota; it provided, in the event the project failed, that the firm could pass on its costs directly to consumers, of which General Motors was one. General Motors was joined in the complaint, which the federal court upheld, by the states of Michigan, Ohio and New York. See author file of clippings and articles.

20. The Galbraith argument is in his *American Capitalism: The Concept of Countervailing Power* (Boston: Houghton Mifflin, 1952); see esp. pp. 108–34.

21. The political role of mass-marketing institutions, including those associated with mass production, is dealt with in Himmelberg, *Origins of the NRA.*

22. See the chapter, "Organize or Perish," which deals more fully with functional group organization, in Samuel P. Hays, *The Response to Industrialism* (Chicago: University of Chicago Press, 1957).

23. A treatment of planners and the politics of planning is in Hays, "Value Premises."

24. The connection between scientific controversy and wider social and political controversy can be followed in several books on pesticide politics. See, for example, Frank Graham, Jr., *Since Silent Spring* (Boston: Houghton Mifflin, 1970); Rita Gray Beatty, *The DDT Myth: Triumph of the Amateurs* (New York: Day, 1973); Georg Klaus and Karen Bolander, *Ecological Sanity* (New York: McKay, 1977); Robert van den Bosch, *The Pesticide Conspiracy* (New York: Doubleday, 1978). See also a case study of asbestos science and politics in Paul Brodeur, *Expendable Americans* (New York: Viking, 1973).

25. The publications of the American Statistical Association are included in its *Proceedings,* especially after 1890.

26. Four major statistical agencies were formed during World War I: the Central Bureau of Planning and Statistics, the Planning and Statistics Division of the Shipping Board, the Planning and Statistics Division of the War Industries Board, and the Research and Tabulation of Statistics Bureau of the War Trade

Board. Edwin F. Gay, Dean of the Graduate School of Business Administration, Harvard University, chaired all four groups.

27. Changes in census occupational classifications are described in Margo Anderson Conk, "The United States Census and the New Jersey Occupational Structure, 1870–1940" (Ph.D. diss., Rutgers University, 1978).

28. Economic analysis has often come to supersede other forms of policy analysis which have a less determinate force. For example, as health matters have come to emphasize low-level, chronic exposures and effects, health scientists have been relatively incapable of identifying adverse health effects clearly, even to their own satisfaction. Hence they are tempted to turn, as many others do, to economic analysis as a substitute in the belief that the numbers, and hence the analysis, in economic data are firmer than in the case of health data.

29. Arguments over "criteria document" assessments can be followed in *Environment Reporter,* Bureau of National Affairs, Washington, D.C. See also two documents pertaining to the assessment of the effects of particulates: W. W. Holland et al., "Health Effects of Particulate Pollution: Reappraising the Evidence," and Carl M. Shy, "Epidemiologic Evidence and the United States Air Quality Standards," both in *American Journal of Epidemiology* 110 (November and December 1979).

30. Environmental assessment was one attempt to break through this overlay of technical detail so that decision makers outside the agency, in other agencies, at other levels of government, in the legislature and in the courts, could know fully the basis of a decision. The judicial elaboration of the form and scope of the environmental impact statement arose primarily from problems of administrative "due process."

31. Few of the contexts of scientific and technical choice outlined here have been investigated. An exception is an account of research choices made recently for the U.S. Forest Experiment Stations, which included a "public participation" process carried out by the Forest Service, with representatives of industry, government, scientific professions, consumers and environmentalists. This has been analyzed by Joseph C. deSteiguer in "Public Participation in Forestry Research Planning" (Ph.D. diss., Texas A&M University, 1979), who makes clear the quite different choices made by each of the five groups as to what research they thought desirable.

32. Both consumer and environmental representation on advisory committees came to be more common in environmental agencies. See the 1978 case of the U.S. Fish and Wildlife Service, note 9.

33. One agency which environmentalists sought to "grab hold" of by delving fairly deeply into its decision-making process was the U.S. Army Corps of Engineers and especially its water project choices. They obtained considerable help in this task from professional economists. Some aspects of this are described in Daniel A. Mazmanian and Jeanne Nienaber, *Can Organizations Change: Environmental Protection, Citizen Participation, and the Corps of Engineers* (Washington, D.C.: Brookings Institution, 1979).

34. For a more extended treatment of the process of centralization of decision making see the author's writings previously mentioned such as "The New Organizational Society," in Israel, ed., *Organizational Society.*

35. State preemption of local authority seems to have been the rule rather than the exception; it involved a "levels of authority" problem which has been obscured amid the preoccupation with the more classic case of state-federal relations.

36. Industry-sponsored market research, though often not open for scrutiny because it was collected as proprietary information, constitutes one of the most significant potential sources of information about social values which historians could utilize. Industry-financed attitude surveys and opinion question surveys seem to be increasing and many of them are publicized. Two massive continuing surveys are noteworthy. One is being carried out by Arnold Mitchell at Stanford Research Institute; it is called the VALS program. See Arnold Mitchell, "Social Change: Implications of Trends in Values and Lifestyles," reprinted from VALS Report No. 3, SRI International, January 1979, and "Vals 1980: Status Report on SRI's Values and Lifestyles Program," SRI International, August 1980. The other is a nationwide content analysis of local and regional newspapers, over 200 of them, beginning in 1970, conducted by John Naisbitt of the Center for Policy Process, Washington, D.C.; see John Naisbitt, "The New Economic and Political Order of the 1980s" (The Foresight Group, Stockholm, Sweden, April 17, 1980).

37. The Final Environmental Impact Statement usually includes copies of all written comments made on the draft and hence becomes an extremely convenient source of documentary evidence about a wide range of political attitudes. See the Final EIS, "Operation of the National Wildlife Refuge System," issued by the U.S. Fish and Wildlife Service, Washington, D.C., in 1976, which contains over 700 pages of written comments from a wide range of political opinion on American wildlife policy.

38. The study of risks is "Risks in a Complex Society," sponsored by insurance broker Marsh and McLennan, conducted by Harris, reported in *Chemical Week*, May 28, 1980, p. 71. An unusual study of the values and attitudes of advocates of solar energy and administrative leaders in the federal agencies contrasts their views on a range of topics, including different concepts of appropriate economic analysis. See Avraham Shama and Ken Jacobs, "Social Values and Solar Energy Policy: The Policy Makers and the Advocates" (Solar Energy Research Institute, October 1979 [SERI-RR-51-329]).

39. The political intelligentsia, for example, has had considerable influence in redefining, in the minds of many decision makers, the "public interest" group into a "special interest" group, and in shaping the concept of the "single issue group." These concepts are applied far more frequently to the post-World War II consumer-environmental groups than to the more longstanding producer groups.

40. My views on the role of "antitrust" ideology are elaborated a bit further in *Response to Industrialism*, esp. pp. 188–93.

41. For the concept of speculative augmentation see Frederick Edward Wood, Jr., "Public Opinion, Interest Groups and Environmental Policy: Incremental Change versus Speculative Augmentation" (Ph.D. diss., Johns Hopkins University, 1980).

Regulation in Perspective

THE "NEW" SOCIAL REGULATION David Vogel

1. The phrase is from an article by Murray Weidenbaum, "The New Wave of Government Regulation of Business," *Business and Society Review*, Fall 1975, pp. 81–86. The distinction between social and economic regulation is important to this analysis. Economic regulatory agencies govern prices, output, terms of competition and entry/exit. Social regulations are concerned with the externalities and social impact of economic activity. The ICC, FPC, and CAB, the FCC, and the SEC are examples of the former; the CPSC, EPA, EEOC, and OSHA illustrate the latter. The FTC falls into both categories. While admittedly this distinction is somewhat artificial, it is nonetheless a useful one. Unless otherwise indicated, the focus of this paper is on *social* regulation and *social* regulatory agencies. Within the category of social regulations, its specific focus is on regulations affecting health, safety, and the environment.

2. Overviews of regulation in the area of consumer protection can be found in Mark Nadel, *The Politics of Consumer Protection* (New York: Bobbs-Merrill, 1971) and *Consumer Protection; Gains and Setbacks* (Washington, D.C.: Congressional Quarterly, 1978). Environmental protection policies are treated in Walter Rosenbaum, *The Politics of Environmental Concern* (New York: Praeger, 1973) and J. Clarence Davies III, *The Politics of Pollution* (New York: Bobbs-Merrill Company, 1980). The best recent overview of contemporary government regulation of business is Murray Weidenbaum, *Business, Government, and The Public* (Englewood Cliffs, N.J.: Prentice-Hall, 1981). This essay draws heavily on each of these works.

3. For a more detailed account of the decline and rise of the political influence of business during the 1960s and 1970s, see David Vogel, "How Business Responds to Opposition; Corporate Political Strategies During the 1970s," unpublished paper presented at the annual meeting of the American Political Science Association, Washington, D.C., 1979.

4. The discussion of the Progressive Era in this paper is drawn from George Mowry, *Theodore Roosevelt and The Progressive Movement* (New York: Hill and Wang, 1946); George Mowry, *The California Progressives* (Chicago: Quadrangle Paperbacks, 1951); and Arthur Link, *Woodrow Wilson and The Progressive Era, 1910–1917* (New York: Harper, 1954).

5. The discussion of the New Deal in this paper is drawn from Arthur Schlesinger, Jr., *The Coming of the New Deal* (Boston: Houghton Mifflin, 1958) and *The Politics of Upheaval* (Boston: Houghton Mifflin, 1960).

6. For a contemporary discussion of the mutual benefits of improved business-government cooperation during this period, see for example, James Quinn, "Next Big Industry: Environmental Improvement," *Harvard Business Review*, September–October 1971, pp. 120–31; Rodman Rockefeller, "Turning Public Problems to Private Account," *Harvard Business Review*, January–February 1971, pp. 130–38; John T. Connor, "The Changing Pattern of Business-Government Relations," *The Conference Board Record*, May 1971, pp. 23–26; *The Corporation in Transition* (Washington, D.C.: U.S. Chamber of Commerce, 1971); and Melvin Anshen, "Changing the Social Contract: A Role for Business," *Columbia Journal of World Business*, November–December 1970, pp. 6–14.

7. For a description of this process, see David Vogel, *Lobbying the Corporation: Citizen Challenges to Business Authority* (New York: Basic Books, 1979), esp. chaps. 2 and 3.

8. For a description of the mood of the business community during this period and the hostility it had developed toward government intervention in the economy, see Leonard Silk and David Vogel, *Ethics and Profits: The Crisis of Confidence in American Business* (New York: Simon & Schuster, 1976), chap. 2.

9. Ralph Nader, *Unsafe At Any Speed* (New York: Pocket Books, 1966); Arthur Kallet and F. S. Schlink, *100,000,000 Guinea Pigs* (New York: The Vanguard Press, 1933); Upton Sinclair, *The Jungle* (New York: Doubleday, Page, 1906).

10. For samples of the former, see Arthur and Lila Weinberg, eds., *The Muckrakers* (New York: Capricorn Books, 1964); the latter are summarized in Morton Mintz, *By Prescription Only* (Boston: Houghton Mifflin, 1967).

11. For importance of the "trusts" to the Progressives' criticisms of business, see Louis Hartz, *The Liberal Tradition in America* (New York: Harcourt, Brace and World, 1955); and Richard Hofstadter, *The Age of Reform* (New York, Vintage Books, 1955). Three of the most controversial and consequential New Deal reforms directly challenged the power of the financial community: the Banking Reform Act, the Securities and Exchange Act, and the law outlawing utility holding companies.

12. One observer commented, "Has there ever been, one wonders, a society that produced more uncertainty more often about everyday life? It isn't much, really, in dispute—only the land we live on, the water we drink, the air we breathe, the food we eat, the energy that supports us. . . . Evidently, a mechanism is at work ringing alarms faster than most of us can keep track of them." Aaron Wildavsky, "No Risk Is the Highest Risk of All," *American Scientist*, January–February 1979, p. 30.

13. See Silk and Vogel, *Ethics and Profits*.

14. The material in this section is primarily based on Ronald Penoyer, comp., *Directory of Federal Regulatory Agencies* (St. Louis: Center for the Study of American Business, 1980).

15. Walter Guzzardi, Jr., "Putting the Cuffs on Capitalism," *Fortune*, April 1975, p. 194.

16. Penoyer, *Directory*, p. 8.

17. Among the highest and most controversial estimates is that of Murray Weidenbaum, who estimated the total cost of compliance with federal regulations at $102.7 billion in 1979. See Murray Weidenbaum, *The Future of Business Regulation* (New York: AMACOM, 1979), p. 23. Weidenbaum's figures, however, primarily include the costs of compliance with economic regulations. For a critique of Weidenbaum's methodology, see Mark Green and Norman Waitzman, "A Challenge to Murray Weidenbaum," *New York Times*, October 26, 1979, and Stephen Kelman, "Regulation That Works," *New Republic*, November 23, 1978.

18. Steven Rattner, "Productivity Lag Causes Worry," *New York Times*, May 8, 1979, p. 22.

19. See, for example, "Consumerism at Bay," *Dun's Review*, May 1978,

p. 96; "How Business Won a Major Victory in Washington," *Nation's Business,* March 1978, p. 86; Walter Guzzardi, Jr., "Business Is Learning To Win in Washington," *Fortune,* March 27, 1978, p. 57.

20. Quoted in Gabriel Kolko, *The Triumph of Conservatism* (Chicago: Quadrangle Paperbacks, 1967), p. 107.

21. Ibid., p. 103.

22. See Samuel P. Hays, *Conservation and the Gospel of Efficiency* (Cambridge, Mass.: Harvard University Press, 1959).

23. Quoted in ibid., p. 145.

24. For an account of consumer politics during the New Deal, see Ellis Hawley, *The New Deal and the Problem of Monopoly* (Princeton: Princeton University Press, 1966), pp. 75–79, 128–32; and Schlesinger, *Coming of the New Deal,* pp. 198–204.

25. See Charles Jackson, *Food and Drug Legislation in the New Deal* (Princeton: Princeton University Press, 1970).

26. Ibid., p. 212.

27. A good overall account of the political strategy of public interest groups can be found in Jeffrey Berry, *Lobbying for the People* (Princeton: Princeton University Press, 1978).

28. See *Public Interest Perspectives: The Next Four Years,* Proceedings from the first major gathering of public interest advocates, Public Citizen, 1977.

29. John Holcomb, "Public Interest Lobbies," *Enterprise,* December 1977, pp. 3–5.

30. Al Gordon, "Public Interest Lobbies: Nader and Common Cause Become Permanent Fixtures," *Congressional Quarterly* **34,** no. 20 (1976): 1197.

31. See "Balancing the Scales of Justice: Financing Public Interest Law in America," a report of the Council for Public Interest Law, 1976.

32. Juan Cameron, "Nader's Invaders Are Inside the Gates," *Fortune,* October 1977, p. 254.

33. Rosenbaum, *Politics of Environmental Concern,* p. 75.

34. Lawrence Mosher, "Environmentalists Question Whether to Retreat or Stay on the Offensive," *National Journal,* December 13, 1980, pp. 2116–21.

35. For a description of Nader's accomplishments, see R. Armstrong, "The Passion That Rules Ralph Nader," *Fortune,* May 1971, pp. 219–28.

36. For an analysis of this phenomenon, see J. David Greenstone, *Labor in American Politics* (New York: Knopf, 1969).

37. For a good summary of the regulatory philosophy of the New Deal see Bruce Ackerman and William Hassler, "Beyond the New Deal: Coal and the Clean Air Act," *Yale Law Journal* **89** (November 1980): 1466–1571.

38. For a more detailed analysis of the movement's strategy, see David Vogel, "The Public Interest Movement and the American Reform Tradition," *Political Science Quarterly,* Winter 1980–81, pp. 607–28. For a good statement of the movement's philosophy and its divergence from that of the New Deal, see Simon Lazarus, *The Genteel Populists* (New York: Holt, Rinehart, & Winston, 1974).

39. For the role of the courts in shaping environmental policy, see Frederick Anderson, *NEPA in the Courts* (Washington, D.C.: Resources for the Future, 1973) and Joseph Sax, *Defending the Environment* (New York: Vintage Books, 1970).

40. Karen Orren, "Standing to Sue," *American Political Science Review,* September 1976, p. 724.

41. See for example, Roger Cramton, "The Why, Where, and How of Broadened Public Participation in the Administrative Process," *Georgetown Law Journal,* February 1972, pp. 525–50, and Ernest Gelhorn, "Public Participation in Administrative Proceedings," *Yale Law Journal* **81** (January 1972): 359–404.

42. For a more complex analysis of the political constituencies affecting regulatory policies, see James Q. Wilson, "The Politics of Regulation," in James Q. Wilson, ed., *The Politics of Regulation* (New York: Basic Books, 1980), pp. 357–94.

43. The clearest example of this is the 1977 amendments to the Clean Air Act, which pitted western against eastern coal interests. See Peter Navarro, "The Politics of Air Pollution," *Public Interest,* Spring 1980, pp. 36–44; also, Ackerman and Hassler, "Beyond the New Deal."

44. For specific examples, see A. F. Ehbar, "Pragmatic Politics Won't Win For Business," *Fortune,* June 4, 1979, pp. 76–80, and "Down With Big Business," *Wall Street Journal,* April 18, 1979, p. 20.

45. For a summary of these proposals see Ralph Nader, Mark Green and Joel Seligman, *Taming the Giant Corporation* (New York: Norton, 1975). In this context, it is striking that five of the eleven corporations singled out by the broad coalition of public interest and trade unions who sponsored Big Business Day as "representative of the impact of Big Business in America" were selected because of some physical injury they had caused to either consumers, employees, or the public. See "Corporate Shadow Boards," Americans Concerned About Corporate Power, Washington, D.C., 1980.

46. The following are quotations from corporate executives at a series of private meetings, held in 1974 and 1975 to discuss business-government relations: "Government agencies don't understand business." "My industry is regulated up to its neck. You are regulated up to your knees. And the tide is coming in." "The harassment of the businessman by the government bureaucracy hampers productivity. I spend a large part of each day with a lawyer or two, protecting myself from possible prosecution." "I spend too much time each day complying with government regulations." "The social responsibility of business should be decided by the boards of directors. But now it is decided by Congress. We're having a major intrusion of government into formerly private decisions." Silk and Vogel, *Ethics and Profits,* pp. 52, 53.

Corporate executives are particularly concerned these days about the additional regulation of private economic activity in such areas as consumer and environmental protection and occupational health and safety. They see new pension regulations as seriously weakening the independence of the private sector.

Not only are the regulations costly, say the businessmen, but they complicate and confuse the process of corporate decision making and have heavy hidden as well as direct costs. They threaten the functioning of a "free" economy and its ability to innovate and respond rapidly and creatively to economic opportunities. Businessmen assert that government regulations made now with the best of intentions will severely limit their future choices; future business earnings will have already been preempted and commited by public policies.

Regulation in Perspective

The government agencies which today bear the brunt of the executives' ire are the new ones whose insulation from business influence makes their decisions unpredictable and, as they see it, hazardous to the ability of business to make adequate profits. It seems that almost every executive has some bureaucratic horror story to relate to his experience with some allegedly unreasonable official from the Consumer Product Safety Commission, the Occupational Safety and Health Administration, or the Environmental Protection Administration. The congressional decision to reverse automobile seat-belt requirements, in response to widespread consumer complaints, was triumphantly cited several times during different conference sessions as a typical example of the lack of foresight in many well-intentioned government actions.

47. For a good overall summary of the criticism of government regulation, see Weidenbaum, *The Future of Business Regulation*.

48. See for example, the various publications of the American Enterprise Institute and the Institute for Contemporary Studies. See also, the "Cost of Government Regulation Study," a study of the direct incremental costs incurred by 48 companies in complying with the regulations of six federal agencies in 1977, published by Arthur Anderson & Co., March 1979.

49. Michael Novak, *The American Vision* (Washington, D.C.: American Enterprise Institute, 1978); Jeanne J. Kirkpatrick, "Politics and the New Class," in B. Bruce Briggs, ed., *The New Class* (New Brunswick, N.J.: Transaction Books, 1979), pp. 37–48; "Business and the New Class," in Irving Kristol, *Two Cheers For Capitalism* (New York: Basic Books, 1977); Herman Kahn, "Some Current Cultural Contradictions of Economic Growth: The Twelve New Emphases," Hudson Institute, 1978; Tom Bethell, "Class War," *New York Times*, May 31, 1978, p. 37.

50. See for example, S. Prakash Sethi, *Advocacy Advertising and Large Corporations* (Lexington, Mass.: Lexington Books, 1977).

51. This paragraph and the one following are based on "Washington's Big Boom," *Dun's Review*, July 1978, pp. 51–52; John Thachery, "How U.S. Business Lobbies," *Management Today*, December 1978, pp. 74–82; "Business Lobbying," *Consumer Reports*, September 1978, pp. 526–31; and Phyllis McGrath, *Redefining Corporate-Federal Relations*, Conference Board Report no. 757 (1979).

52. McGrath, *Redefining Corporate-Federal Relations*, p. 2. See also Kim McQuaid, "Big Business and Public Policy in Contemporary United States," *Quarterly Review of Economic Business* 20, no. 2 (Summer 1980): 57–68.

53. Phyllis McGrath, *Management Corporate External Relations: Changing Perspectives and Responses*, Conference Board Report no. 679 (1976); Robert L. Fegley, "New Breed of Top Executive Takes Charge," *Los Angeles Times*, December 31, 1976, pt. 4, p. 6.

54. From a speech by Irving Shapiro quoted in Peter F. Drucker, "Coping with those Extra Burdens," *Wall Street Journal*, May 2, 1979. This development has led some firms to appoint two chief executives—one to deal with the public and the other to manage the business.

55. James W. Singer, "Business and Government—A New 'Quasi-Public' Role," *National Journal*, April 15, 1978, p. 596.

56. For a discussion of this later phenomenon, see Edwin M. Epstein, "Business and Labor in the American Electoral Process," in Herbert Alexander, *Sage Electoral Studies Yearbook* 4 (1979). See also Neil Ulman, "Companies Organize Employees and Holders Into a Political Force," *Wall Street Journal*, August 15, 1978, pp. 1, 15.

57. Among the most important changes in corporate political activity that did take place during the Progressive Era was the establishment of the Chamber of Commerce of the United States and the National Industrial Conference Board. The emergence of corporate public relations also dates from this period. Business opposition to the New Deal primarily took place through the Republican Party, though the utility industry did organize a "grass roots" campaign in opposition to the Public Utility Holding Company Act. The Business Council was also established during the 1930s. For a good historical overview of business political activity in the United States, see Philippe C. Schmitter and Donald Brand, "Organizing Capitalists in the United States: the Advantages and Disadvantages of Exceptionalism," presented at American Political Science Association Meeting, Washington, D.C., 1979. For the political response of business to the Progressive Era, see Robert H. Wiebe, "Business Disunity and the Progressive Movement, 1901–1914," *Mississippi Valley Historical Review*, March 1958, pp. 664–85. On the New Deal, see Kim McQuaid, "The Frustration of Corporate Revival During the Early New Deal," *The Historian* 41 (August 1979): 689–704. Schlesinger, *Coming of the New Deal*, pt. 7, and Schlesinger, *Politics of Upheaval*, pp. 302–24. For an overview of the development of corporate public relations during the twentieth century, see Richard S. Tedlow, *Keeping the Corporate Image: Public Relations and Business, 1900–1950* (Greenwich, Conn.: JAI Press, 1979).

58. McGrath, *Redefining Corporate-Federal Relations*, p. 1.

59. "Washington's Big Boom," *Dun's Review*, July 1978, p. 11.

60. See for example, "Pollution in Europe," *European Community*, October 1973, p. 19, and Adam Meyerson, "Japan: Environmentalism with Growth," *Wall Street Journal*, September 5, 1980. Claude Fischler, "The Ecological Movement and Its Contradictions," *European Business*, Winter 1974, pp. 30–39.

61. Adrien Sapiro and Jacques Lendrevie, "On the Consumer Front in France, Japan, Sweden, U.D., and the U.S.A.," *European Business*, Summer 1973, pp. 43–52; S. D. Brooks and J. J. Richardson, "The Environmental Lobby in Britain," *Parliamentary Affairs*, Summer 1975, pp. 312–29; Jeff Bridgford, "The Ecologist Movement and the French General Election 1978," *Parliamentary Affairs*, Summer 1978, pp. 314–22; Jean Vinocur, "Environmentalists in Bonn Plan a National Party," *New York Times*, November 7, 1979, p. A9; "New West German Party Attracts Coalition of Protesters," *Washington Post*, January 14, 1980, p. A4; Timothy O'Riordan, "Public Interest Environmental Groups in the United States and Britain," *American Studies*, 13: 409–38.

62. See Floyd Lawrence, "Where on Earth Does Industry Stand in Pollution Control?" *Industry Week*, February 14, 1977, pp. 43–51; Ernest Stern, "The Impact of Pollution Abatement Laws on The International Economy: An Overview of the Hydra," *Law and Policy in International Business* 7 (1975): 203–73; Robert Lutz II, "The Laws of Environmental Management: A Comparative Study," *The American Journal of Comparative Law* 24 (1976): 447–520.

63. Norman Lee and Christopher Wood, "The Assessment of Environmental Impacts in Project Appraisal in the European Communities," *Journal of Common Market Studies,* March 1978, pp. 189–210; *European Communities Environmental Policy,* Brussels, Commissioner of the European Communities, 1978; John Frey and F. Joseph Warin, "European Consumer Protection: The Council of Charter Initiative," *Law and Policy in International Business* 6 (1974): 1107–31.

64. See for example, Meyerson, "Japan"; Roger Williams, "Government Regulation of the Occupational and General Environments in the United Kingdom, the United States and Sweden," Science Council of Canada, Background Study no. 40 (October 1977); "Europe's Coming Liability Explosion," *Economist,* July 30, 1977.

65. See for example, Edward Mason, "Interests, Ideologists and the Problem of Stability and Growth," *American Economic Review* 53 (1963): 1–18; Andrew Schonfield, *Modern Capitalism* (New York: Oxford University Press, 1965), and Alfred D. Chandler, Jr., "Government Versus Business: An American Phenomenon," in John Dunlop, ed., *Business and Public Policy* (Boston: Harvard University Graduate School of Business Administration, 1980), pp. 1–11.

66. This argument is based on the analysis developed in David Vogel, "Why Businessmen Distrust the State: The Political Consciousness of American Corporate Executives," *British Journal of Political Science,* January 1978, pp. 45–78.

67. A particularly dramatic example of this has occurred in France. When environmental issues became an important focus of government policy, the Corps des Mines, one of the Grands Corps, became the source of recruitment for the key ports in the Ministry of Environment. See Ezra Scleiman, *Elites in French Society* (Princeton: Princeton University Press, 1978), pp. 214–15.

68. See Echard Rehbinder, "Controlling the Environmental Enforcement Deficit: West Germany," *American Journal of Comparative Law* 24 (1976): 373–91. Also P. F. Tenlère-Buchot, "The Role of the Public in Water Management Decision in France," *Natural Resources Journal* 16 (January 1976): pp. 159–76.

69. See for example, the chapters on enforcement in *Air Pollution Control: National and International Perspectives,* American Bar Association, Standing Committee on Environmental Law, 1980.

70. The relative informality of the European regulatory process was captured in an interview with Philip Caldwell, the chairman of Ford Motor Company. Caldwell recalled a conversation he had had with the Secretary of Transportation, Neal Goldschmidt. "I said to him that time, 'Does it strike you as odd, on fuel economy standards, that ours are all written into law and you have hundreds and perhaps thousands of people down there refining and supervising their application? Did you know we have verbal agreements with the governments of the United Kingdom, France, and Germany and that we're going after fuel economy improvement in our vehicles in Europe and working on them just as hard as we are here in the United States? And we're using all the technology we have in the United States over there and vice versa, and there we don't have any rules except the agreement that we'll do it.'" ("The Automobile Crisis and Public Policy," *Harvard Business Review,* January–February 1981, p. 80.)

71. François M. Flessinge and P. F. Tenlère-Buchot, "Pollution Fees Are For Real in France," *Water Spectrum,* Spring–Summer 1976, pp. 29–35.

72. See June Kronholz, "Consumerism: European-Style," *Wall Street Journal,* November 20, 1979, p. A22.

73. For a comparison of the establishment and enforcement of auto emission standards in Sweden and the United States which illustrates this point, see Lennart Lundquist, *The Hare and the Tortoise: Clean Air Policies in the United States and Sweden* (Ann Arbor: University of Michigan Press, 1980). See also *Air Pollution Control* (A.B.A.), for examples of the sensitivities of government officials in Europe to the economic impact of their regulatory efforts. A primary purpose of the European Community's growing interest in the regulation of environmental and consumer protection has been to reduce the possibility that members of the Community will suffer a competitive disadvantage as a result of their efforts to regulate in this area. A comparable sensitivity to the effects of regulation on international competition has generally been lacking in the United States.

THE CONTRIBUTORS

Thomas K. McCraw teaches at the Harvard Business School. His research has focused on business-government relations from the nineteenth century to the present, and his publications include *Morgan vs. Lilienthal: The Feud within the TVA* (Chicago: Loyola University Press, 1970); *TVA and the Power Fight, 1933–1939* (Philadelphia: J.B. Lippincott, 1971); and "Regulation in America: A Review Article," *Business History Review*, Summer 1975.

Morton Keller was Harmsworth Professor of American History at Oxford during 1980–81, prior to returning to his post at Brandeis University. He has investigated numerous aspects of American political, legal, and economic history in the nineteenth and twentieth centuries, and has written *In Defense of Yesterday: James M. Beck and the Politics of Conservatism* (New York: Coward-McCann, 1958); *The Life Insurance Enterprise, 1885–1910* (Cambridge, Mass.: Harvard University Press, 1963); *The Art and Politics of Thomas Nast* (New York: Oxford University Press, 1968); and *Affairs of State: Public Life in Late Nineteenth Century America* (Cambridge, Mass.: Harvard University Press, 1977).

Ellis Hawley is a professor of history at the University of Iowa. He has written widely about Herbert Hoover and about the inherent tensions in the evolution of economic policies in twentieth century America. Among his publications are *The New Deal and the Problem of Monopoly* (Princeton: Princeton University Press, 1966); *The Great War and the Search for a Modern Order* (New York: St. Martin's Press, 1979); and *Herbert Hoover and the Crisis of American Capitalism* (Cambridge, Mass.: Schenkman, 1973), which he co-authored.

Samuel P. Hays teaches at the University of Pittsburgh. His special field of interest is the relationship between society and politics in twentieth century America; he is author of *The Response to Industrialism* (Chicago: University of Chicago Press, 1957); *Conservation and the Gospel of Efficiency: The Progressive Conservation Movement, 1890–1920* (Cambridge, Mass.: Harvard University Press, 1959); and a collection of essays, *American Political History as Social Analysis* (Knoxville: University of Tennessee Press, 1980), many of which have been extremely influential.

David Vogel teaches in the School of Business Administration at the University of California, Berkeley. A political scientist, he has specialized in the structure of business-government relations. He has written a number of articles in addition to *Lobbying the Corporation: Citizen Challenges to Private Business Authority* (New York: Basic Books, 1979); and has co-authored with Leonard Silk *Ethics and Profits* (New York: Simon and Schuster, 1976), and with Thornton Bradshaw *Corporations and Their Critics* (New York: McGraw-Hill, 1981).